Modular Narratives in Contemporary Cinema

Modular Narratives in Contemporary Cinema

Allan Cameron

First published 2008 by
PALGRAVE MACMILLAN
Houndmills, Basingstoke, Hampshire RG21 6XS and
175 Fifth Avenue, New York, N.Y. 10010
Companies and representatives throughout the world

PALGRAVE MACMILLAN is the global academic imprint of the Palgrave Macmillan division of St. Martin's Press, LLC and of Palgrave Macmillan Ltd. Macmillan® is a registered trademark in the United States, United Kingdom and other countries. Palgrave Is a registered trademark in the European Union and other countries.

ISBN-13: 978-0-230-21041-7   hardback
ISBN-10: 0-230-21041-4   hardback

This book is printed on paper suitable for recycling and made from fully managed and sustained forest sources. Logging, pulping and manufacturing processes are expected to conform to the environmental regulations of the country of origin.

A catalogue record for this book is available from the British Library.

Library of Congress Cataloging-in-Publication Data

Cameron, Allan, 1973–
Modular narratives in contemporary cinema / Allan Cameron.
     p. cm.
  Includes bibliographical references and index.
  ISBN 0-230-21041-4 (alk. paper)
  1. Motion pictures and literature. 2. Narration (Rhetoric) I. Title.

PN1995.3.C36 2008
  791.43'6—dc22   2008015892

10   9   8   7   6   5   4   3   2   1
17 16 15 14 13 12 11 10 09 08

Printed and bound in Great Britain by
CPI Antony Rowe, Chippenham and Eastbourne

For Bridget and Duncan

Contents

Illustrations

Acknowledgements

I would like briefly to express my gratitude to those who have aided me, in whatever way, with the completion of this work.

Thanks, first of all, to Angela Ndalianis, my PhD supervisor at the University of Melbourne. Her comments and advice were much appreciated, as was her patience with a project that went through a great deal of shape-shifting in its early stages. I have also appreciated the input (direct or indirect) of other staff and postgraduate students at the University of Melbourne. Particular thanks are due to Richard Misek, whose comments on earlier drafts were invaluable. His keen intellect and passion for cinema have benefited this work a great deal.

More recently, Sean Cubitt, Glenn Man, Roberta Pearson and Warren Buckland have all contributed illuminating and useful feedback, for which I am very grateful. I am also grateful to my colleagues in the Screen Studies Department at the Australian Film, Television and Radio School for their responses to the project.

Finally, this work would not have been possible without the support of my wife Bridget and son Duncan. I thank them both for their patience, love and understanding.

Parts of Chapter 3 originally appeared as 'Contingency, Order and the Modular Narrative: *21 Grams* and *Irreversible*', in *The Velvet Light Trap*, no. 58: 65–78. Copyright 2006 by the University of Texas Press. All rights reserved.

1
Modular Narratives in Contemporary Cinema

Since the early 1990s, popular cinema has displayed a turn towards narrative complexity. In many cases, this complexity has taken the form of a database aesthetic, in which the narrative is divided into discrete segments and subjected to complex articulations. These films, which I am calling 'modular narratives', articulate a sense of time as divisible and subject to manipulation. They suggest both the pleasures and the threats offered by a modular conception of time. 'Modular narrative' and 'database narrative' are terms applicable to narratives that foreground the relationship between the temporality of the story and the order of its telling. For Marsha Kinder, 'Database narrative refers to narratives whose structure exposes or thematizes the dual processes of selection and combination that lie at the heart of all stories' (2002a, 6). This description, suggests Kinder, applies to interactive computer-based narratives as well as to the cinematic experimentation of European art cinema. In its cinematic form, database or modular narrative goes beyond the classical deployment of flashback, offering a series of disarticulated narrative pieces, often arranged in radically achronological ways via flashforwards, overt repetition or a destabilization of the relationship between present and past.

The resurgence of this type of formal experimentation became particularly prominent following the success of Quentin Tarantino's *Pulp Fiction* (1994). It coincided with the wide dispersal of the personal computer and digital consumer technologies throughout the 1990s, and with the rapid growth of the Internet as a cultural medium. While many of the films I discuss do not address such techno-cultural changes directly, digitality has arguably shaped the cultural landscape in which these films are produced and make meaning. As theorists such as Marsha Kinder (2002a) and Lev Manovich (2001b) have argued, the

1

conceptual structure of the digital database has profoundly influenced the way in which we think about narrative. I suggest that contemporary modular narratives, however indirectly, address the rise of the database as a cultural form, while also gesturing towards broader shifts in the conceptualization of time.

The trend towards narrative modularity has traversed mainstream Hollywood and independent and international cinemas, despite the clear differences among these industries. Yet these films do not constitute a new norm in narrative cinema. Rather, it would seem that the majority of both Hollywood and international films follow a narrative structure that is largely traditional and tends towards the chronological. However, the relative popularity of such modular narratives as *Pulp Fiction* and *Memento* (Christopher Nolan, 2000) suggests that audiences are now acclimatized to achronological narrative structures. *Groundhog Day* (Harold Ramis, 1993), for example, demonstrated that a non-linear, iterative structure could be used in the service of a romantic comedy, while the radically fragmented narrative of *21 Grams* (Alejandro González Iñárritu, 2003) was granted the mainstream recognition of two Academy Award nominations in 2004.[1]

Although the pleasure of navigating the narrative structures of these films is undoubtedly central to their appeal, many modular narratives also evoke a mood of temporal crisis by formally enacting a breakdown in narrative order. This mood of crisis is not simply a response to the mediating role of digital technology in contemporary society, or to the rise of the database as a cultural model.[2] It also serves as one of the most recent extensions of a modern and postmodern discourse that continues to rethink the human experience of time in relation to science, technology and social and industrial organization.[3] Paul Ricoeur describes the modernist novels of Marcel Proust, Virginia Woolf and Thomas Mann as 'tales about time', in the sense that they make time the subject of their diegetic and narrational configurations (1984–8, 2:101).[4] Contemporary modular narratives, by extension, are our own 'tales about time'.

Certain modular narratives connect database structures to a crisis of the past, in which both memory and history are refigured as archival materials, subject to easy access but also to erasure: examples include *Memento, Eternal Sunshine of the Spotless Mind* (Michel Gondry, 2004), *Ararat* (Atom Egoyan, 2002) and *Russian Ark* (Aleksandr Sokurov, 2002). Another group, including *21 Grams, Irreversible* (Gaspar Noé, 2002) and *Run Lola Run* (Tom Tykwer, 1998), uses modular narrative structures to highlight the roles of order and contingency in shaping narrative futures. Others query narrative's ability to represent the simultaneous present: in such films as *Code Unknown* (Michael Haneke, 2000) and *Time Code* (Mike Figgis, 2000), disjunctive temporal structure and the spatial segmentation of the screen, respectively, throw into question narrative's attempt to synthesize technologized and/or globalized urban spaces.

Approaching modular narratives

A working definition of narrative might label it the *temporal arrangement of causally linked events*. Note that this definition, although broad, already depends upon the separation of past, present and future. Modular narratives place this separation into question by foregrounding temporal configuration, creating a play among duration, frequency and order. These formal games constitute a departure from 'classical' narrative norms. In particular, they focus attention upon the relationship between story and plot. Adapting the work of Russian formalist critics to a cinematic context, David Bordwell borrows the terms *syuzhet* and *fabula* to describe the construction of narrative. The fabula (or story) 'embodies the action as a chronological, cause-and-effect chain of events occurring within a given duration and a spatial field' (Bordwell 1985, 49). The fabula is never materially present; rather, readers, viewers or auditors construct the fabula 'through assumptions and inferences' (49). The syuzhet (or plot), by contrast, refers to the way the story is presented in the telling; it 'is the actual arrangement and presentation of the fabula in the film' (49).[5] The relationship between syuzhet and fabula is determined by three principles: narrative 'logic' (largely referring to causality), time and space. Bordwell notes that the syuzhet can arrange events (in terms of order, duration or frequency) so as to aid or impede the operations of narrative logic and the construction of fabula time (51).[6]

Theories of classical narrative have an important stake in the relationship between syuzhet and fabula, and place particular emphasis on its stability. The definition of a *classical* narrative can be built upon Aristotle's demands for a structure with a beginning, middle and end, a unified plot and character focus. For Aristotle, a 'well-constructed plot' may not 'begin at some chance point nor end at some chance point' (52). Only events relating to a central, unified plot should be included, and these must form a single progression from beginning to middle to end. Aristotle's injunctions still have currency today, and perhaps nowhere more so than in the world of Hollywood filmmaking.

Aristotle's call for a unified plot is echoed in the popular screenwriting manuals of writers such as Robert McKee (1999) and Syd Field (1994), and in countless script development workshops and readers' reports. In these cases, the recipe for a successful script involves dramatic conflict, a protagonist with clearly defined goals and a narrative 'arc'. These unified elements are generally organized in a 'three-act structure', fulfilling Aristotle's requirement for a clear beginning, middle and end.

This model of unity and order is also described and canonized by Bordwell, Staiger and Thompson in their landmark formal and industrial study *The Classical Hollywood Cinema*, which focusses on Hollywood cinema until 1960. In describing the narrative patterning of Hollywood cinema, they emphasize, like Aristotle, chronology, clarity and forward movement. The spectator of a classical Hollywood film proceeds 'by casting expectations in the form of hypotheses which the text shapes' (Bordwell, Staiger and Thompson 1985, 40). This process is aided by a 'relatively close correspondence between story order and narrational order' (44), in other words between the fabula and the syuzhet. Where the narration departs from story order, it does so in order to integrate the present, past and future in a coherent way, allowing for the forging of causal connections, and thereby facilitating the 'search for meaning' (43). Leaps into the past are generally 'motivated through characters' memory' (30), while flashforwards are avoided altogether (374), as they cancel out narrative suspense: 'Classical narration admits itself to be spatially omnipresent, but it claims no comparable fluency in time. The narration will not move on its own into the past or the future' (30).[7]

Contemporary modular narratives do not adhere to this definition of classical narrative. Many of the films I will be discussing create their narrative effect by structuring the syuzhet in radically achronological, elliptical or repetitive ways. The characteristic structures of modular narratives can be created through temporal fragmentation, through the juxtaposition of conflicting versions of events or through the organization of narrative material by non-narrative principles. In these films, narrational order (presented by the syuzhet) may differ radically from story order (that of the fabula). These divergences may even impede audiences' efforts to establish causal, spatial and temporal relations within the story. In many cases, they offer 'flashforwards' (rare in classical cinema) or flashbacks that are not, strictly speaking, motivated by characters' memories. Arguably, non-narrative spatial and temporal systems are granted a role in structuring these films. In this respect, the term 'modular narrative' could be applied to digital media including computer games, hypertext narratives and the Internet, all of which provide a more literal instance of modularity. It should be emphasized that the films are modular on a *conceptual* level. In a literal sense, they continue to display the linear form that has long been integral to narrative cinema. Nonetheless, these films present themselves as made up of discrete temporal or narrative units, arranged in ways that gesture towards non-linearity.

David Bordwell has argued that complex narratives in contemporary Hollywood cinema should be seen merely as a limited instance of innovation within a system of tradition. Pointing out that mainstream cinema has frequently been overlooked as a source of innovation, he connects these films to Hollywood's past formal movements. 'As with the experiments of the 1940s and 1960s', he comments, 'most storytelling innovations since the 1990s have kept one foot in classical tradition' (2006, 73). He is keen to point out, for example, the way that high levels of redundancy smooth over the narrative disruptions of *Run Lola Run* and *Memento*. Although these comparisons are certainly valid (I dwell on them at greater length in Chapter 2), Bordwell downplays the characteristics that distinguish contemporary examples from their earlier counterparts. Formally, modular narratives go further than the *films noirs* of the 1940s or the French New Wave-influenced Hollywood films of the late 1960s. These films aggressively foreground the relationship between time and narrative, making temporal codes and narrative rules into an important source of audience pleasure.

Furthermore, by focussing his attention more or less exclusively on Hollywood films, Bordwell glosses over a key feature of the contemporary complex narrative, namely its international reach. It is, of course, important to acknowledge the distinct national and industrial contexts in which these films emerge. However, there have been clear formal and thematic parallels among complex narratives produced in different countries. In subsequent chapters, for example, I look closely at modular narratives from France, Germany, Canada and South Korea.[8] Hollywood's modular narratives are closely related to these examples of 'art cinema'. Indeed, the Hollywood examples are both inside and outside mainstream cinema, which continues to produce, as a rule, traditionally conceived and executed stories. In this respect, then, I disagree with Bordwell's contention that 'offbeat storytelling' has become 'part of business as usual' in Hollywood (2006, 73). Finally, Bordwell ignores the way that such modular narratives address broader questions of time and mediation. In the following section, I go on to discuss the formal qualities of the contemporary modular narrative. In the chapters that follow, I will explore the thematics of time articulated through these formal operations.

A typology of the cinematic modular narrative

Although the terms 'modular narrative' and 'database narrative' have been connected with contemporary cinema, most notably by Marsha Kinder (2002a) and Sean Cubitt (2004), attempts at a systematic classification of the formal variations among these films have been tentative at best.[9] Here, I propose a taxonomy of the cinematic modular narrative. Although all of these films can be designated as 'tales about time', it should be noted that the aspects of temporality dealt with by these films are not directly determined by formal factors. The thematics of time therefore cut across formal divisions. Cinematic modular narratives fall into a number of groups, generally taking one (or more) of the following forms: (1) anachronic (involving the use of flashbacks and/or flashforwards), (2) forking paths (invoking divergent or parallel narrative possibilities), (3) episodic (organized as an abstract series or narrative anthology) and (4) split-screen (dividing the narrative flow into parallel, spatially juxtaposed elements).

Anachronic narratives

The most common type of modular narrative is the anachronic modular narrative. Anachronic modular narratives modify the flashback structure of classical Hollywood cinema, undermining the traditional hierarchy between primary and anterior narrative temporality. As narratologist Gérard Genette describes it, anachrony involves a departure from the 'first' temporality of the narrative, a departure that establishes the analepsis (flashback) or prolepsis (flashforward) as 'subordinate' to it (Genette 1980, 48). The first narrative, then, provides a temporal grounding for any secondary narratives. Only in the most extreme cases, such as the work of French novelist Alain Robbe-Grillet, is this hierarchy undermined (49). For example, in Robbe-Grillet's *Jealousy* (originally published in French in 1957), a husband's suspicions regarding his wife's infidelity are conveyed through perspectives that conflate the present and the past, to the point where the reader is unsure whether to view a given scene as dream or reality.

However, recent modular-narrative films display temporal ordering that, while not achieving the disorienting effect of a Robbe-Grillet novel, creates a sense of uncertainty regarding the primacy of one narrative temporality in relation to another. These films destabilize the hierarchy of first narratives and second narratives, so that no one temporal thread is able to establish clear dominance. This distinguishes them from the classical cinema and its use of flashback; rather than simply 'interven[ing] within the present flow of film narrative' (Turim 1989, 2), segments of the past may interrupt the ordering of chrono- logical time, establishing themselves at the head of the hierarchy, or dispensing with it altogether. In some cases, this relationship between present and past is naturalized in mimetic terms (that is, it is coded as subjective, constituting a representation of memory), but this is not always the case. Although Genette acknowledges that complications often occur (an anachrony can become a first narrative in relation to another anachrony nested within it, for instance [1980, 49]), he does not fully account for this particular destabilization, referring only in passing to Robbe-Grillet's 'sabotage' of temporal reference (35). This may have something to do with the fact that he is addressing written narratives, which mark tense directly in the form of language. As Brian Henderson points out, 'Cinema has no built-in tense system' (1983, 6). Thus, anachrony in cinema has a potentially more drastic effect than it does in a literary context. This fact also explains its relative scarcity: while Genette remarks that anachrony is common in literature, Henderson points out that most films display chronological narrative order (1983, 5).

Pulp Fiction (Quentin Tarantino, 1994) provides an example of anachronic modularity. In this film, we follow three stories that overlap in terms of characters, events and time. Each story is assigned a distinct part or 'chapter' within the overall structure. The third of these chapters (excluding the prologue) takes place, in diegetic terms, before the first and second. Thus, the character of Vincent, who is killed in the second chapter, is still alive in the final one. There is no obvious internal moti- vation for this achronological arrangement. As Bordwell, Staiger and Thompson note, classical narrative justifies movements into the past in psychological terms, by presenting flashbacks as the memory of one (or sometimes more) characters (1985, 30). In the case of *Pulp Fiction*, no such justification is offered.

In addition, it is difficult to determine whether the structure of the film is best described in terms of analepsis (flashback) or prolepsis (flashforward). The first major chapter involves Vincent's date with his employer's wife, Mia, and his attempt to deal with the aftermath of her heroin overdose. If we assume that this is the 'first' narrative of the film, then the third chapter can be described as analeptic. In the third chapter, Vincent and his partner Jules must clean up the mess after Vincent accidentally kills a young man they have been holding captive. This episode 'flashes back' to a confrontation Vincent and Jules had at the beginning of Chapter One, in which they kill some young men who owe them money. Effectively, the third chapter fills in the gaps in the first one by showing us more detail regarding the confrontation (in which one young man tries and fails to shoot them), and showing the aftermath of the confrontation (the death of the captive and the subsequent clean-up). It also shows us Vincent and Jules defusing a hold-up at a diner. These events all take place between the two key episodes in Chapter One: the shoot-out and Mia's overdose. This filling in of previous gaps is dubbed 'internal analepsis' by Genette.

However, the temporal orientation of the film changes somewhat if we are prepared to view the film's opening sequence as establishing the primary narrative temporality. In this prologue scene, two British petty criminals hold up a diner. Effectively, this scene establishes the end of the movie (the Mexican stand-off between Jules and the British couple) at the beginning: the final scene is the continuation of the prologue. The opening scene, in story terms, also occurs *after* the confrontation between Vincent, Jules and the young men in the apartment (at the beginning of the first story). Thus, it potentially establishes the latter scene, in Chapter One, as a prolepsis (flashforward). Clearly, there is no way to resolve these temporal questions in a straightforward way. *Pulp Fiction* throws the very notions of analepsis and prolepsis into question through its complex non-linear structure.

Memento (Christopher Nolan, 2000) also employs a non-classical anachronic structure. The film organizes a series of analepses in reverse chronological order, to tell the story of a man with short-term memory loss who is trying to track down his wife's murderer. In this case, the analepses are closer to Bordwell, Staiger and Thompson's definition of a classical flashback, because they are used to represent the main character's short-term memory disorder. Yet in a sense, they are the *inverse* of a classical flashback – rather than showing us what the character remembers, they progressively reveal what he is *unable* to remember. Interpolated between these 'flashbacks' are scenes presented in black and white. These appear to be in linear order, and we later discover that they lead up to the final scene of the film (in terms of the story, this is in fact the earliest of the scenes presented in colour). Yet for most of the film, it is unclear when these scenes are set, and how they relate to the other (colour) scenes. For these reasons, the black-and-white scenes cannot be considered a 'first' narrative. In fact, *Memento*'s disorienting effect depends upon this temporal instability. A similar breakdown in narrative hierarchy is evident in other 'reversed' narratives such as *Irreversible* and *Peppermint Candy* (Lee Chang-dong, 2000), as well as in the 'shuffled' narrative of *21 Grams* (Alejandro González Iñárritu, 2003).

When departing from chronological order, cinema has largely done so in the form of flashbacks (or analepses, in Genette's terms); flashforwards (or prolepses) 'are relatively rare in the novel but they are even rarer in cinema' (Henderson 1983, 5). As Genette points out, prolepsis is at odds with the 'classical' narrative of the nineteenth-century novel, which is concerned with maintaining suspense (1980, 67). *21 Grams* is a cinematic example of narrative prolepsis. The opening of the film darts into the future to show us scenes from the very end of the story as well as from the middle and the beginning. We see the characters Cristina and Paul in bed together (from the latter part of the story), Cristina's husband and children (from the beginning), then Cristina in drug rehabilitation (from the very end of the story). This abrupt movement from past to present to future is a structural feature of the entire film. In terms of classical norms, the most notable aspect of this structure is that we are offered narrative information regarding the end of the film well before the events leading up to it have been established. The classical-era *film noir Sunset Boulevard* (Billy Wilder, 1950), which begins by revealing the main character's death, provides an antecedent of sorts for this approach. However, *Sunset Boulevard*'s brief excursion into the future is heavily regulated: the main character's (post-mortem) voiceover narration establishes the opening scene as a framing device, in relation to which the rest of the film is an explanatory flashback, and very little extra narrative information is communicated via this device. By contrast, the unmotivated, unregulated flashforward associated with European art cinema is, as Bordwell, Staiger and Thompson argue, 'unthinkable' in a classical Hollywood narrative (1985, 374). *21 Grams*, in its use of unmotivated flashforwards, departs from this classical model. Moreover, Genette's notion of a 'first' narrative is, in straightforward terms, unworkable here, because we seem to have equal access to a multitude of times. In practice, the narrative of *21 Grams* (as in the similarly structured *Bad Timing* (Nicolas Roeg, 1980) does not eschew suspense altogether, as it holds back a great deal of narrative information that links together the segments from the present, past and future. Nonetheless, it goes a long way towards undermining the temporal hierarchy of classical narrative.

Anachronic narratives may also repeat scenes, directly or via different perspectives. In cinematic modular narratives, repetition is used to show time elapsing, to allow audiences to establish the temporal order of events, or even to throw such temporal relations into doubt. Arguably, repetition is a building block of narrative: it is certainly an important structuring element in many fairytales, and relations of repetition and variation contribute to most narratives, including filmic ones. Yet classical narrative is opposed to *excessively overt* displays of repetition, as it undermines the linear progression and unity of the story. Certain modular narratives foreground repetition, thereby drawing attention to repeated scenes or situations as discrete elements. These relations of frequency interact in turn with those of order and duration. In *Elephant* (Gus Van Sant, 2003), the events leading up to a high school shooting are visited and revisited in a series of overlapping temporal segments. Thus, certain narrative events are presented from a number of perspectives. In this case, the temporal shifts are not directly motivated by character memory. Although the overall narrative progression moves from the beginning of the day towards the climactic shootings, the various segments are not organized hierarchically.

Forking-path narratives

Some modular narratives create disjunctive leaps, not just between present, past and future, but between alternative temporalities. Commonly, these different versions are introduced via a 'forking paths' conceit. Forking-path narratives juxtapose alternative versions of a story, showing the possible outcomes that might result from small changes in a single event or group of events. Examples include *Groundhog Day* and *Run Lola Run*. Whereas anachronic narratives are modular at the level of the syuzhet (plot), forking-path narratives introduce modularity at the level of the fabula (story). Anachronic narratives generally allow audiences to reconstruct a linear story from the jumbled temporal order of the syuzhet. The forking-path narrative, on the other hand, introduces a number of plotlines that usually contradict one another. It is this type of film that appears to cleave most closely to Marsha Kinder's notion of 'database narrative', which emphasizes 'the selection of particular data (characters, images, sounds, events) from a series of databases or paradigms, which are then combined to generate specific tales' (2002a, 6). If the ordering of plot events can be designated the syntagm, then the paradigm refers to the list of narrative elements that may be selected for presentation in the plot. Whereas anachronic tales generally rearrange plot elements in syntagmatic terms, the multiple draft narrative 'projects' the paradigm 'onto the syntagmatic plane' (Kinder 2002a, 12). The paradigm is made manifest, so that various narrative possibilities are allowed to confront one another in the body of the text.

Figure 1.1   Run Lola Run. Sony Pictures Classics/The Kobal Collection/Bernd Spauke

Recent examples of forking-path narratives tend not to overlap with anachronic structures, although this is not impossible. Flashback has been combined with limited forking-path structure in classical Hollywood cinema (see the 'lying flashback' in Hitchcock's *Stage Fright* [1950]) and, in more emphatic fashion, in high modernist cinema: *Last Year at Marienbad* (Alain Resnais, 1961) offers a variety of conflicting narrative possibilities that are indistinguishable from the characters' memories of past events. Similar examples are rare in the present context, although David Lynch's *Lost Highway* (1997), *Mulholland Drive* (2001) and *Inland Empire* (2006) all venture some way into this territory. Arguably, these and other recent films, including *Donnie Darko* (Richard Kelly, 2001) and *Fight Club* (David Fincher, 1999) create ontological uncertainty between 'subjective' and 'objective' narrative modes. In doing so, they introduce a limited degree of modularity, and blur the boundaries between anachronic and forking-path narratives: we are not always sure whether we are witnessing a memory, a hallucination or an alternative reality.

Run Lola Run combines a forking-path structure with some rapid flashforwards, but these do not play a major part in the core narrative. Nonetheless, anachronic and forking-path narratives share certain qualities. Just as the anachronic narrative invites reflection upon the organization and experience of time (by raising questions around the notions of past, present and future), the forking-path narrative presents us with ways of thinking of time in terms of simultaneity and causal linkage. Rather than dispensing with the temporal, the forking-path narrative allows us to view time at once as linear (a progression from past to present to future), and as non-linear (a selection of parallel possibilities).

Contemporary forking-path narratives can be linked to Jorge Luis Borges's short story 'The Garden of Forking Paths' (first published in English in 1958), which posits a mystery plot riven by multiple bifurcations, as well as to more mainstream fare such as the film *It's a Wonderful Life* (Frank Capra, 1946), in which a man is given a chance to see how the people around him would be affected had he not been born. Forking-path narratives may adhere to the rules of classical narrative to varying degrees. David Bordwell claims that such stories generally limit the potential for audience disorientation by restricting their stories to 'a very, very few options and no ontological differences between the futures displayed' (2002, 91). This sense of order is maintained through the linearity of each narrative thread, the common elements among threads and the use of 'traditional cohesion devices' (95) such as appointments and deadlines that allow us to link scenes spatially, temporally and causally. Furthermore, such narratives offer a sense of closure by privileging the final iteration of the narrative over the earlier versions (100). Kristin Thompson makes a similar argument, suggesting that the looping story of *Groundhog Day* belies the fact that the film is a 'panegyric to linear causality' (1999, 140). However, while it is true that forking-path stories generally fulfil narrative requirements of coherence and causality, both Bordwell and Thompson neglect to address fully their temporal implications.

These films articulate a modular sense of time that is distinct from that of the classical narrative. Significantly, recent forking-path narratives tend not to motivate their iterative structures from within the diegetic world. No guardian angel is deployed, for example, to explain the looping mechanisms of *Run Lola Run* or *Groundhog Day*. *Run Lola Run* follows three alternative paths, with the main character Lola trying in each case to acquire DM 100,000 by noon in order to save her boyfriend Manni. With each iteration of the narrative, a small difference in timing leads to a wildly different outcome: the death of Lola, the death of Manni and, with the final iteration, her success. The same characters and locations show up in each version, allowing us to compare the differences and similarities. Each 'fork' is presented as linear, and events are ordered temporally, spatially and causally. Yet although the film restricts the potential for confusion by heavily regulating each bifurcation and by offering a single definitive ending, its forking-path structure gestures beyond the bounds of the narrative, implying a potentially infinite series of possibilities.

Episodic narratives

Aristotle defined episodic plots as those 'in which the episodes follow one another in no probable or inevitable sequence', and declared these to be 'the worst' of all types of plot (1982, 55). For the purposes of this discussion, 'episodic' refers to structures that critically weaken or disable the causal connections of classical narrative. I propose dividing episodic modular narratives into two groups: abstract series and anthology.

Abstract series

This type of modular narrative is characterized by the operation of a non-narrative formal system which appears to dictate (or at least overlay) the organization of narrative elements. The conventional relationships of narrative time, space and causality may be disrupted by this type of structure, which acts independently or semi-independently of them. The clearest example of this tendency is perhaps the work of Peter Greenaway. In *A Zed and Two Noughts* (1985), the narrative follows two zoologically obsessed brothers, but is organized in relation to an alphabetical list of animals. *Drowning By Numbers* (1988) is also a narrative (it is to do with a woman who has a history of drowning her previous husbands), but the audience's attention is continually drawn to the presence of numbers within the frame, which progress from 1 to 100 throughout the film. In each case, an alphabetical or numerical progression implies a database structure that may not depend strictly upon narrative causality.

This type of structure is not common in mainstream cinema (or contemporary narrative cinema in general). However, there are recent films that gesture towards it. *32 Short Films About Glenn Gould* (Francois Girard, 1993) tells the life story of the Canadian pianist and recording pioneer Glenn Gould in linear fashion, but breaks up the unity of the narrative by structuring it as a series of 32 vignettes that differ radically in style and approach. In these cases, narrative has certainly not been abandoned. However, the use of a database structure foregrounds syntagm (the way the material is ordered) as well as paradigm (the choice of material), and suggests that the material could have been ordered and selected differently.

Anthology

The modular narrative, in its anthology form, consists of a series of shorter tales which are apparently disconnected but turn out to share the same diegetic space. In this case a very fine line separates the modular narrative from the portmanteau film, which simply consists of a collection of short films that are not diegetically connected. In a sense, this type of film marks the outer limit of the modular narrative.

For example, Krzysztof Kieślowski's *Dekalog* (1988–9) is a series of separate stories presented as discrete episodes (this series of ten episodes was originally shown on Polish television). Nonetheless, most of the characters live in or visit the same Warsaw apartment building, and at times characters appear, cameo-fashion, in stories that do not principally concern them. Similarly, in his *Three Colours* trilogy (1993–94), Kieślowski has most of his principal characters appear as survivors of a shipwreck, despite the fact that each of the three narratives is otherwise unconnected to the others. Jim Jarmusch's *Mystery Train* (1989) fits more easily within the category of modular narrative, as the three tales are presented within the context of a single feature-length film, and shows us a variety of characters who cross paths briefly in the same city. In *Night on Earth* (1991) Jarmusch offers us five stories based around five taxi rides in different cities around the world. He links these temporally by presenting us with a series of clocks showing the time in each city. These tenuous links between narratives invite us to think about them both as separate episodes and as a narrative whole.

In another form, this type of modular narrative takes on a forking structure, with each new narrative segment emerging from the last. However, unlike the forking-path narratives described above, this type of film does not linger over alternative versions. For example, in *Slacker* (Richard Linklater, 1991), we follow a character for a few minutes before branching off to follow another. Although the emphasis is on temporal flow, in narrative terms the film is made up of a series of short, virtually self-contained segments. Similarly, *Chungking Express* (Wong Kar-wai, 1994) uses a forking-path device to connect two unconnected stories of lovelorn cops. The protagonist of the first episode walks past a young woman who will play an important role in the romantic plot of the second episode. Apart from this chance encounter, and certain similarities between the two plotlines, they are otherwise not linked. A similar structure is evident in the Iranian film *The Circle* (Jafar Panahi, 2000).

Recent years have seen a number of films deploying several main plotlines within the same film. Such films as *Short Cuts* (Robert Altman, 1993) and *Magnolia* (Paul Thomas Anderson, 1999) follow a large number of loosely connected characters without privileging one narrative thread over the others. This type of structure might be considered a relatively recent departure for cinema, if one excludes such notable exceptions as *Intolerance* (D.W. Griffith, 1916), *Grand Hotel* (Edmund Goulding, 1932) and *Nashville* (Robert Altman, 1975). Yet one might also suggest that these narratives are consistent with the tradition of *literary* narrative unity. For example, George Eliot's *Middlemarch* (1872), perhaps the quintessential example of the realist novel, incorporates a large number of protagonists and plotlines. The key difference between *Middlemarch* and contemporary multiple-protagonist films is the looseness of the character and plot connections in the latter group. It is a long way, one must admit, from the small community of *Middlemarch* to the sprawling, disconnected Los Angeles of Altman's *Short Cuts*. Yet by interleaving the stories in fluid fashion, these films downplay modular form. In films such as *Night on Earth*, by contrast, the discrete nature of each episode places the disconnectedness of the fabula (story) on the level of the syuzhet (plot). For this reason, films such as *Magnolia* and *Short Cuts* should not be considered modular narratives, even though they bear some elements in common.

Split-screen narratives

Split-screen narratives are distinct from the other types of modular narrative discussed here, because their modularity is articulated along spatial rather than temporal lines. These films divide the screen into two or more frames, juxtaposing concurrent or anterior events within the same visual field. Here, I am including films that pursue this formal path in a sustained fashion, as opposed to those films that display multiple frames briefly or sporadically, such as *Blow Out* (Brian de Palma, 1981) or *The Boston Strangler* (Richard Fleischer, 1968). Although experimental films have long made use of split-screen aesthetics, it is rare in narrative cinema. One conspicuous example is the film *Time Code* (Mike Figgis, 2000), which follows a number of characters simultaneously by splitting the screen into four quadrants. In this case, each quadrant consists largely of a single shot unbroken by edits of any kind. This durational aesthetic is far removed, in the formal sense, from the temporal segmentation of most modular narratives. Yet the spatial modularity of such split-screen narratives allows for an exploration of such temporal concerns as memory and simultaneity (*Time Code* is particularly concerned with the latter). As its title suggests, *Time Code* is, as much as any of the films discussed here, a tale about time. Other examples include *AKA* (Duncan Roy, 2002), which is designed to be projected on three screens simultaneously, and *Pretend* (Julie Talen, 2003), which employs a shifting array of split-screen techniques in order to tell the story of two children who fake a disappearance in order to bring their parents back together.

Modular narratives as tales about time

In pursuing the temporal thematics of the modular narrative, this study will cut at an angle across the formal designations detailed above. While some formal categories may lend themselves to certain themes (for example, anachronic narratives are particularly suited to the representation of memory), the correspondences are not direct or straightforward. This thematic exploration also produces intersections with the temporal discourse of modernism and postmodernism. I will be suggesting that modular narratives are a particular instance of narrative in the postmodern era, but that they display strong connections with the formal and thematic concerns of the modernists.[10] Here, the intention is not to argue for the emergence of a 'neo-modern' aesthetic, but to demonstrate the way that ostensibly 'modernist' concerns have persisted and developed within the postmodern. By extension, this argument challenges the notion of a distinct 'rupture' between the modern and postmodern. At the same time, these narratives are closely linked with the rise of digital media. In some cases, this connection surfaces explicitly within the diegesis; in others, digitality can be seen as part of the cultural backdrop that has endowed modular narratives with their cultural currency and legibility. Indeed, what is notable about these films is not so much that they mark a new departure in narrative aesthetics (in most cases, they are more formally conservative than their modernist predecessors), but that they signal the point at which these aesthetics have been accepted by popular culture at large.

Any study of narrative and temporality must confront the variety of theoretical approaches that have been applied in this area. In broad terms, this work is grounded in the structural analysis of narrative, but also reads beyond structure, showing the way that these films articulate complex ideas regarding time and narrative. Furthermore, my approach takes into account postmodernism and post-structuralism's interrogation of narrative, and the more recent efforts of new media theorists either to reject narrative in favour of other structural models, or to enshrine it as the goal of new media's aesthetic aspirations. In considering the implications of the modular narrative in relation to time and narrative, this book will also initiate encounters with theories of memory, identity, temporality and globalization.

This book's particular contribution is therefore based upon a combination of formal analysis with theoretical approaches to narrative, time, culture and technology. In this sense, formal and conceptual categories cut across each other at an angle, offering a perspective on the way that certain formal approaches may have distinct implications across a variety of conceptual zones. While other articles and books have dealt with aspects of these films, most have tended to focus on a relatively narrow area: addressing formal factors only, drawing easy causal links with new media or engaging with an isolated theoretical paradigm (Deleuzian theories spring to mind). By contrast, this work aims to create a broader set of connections among the formal, the technological and the theoretical, focussed around the question of temporal representation.

In Chapter 2, I argue that modular narratives' overt play with narrative form offers audiences an analytic perspective on narrative that is also, in a number of films, figured as an analytic perspective on time itself. This perspective offers both a sense of pleasure and of crisis, and positions modular narratives within a formal and discursive history extending from the early twentieth century to the present day. I suggest that these modular narratives make the analytic perspective the object of both challenge and reconciliation. In doing so, they suggest a new, modular temporal mode that both overtakes and combines with the subjective and schismatic modes associated with modern and postmodern literature and cinema. The following chapters explore the implications of this analytic perspective for conceiving of the past, present and future.

Chapter 3 explores the way that such modular narratives as *21 Grams*, *Irreversible* and *Run Lola Run* address the possibility of conceiving of the future by raising questions of contingency and order. The narrative structures of these films invoke determinism by offering the ending of the story at the beginning, but also mimic the unpredictable, chaotic movements of contingency. Contingency in these films is associated both with the violent chance events that befall the characters, and with the open possibilities offered by chance encounters and free, unstructured time. These formal and thematic negotiations are related to the modernists' elevation of narrative contingency for its resistance to rationalized, industrialized time, and to postmodern explorations of chaos and order. Here, modular narrative becomes a vehicle for reconciling narrative order and meaning with the threat and promise of the chaotic.

Modular representations of memory are the main focus of Chapter 4. Drawing upon Andreas Huyssen's notion of 'temporal anchoring', I suggest that certain contemporary modular narratives are concerned with memory's ability to orient the subject in time. In *Eternal Sunshine of the Spotless Mind* and *Memento*, memory is placed into crisis, in one case by a technologized erasure process, and in the other by physical injury. In both cases, the modular narrative structure attempts to represent the fracturing of memory experienced by the characters, but also sets up a formal game addressed towards the audience. This self-conscious attention to questions of representation establishes an interplay among narrative, memory and forgetting. *Eternal Sunshine* insists upon the necessity of temporal anchoring in the digital era, even as it displays an attraction to digital technology's ability to invoke temporal drift and romantic forgetting. *Memento*, by comparison, is concerned with *pragmatic* forgetting, which enables the main character to establish a modular subjectivity.

Chapter 5 builds upon the previous chapter's discussion of memory to examine the way that such films as *Russian Ark* and *Ararat* use modular structures to examine history's status as narrative. In doing so, they suggest that history, like memory, is unstable and mutable. Again, forgetting plays a dual role, both aiding with the establishment of narrative order, and working to disarticulate temporal relations. In these films, the dialectic between temporal anchoring and floating time is made manifest in the references to water and land, and to the image of the ark as archive. The ark/archive, as a repository for cultural and ethnic memory, raises questions regarding the narrative structure underpinning identity. These films affirm the notion of national or communal identity, while acknowledging in their very narrative structures the disjunctive processes that produce it.

Certain modular narratives, I argue in Chapter 6, utilize a modular aesthetic in order to represent coexisting spaces and narrative threads. Here, the modernist discourse regarding the relationship between simultaneity and succession is renovated for the era of globalization, digital technology and omnipresent surveillance. Focussing on the episodic narration of *Code Unknown* and the split-screen narration of *Time Code*, I show the way that both films combine long-take and modular aesthetics to explore the codes that structure temporal experience. At stake in both films, as indicated by the presence of the word 'code' in the title, is the notion of time as a communicable dimension. Exploring alternative (technological, linguistic and musical) modes of temporal mediation, *Code Unknown* and *Time Code* reach differing conclusions regarding narrative's suitability as a temporal code.

Finally, Chapter 7 addresses a number of new media works that directly address the representation of time by engaging with cinematic temporality. I argue that these multilinear structures do not simply supersede 'linear' cinematic time, but enter into complex relations with it. Collectively, they touch upon many of the key concerns of cinematic modular narratives, including chaos and order, memory and history and simultaneity and succession. Ultimately, these works may suggest a ghostly afterlife for cinematic narrative time.

Contemporary cinematic modular narratives explore different aspects of the representation of time. In particular, they articulate anxieties regarding the relationships between present and past, present and future, and even between different versions of the present. In this respect, they constitute the most recent iteration of a fraught temporal discourse that established itself with the advent of the modern era and has developed throughout the postmodern. With the digital era comes a new set of possibilities and anxieties regarding temporal representation. Cinematic modular narratives, then, both reflect and respond to changes in our perspectives on time and space, and constitute a valuable tool for analysing the role of narrative in contemporary culture.

2

The Shape of Narrative Time: Subjective, Schismatic and Modular

Modular narratives, by directly foregrounding their formal articulation of narrative temporality, invite comparison with earlier and concurrent developments in the representation of time. In this chapter, I plot a course through the modern and postmodern approaches to time, suggesting the ways in which modular narratives both take up and depart from these approaches. Although the connections between modular narratives and their forebears are at times indirect, these separate movements are profoundly linked by the way they reflect and respond to changes in the experience of time wrought by technological and social shifts. In broad terms, I suggest that the literary and cinematic tradition of temporal representation has undergone a series of changes throughout the twentieth century. It is possible to discern three modern phases in narrative temporality, each querying the relationship between time and narrative. The early modernists tended to oppose the mysterious movements of private, subjective time to the analytically defined, measurable parameters of public time. Certain later modernists, by contrast, articulate a schismatic temporality, in which time loses its human dimension and becomes indecipherable and fractured. Finally, contemporary modular narratives explore an emergent modular temporality, in which time is regarded analytically. This analytic perspective on time not only reconfigures past narrative innovations from cinema and literature; it also displays formal parallels with electronic media. I argue, therefore, that the increasing prominence of digital media technologies accompanies a further examination of time in relation to representation, and offers another chance to articulate the concomitant crises and opportunities.

In approaching the modular narrative, it is necessary to avoid two potential misreadings of its contextual significance: the first of these involves overstating the novelty of these narrative forms, and the second involves dismissing them as a straightforward recycling of forms from the past. It is important to emphasize what links the modular narrative to its antecedents, as well as what distinguishes it from them. In regarding the relationships among the modular narrative, its modernist forebears, and concurrent developments in digital media, it is possible to identify an emergent conception of time that builds upon and renovates earlier models. This emergent modular temporality, however, should not be viewed as an unprecedented phenomenon; rather, it has its roots in modernist ideas regarding space and time, and is a further development of those ideas. Furthermore, the analytic perspective associated with many contemporary narratives does not make subjective or schismatic models obsolete; rather, it is entwined with these earlier modes and can favour one or the other to varying degrees. Cinematic modular narratives chart the interactions among modular, schismatic and subjective time in a variety of ways, often implying divergent conclusions as to the threats and pleasures of modular time and the relative value of narrative as a temporal code.

By exploring the recent history of narrative time, this chapter reflects upon the changing uses and connotations of formal non-linearity. Non-linearity, in this context, can be understood as the departure from chronological time and/or narrative causality. In terms of the digital era, it signifies the ability to access segments of represented time instantly, as with a DVD or computer file. In plotting a trajectory of non-linearity's associations through modernism and postmodernism, one observes a shifting emphasis between connotations of liberation on the one hand, and connotations of schism, paranoia and disorder, on the other. The non-linear treatment of time in modular narratives thus varies between the schismatic and the schematic, between fragmentation and segmentation. However, coincident with the adoption of non-linear narrative forms by popular cinema is an overall tendency towards the latter term in each of these pairs. In other words, contemporary modular narratives tend to reconcile themselves with an analytic perspective on time.

Narrative complexity and the operational aesthetic

Modular narratives' analytic perspective on time can, first of all, be contextualized in relation to a broader acceptance of complex narrative forms in contemporary media. Certainly, there are earlier examples of narrative structures that embellish or go beyond linearity. Geoffrey Chaucer's *Canterbury Tales* (c. 1387–1400), for example, consists of a series of separate stories recounted by characters on a pilgrimage.

Similarly, the Middle Eastern epic *The Book of One Thousand and One Nights* (c. 850) builds upon a structure of serial recounting. Classical Chinese literature offers a further alternative to the unity and linearity of Western narratives. In *Dream of the Red Chamber* (c. 1760) the story of the Chia family is rendered as an interlinked series of micro-narratives, in which we follow certain characters (family members, servants or associates) for a chapter or two before moving on to another narrative thread. One can detect broader patterns in the story (such as the rise and fall of the family's fortunes) and some characters are more prominent than others. Nonetheless, the story never resolves itself firmly into a hierarchical structure in which subplots are decisively subordinated to a single unified action or central character. Among Western narratives of more recent vintage, *The Life and Opinions of Tristram Shandy, Gentleman* (Laurence Sterne, 1759–69) is one of the most famously convoluted. The titular character attempts to recount his life story, but is constantly sent off course by a series of comic digressions, to the point where narrative form almost overtakes narrative content as the centre of interest. The episodic or divergent dimension of these earlier examples, however, is distinct from more recent narrative developments. Contemporary modular narratives belong in a modern context, in which storytelling as a practice and tradition can no longer be taken for granted after the narrative convulsions of literary modernism. There is a quite distinct sense that, with the advent of the modern, conventional narrative forms were not sufficient to cope with the synchronic complexity of contemporary life. As I argue here, however, current examples encourage audiences to view narrative structures with an analytic formal eye and to take pleasure in these formal workings.

The contemporary media landscape offers an unprecedented profusion of narrative material. Yet it should not be assumed that narrative is disabled in this context; rather, it overflows its traditional containers and is multiplied across media, from commercials to video games. Audiences are thus, I suggest, hypersensitized to the rules and forms of narrative. If contemporary media texts display a tendency to expose the mechanics of narrative, then this does not necessarily produce a modernist 'rupture' or a critical perspective upon narrative itself. Rather, such games can produce new types of narrative pleasure. Writing on the growth of complex plots and story situations in contemporary television, Jason Mittel argues that many contemporary narratives foster an 'operational aesthetic', in which audiences take pleasure not only in the story but in the technical craft through which the story is conveyed (2006, 35).[1] Mittel sees a similar formal game played out in 'puzzle films'. He includes under this designation such films as *The Sixth Sense* (M. Night Shyamalan, 1999), *Pulp Fiction* (Quentin Tarantino, 1994), *Memento* (Christopher Nolan, 2000), *The Usual Suspects* (Bryan Singer, 1995), *Adaptation* (Spike Jonze, 2002), *Eternal Sunshine of the Spotless Mind* (Michel Gondry, 2004) and *Run Lola Run* (Tom Tykwer, 1998). Although he does not unify these films according to specific formal parameters, Mittel suggests that they embrace 'a game aesthetic, inviting audiences to play along with the creators to crack the interpretive codes to make sense of their complex narrative strategies' (38). In this way, an analytic perspective on narrative is reconciled with a more traditional immersion in the storyworld: 'we want to enjoy the machine's results while also marveling at how it works' (38). This perspective on narrative traverses a number of story types, all of which overlap with the formal category of the modular narrative.

To the puzzle films identified by Mittel, one can add the related category of the 'psychological puzzle' films in which 'the deceptive narration is a manifestation of an aspect of the protagonist's mind' (Panek 2006, 86). Examples of this type would include *Fight Club* (David Fincher, 1999), *Identity* (James Mangold, 2003), *The Jacket* (John Maybury, 2005), *The Butterfly Effect* (Eric Bress and J. Mackye Gruber, 2004), *Donnie Darko* (Richard Kelly, 2001), *Waking Life* (Richard Linklater, 2001), *Jacob's Ladder* (Adrian Lyne, 1990), *12 Monkeys* (Terry Gilliam, 1995), *Pi* (Darren Aronofsky, 1999), *Open Your Eyes* (Alejandro Amenábar, 1997), *Lost Highway* (David Lynch, 1997), *Mulholland Drive* (David Lynch, 2001) and *Memento*. Not all of these definitively display a modular structure (some cleave more closely to the 'deceptive flashbacks' of *film noir*, for example), yet all display a modular tendency, in which story elements and events are imbued with a high degree of uncertainty, and are subject to revision and rearticulation. For example, in *Identity* a series of murders takes place in a cheap motel. Later in the film, it is revealed that the characters, victims and perpetrator alike, are all multiple personalities in the mind of a psychopath. The schematic nature of the plot is emphasized by the numbered room keys that are discovered near each of the victims, a gesture reminiscent of the enumerative pattern in Peter Greenaway's *Drowning by Numbers* (1988). Like Mittel, Elliot Panek describes puzzle films as allowing audiences to inhabit a dual perspective, both immersed in the story and observing it from the outside. He also, like Mittel, emphasizes the game element in these works. Thus, these films do not simply represent the mental instability of their protagonists; they also invite us to 'take pleasure in trying to figure out the rules of the narration that presents the story to us' (87). In the case of *Identity*, the psychoanalytic explanation offered by the killer's psychiatrist serves more to reveal the film's narrative game than to offer a genuine character revelation. In this respect, the film contrasts with Hitchcock's *Psycho* (1960), in which the motel killer's neurosis is helpfully explained for the characters and the audience by a psychiatrist at the end of the film. In *Identity*, both the narration and character subjectivity itself are transformed into a game.

Modular narratives also overlap with other prominent story types, all of which may invite an analytic focus on narrative form: multiple protagonist films, time travel films and metafictions. Multiple protagonist narratives such as *Magnolia* (Paul Thomas Anderson, 1999) and *Syriana* (Stephen Gaghan, 2005), for example, create dense networks of relationships among characters, events and locations, so that viewers must exert focussed analytic effort to resolve them. For the most part, however, these films do not pursue a modular temporal structure. Notable exceptions include *21 Grams* (Alejandro González Iñárritu, 2003), *Pulp Fiction* and *Babel* (Alejandro González Iñárritu, 2006). Initially, *Babel* allows its viewers to assume that its network of globally connected tales is unfolding in a linear temporal mode, until a phone call near the end of the film reveals that the separate plot lines are not contemporaneous. Time travel films also overlap with modular narratives, although most tend not to exploit the inherent possibilities for disjuncture and confusion (see *The Time Machine* [George Pal, 1960], *Back to the Future* [Robert Zemeckis, 1985] and the *Terminator* films [James Cameron, 1984 and 1991, and Jonathan Mostow, 2003]). *12 Monkeys* and *Primer* (Shane Carruth, 2004), by contrast, are genuine modular narratives, in which the mechanics of story are exposed by their protagonists' movements through time. Indeed, these films appear to suggest that narrative itself may be unable to contain such traumatic temporal upheavals. Finally, modular narratives are closely connected to the tradition of metafictional narrative. Recent films such as *American Splendor* (Shari Springer Berman and Robert Pulcini, 2003), *Adaptation* and *Suzhou River* (Lou Ye, 2000) tell stories within stories, engaging overtly with the process of narration. These films are related to earlier cinematic examples such as *The French Lieutenant's Woman* (Karel Reisz, 1981), *Céline and Julie Go Boating* (Jacques Rivette, 1974) and *The Saragossa Manuscript* (Wojciech Has, 1965), all of which are related in turn to the literary metafictions of Borges, Fowles, Cortazar and Calvino. By definition, metafictions tend heavily towards a modular aesthetic, in which fragments of story are linked, separated and rearticulated via the formal operations of the narration. As with the puzzle films described earlier, viewers may find themselves both inside and outside the story, taking pleasure in its operational aesthetic.

In relation to these various modes of narrative complexity in contemporary cinema, all of which foster an analytic perspective on *narrative*, I argue that modular narratives also deploy an analytic perspective on *time*. On the whole, anachronic, forking path, episodic and multiscreen modular narratives go further than their complex counterparts in separating time and narrative. As I will argue, they do so in a way that is both related to and distinct from earlier literary and cinematic experiments with time. These films test the limits of narrative's hold upon time, through operations of segmentation, resequencing and repetition, while encouraging us to view time itself as a type of information. In many of these films, the syntagmatic structure of the plot seems dictated by external forces rather than motivated by the internal demands of the story. There is the sense, at least, of an external logic that exceeds the requirements of conventional storytelling (even if such requirements are ultimately satisfied). Whatever their relative merits in other respects, these films represent some of the best attempts to come to terms with the experience of temporality in contemporary culture.

Amongst the films that I go on to discuss in later chapters, there is a persistent concern with the mediation of time. This mediation includes technological mediation (films, photographs and digital media) but also the less tangible mediation offered by the codes and measurements that orchestrate the simultaneity of urban and global spaces (actualized in turn through technology). By foregrounding such codes and systems, these films invite a questioning of narrative's claim upon time. They play upon the notion that narrative itself may be simply another form of temporal mediation, by foregrounding the mediating function of structure. Thus, the operational aesthetic described above also functions to reveal the narrative mechanics of temporal mediation. Writing about the parallel development of industrial technologies and modernist literary techniques, David Nye argues that 'the inseparability of machines and modern narratives ... suggests that most fiction has a technological underpinning, even if it is not explicit' (1997, 180). I suggest, in turn, that modular narratives tend to make explicit, to varying degrees, the technological underpinnings of the narrative mechanism. As Nye points out, such an argument is based not upon technological determinism but upon the notion that 'machines are social constructions' that modern societies have embedded in both their narratives and their sense of place (1). In this way, both narratives and new technologies reveal much about the shape of temporality in contemporary society. Modular narratives reflect upon the contemporary experience of (mediated) time, but also themselves mediate temporal experience, contributing to the ways in which we conceptualize time. These are not simply facile 'zeitgeist' arguments. Rather, they suggest that technological and sociocultural changes are driven by relations of mutual causality. My argument is, therefore, that modular narratives reveal both the projection of subjectivity into the domain of technology and the projection of technology into the domain of narrative. Thus, the uptake of modular narrative structures has implications both for the representation of character psychology, and for the representation of technology as a disruptive or bonding force.

In this context, the term 'modular' may have different resonances. On the one hand, it is a technical concept based in engineering, denoting a system in which the parts can be rearranged with maximum efficiency and flexibility. On the other, it may also be associated with the 'rhizome', which Deleuze and Guattari identify as a non-hierarchical structure resistant to systemic laws and controls (1987, 7). These two denotations are in conflict, because the former is predicated upon systemic control while the latter emphasizes resistance and unpredictability. In the first instance, my use of the term 'modular' is inspired at least in part by Lev Manovich's characterization of new media as modular (2001). Manovich's description is both a formal and a technological one, and it cleaves closely to the systemic modularity covered by the first denotation. In this sense, I am (with Manovich) referring to a technologically based system allowing both control and flexibility. It is worth noting, however, that the Deleuzian approach to modularity is a conspicuous thread both in techno-cultures and in techno-theories. In other words, technological modularity is often tied together with rhizomatic modularity, while the mutual tension between them is overlooked. The tension between these two notions of modularity is, I would argue, a central animating force in contemporary narrative cinema. One of the most interesting things about these films is the way that they oscillate between instability and uncertainty on the one hand, and schematic structures on the other. I further explore this pattern of oscillation in the later chapters, which investigate, for example, the modular narrative's contradictory impulses towards order and chaos, towards temporal anchoring and temporal drift. It is also worth noting that the term modular, when applied to narrative, is not a straightforward and literal fit. Although all of these films foreground their narrative seams, suggesting that the story might have been assembled in a number of different ways, most of them obey a set of narrative rules (however minimal) that are predicated upon a degree of linearity. Thus, there is another tension in play here, between the demands of narrative sequence and the formal impulse towards a non-linear articulation of time.

By placing an emphasis upon literary and cinematic precursors of the modular narrative, I suggest that literature and cinema are key zones for conceptualizing time and space. Cinema, it may be argued, is a particularly interesting zone, because of its technological grounding: it expresses narrative and subjective temporality through the machine-time of the camera/projector and the technical means of the flashback. In the following sections, I argue that certain strands within literature and cinema over the past century explore and sometimes challenge narrative's role as the privileged medium for temporal representation. Contemporary modular narratives allow their characters and their viewers to take pleasure and solace in the manipulation of time, but also associate such manipulation with crises of narrative order, history and subjectivity. In many cases, modular narratives attempt to reconcile the notion of time as information with more traditional types of human-centred temporality (including narrative and the experience of duration). More specifically, they display the interactions among three distinct but intertwined temporal modes: subjective, schismatic and modular.

Modern temporality and non-linear narrative

The question of time and temporal experience has been a particularly persistent concern since the advent of modernity in the late nineteenth century, and it is a concern that emerges in the thematic and formal workings of modernist literature. The dawning of the industrial era had ushered in a series of drastic changes in the ways that time and space were conceived. The development of the wireless, the telephone, the cinema and also high-speed printing presses linked disparate spaces in a single moment, fostering a heightened awareness of simultaneity (Kern 1983, 68). Meanwhile, increased global trade and travel offered Europeans and Americans a perspective on different cultures and their ways of thinking about time, thereby challenging the universality of Western conceptions of time (34–5). In addition, Einstein's special and general theories of relativity (1905, 1916) suggested that time itself could run at different speeds depending upon the velocity of a given reference system. Yet the predominant modern discourse was predicated upon a division between two types of time: public (linear) and private (non-linear). Whereas public time continued to be thought of as homogeneous and continuous, private time came to be seen as heterogeneous and multiple. This division was reinforced by the introduction of World Standard Time, which synchronized global time in order to better enable the conduct of trade, communication and transport.[2]

By contrast, the modernist novel epitomized by the work of Marcel Proust, James Joyce and Virginia Woolf emphasized the workings of private temporal experience, and its divergence from rational, linear social temporality (Heise 1997, 36). Woolf, for example, announced her wish to 'go beyond "the formal railway line of a sentence"', declaring Aristotelian narrative theory, and the conventional ordering of beginning, middle and end, to be a thing of the past (Kern 1983, 31).[3] In Marcel Proust's *A la récherche du temps perdu* (*In Search of Lost Time*, 1913–27), the time of the narrator, Marcel, 'moves at an irregular pace that is repeatedly out of phase with that of the other characters and defies reckoning by any standard system' (Kern 1983, 16). The narrative uses iterative descriptions which telescope different instances of the same action, and complex analeptic structures, including flashbacks within flashbacks. In Joyce's *Ulysses* (1922), the story takes place over the course of a single day, while Joyce gives us a minutely detailed account of the character Leopold Bloom's thoughts and feelings. However, time extends outwards from the present via Bloom's internal monologues and references to the scope of cosmic time. In formal terms, varied textual rhythms and prose styles serve as a formal analogue for the heterogeneity of temporal experience. As with Proust, temporal discontinuity is an important narrative element. Approaching a brothel, notes Kern, Leopold Bloom 'steps back to avoid a street cleaner and resumes his course forty pages and a few seconds later' (31). These works, then, articulate a temporality that is more complex and heterogeneous than that of the public sphere.

In their formal articulations, these works can be identified as 'tales about time' in two respects: one theoretically grounded, and one historically grounded. Philosopher and theorist Paul Ricoeur uses this term to describe the fiction of Proust, Woolf and Thomas Mann. Whereas all fictional narratives show the effect of 'structural transformations' on characters and situations over time (making them 'tales in time'), these 'tales about time' are distinctive because 'in them it is the very experience of time that is at stake in these structural transformations' (Ricoeur 1984–8, 2:101). Each of these novels explores 'uncharted modes of discordant concordance, which no longer affect just the narrative composition but also the lived experience of the characters in the narrative' (101). By connecting Ricoeur's ideas to the historically grounded analysis of Kern and Heise one can suggest that these novels are not only tales about time but also tales about *modern* time.

Concurrent with the development of these new modes of narrative was the emergence of cinema as a popular medium. Indeed, certain novelists (including James Joyce) were inspired by the formal possibilities of cinema, which refigured time through such techniques as montage, camera tricks and backwards projection (Kern 1983, 29).[4] From the twentieth century's second decade, filmmakers, like their literary counterparts, began to explore the narrative possibilities of the flashback. The flashback appears as a narrative device in a number of early American films, including D.W. Griffith's *The Birth of a Nation* (1915). Subsequently, European and Japanese filmmakers began to experiment with the flashback's potential for representing mental processes. For the German Expressionists, the flashback tended to work along psychoanalytic lines, as in *The Cabinet of Dr Caligari* (Robert Wiene, 1919), in which a concluding segment reframes the preceding events as the visions of a madman in an asylum. French and Japanese filmmakers, by contrast, used the flashback in a more poetic, associative mode (Turim 1989, 101). *A Page of Madness* (Kinugasa Teinosuke, 1926), for example, also represents mental illness, but its temporal leaps and reversals are not made legible by a symptomatic reading and therefore retain their poetic sense of mystery. Like their literary counterparts, these filmmakers linked temporal shifts closely to subjective processes.

This tendency was borne out by mainstream narrative cinema. The possibilities of the flashback were explored at various times by the Classical Hollywood cinema, but most emphatically in the period between 1941 and 1955. For example, Orson Welles's *Citizen Kane* (1941) offers the life story of its main character told as a series of flashbacks, from the perspectives of a variety of characters, and linked by a frame-narrative (a journalist's investigation of Kane's life) set in the diegetic present. During this period, a number of *films noirs* evoked a sense of psychological crisis by moving backwards and forwards in time, sometimes in quite complex ways that could include flashbacks within flashbacks or even 'lying' flashbacks, as in *Stage Fright* (Alfred Hitchcock, 1950). *The Killing* (Stanley Kubrick, 1956) tells the tale of a bank heist gone wrong via a series of flashbacks, cued overtly by voiceover, dialogue cues, facial close-ups and optical effects (Bordwell, Staiger and Thompson 1985, 43). For David Bordwell, the fashion for psychologically motivated flashbacks during this period is connected to a 'changing conception of psychological causality' at the time, and in particular to an 'increasing interest in vulgarized Freudian psychology' (43). For the great majority of these flashback films, analeptic (flashback or flashforward) sequences are followed by a return to the framing narrative.[5] Linguistic, visual or musical cues all allow these classical films to make temporal transitions without disorienting audiences. Crucially, they also anchor temporal shifts in character psychology.

By contrast, cinematic modular narratives often make transitions without overtly signifying a temporal shift or anchoring such a shift subjectively. For example, in *21 Grams* the shifts between present, past and future are presented in disjunctive fashion, with nothing to signify their temporal relationships other than our knowledge of the events. This technique is potentially more disruptive than novelistic time-shifts, because cinema, unlike language, lacks a direct means of marking tense (Henderson 1983, 6). In classical Hollywood cinema, 'the cut to another sequence is read as straight chronological order, unless otherwise marked' (6). Contemporary audiences, however, cannot make sense of modular narratives by assuming a direct relation between plot succession and narrative chronology. The contemporary modular narrative shares *film noir*'s exploration of temporal experience, but in formal terms it comes closer to the experimental narratives of literary and filmic modernism. It would be stretching the links too far to suggest that modular narratives in general draw *directly* upon modernist literature for formal inspiration. However, both bodies of work respond to ongoing changes in the personal and social experience of time and space. Just as the modern novel was implicated in a dialogue regarding the changes to time and space wrought by industrialization, the modular narrative in its own way reflects upon time in the digital era. Later movements, however, have tended to depart from the modernists' affirmation of subjective time in the face of public time's analytic perspective.

Schismatic form and the limits of narrative

Modular narratives are closely related to subsequent developments in the modern and postmodern discourse relating to time, a discourse characterized by an increasing emphasis upon temporal schism. In particular, modular narratives bear much in common with the narrative experiments of 1950s and 60s literature and cinema, which straddle the ambiguous boundary-line between received definitions of 'modern' and 'postmodern' art.[6] For the purposes of this argument, it should be noted that a broad consensus links most accounts of the role of time in late modernist and postmodernist art and literature. This consensus coheres around the notion of schismatic temporality. In this respect, my aim here is to suggest an underlying thematic continuity between the two periods, rather than an abrupt disjuncture. Frank Kermode, in his landmark 1967 book *The Sense of an Ending*, points towards a tendency in mid-to late-modernist literature (or 'new modernism', as he calls it) to represent time in terms of schism. The new modernism is distinguished from the older version by its differing attitude to the past: 'To the older it is a source of order; to the newer it is that which ought to be ignored' (Kermode 1967, 115). While contemporary modular narratives function within a cultural environment that might still be identified as 'postmodern', they can also be linked to the formal games of this late or 'new' modernism.

The sense of temporal rupture in Kermode's definition of the new modernism is similar to that found in later theorizations of the *postmodern*, perhaps most notably in Fredric Jameson's formulation, in which temporal rupture has become a cultural way of life.[7] Indeed, Jameson argues that temporal experience has become schizophrenic, in the Lacanian sense of 'a breakdown in the signifying chain', in which signifiers are unmoored from their customary order, producing a 'mirage of signification' (26). The temporal unification of past, present and future (and, by extension, identity itself) is radically undermined by this breakdown of order, which presents experience as 'a series of pure and unrelated presents in time' (27). This postmodern crisis of time can also be linked, argues Ursula Heise, to a general 'shortening of temporal horizons' since the 1960s and a growing awareness of time-scales beyond immediate human experience (1997, 6–7). The shortening of temporal horizons is produced by postmodern culture's insistence on the present as the true locus of experience, and is aided by the instantaneity of global communications networks and television (25). Similarly, Helga Nowotny goes so far as to suggest that 'the temporal category of the future is being abolished and replaced by that of the extended present' (1994, 51; see also Hayles 1990 and Jameson 1991). The sense of alternative temporalities derives from the scientific revelation of time-scales that lie outside of human experience, 'from the nanoseconds of the computer to the billions of years in which contemporary cosmology calculates the age of the earth and the universe' (Heise 1997, 7). On the one hand, time appears to lose its sense of flow; on the other, it exceeds human experience and understanding altogether; human time is 'dwarfed in importance compared to the realm of the very large and the extremely small' (40), while computerization removes technological time from the realm of human perception (44). These phenomena can be described in terms of a hypertrophy of the analytic perspective on time, in which time viewed analytically becomes unassimilable to human experience.

This sense of temporal schism and indecipherability is evident in the narrative experiments of a number of post-war authors, particularly Samuel Beckett, Alain Robbe-Grillet, Julio Cortazar and Thomas Pynchon, as Heise argues.[8] In these schismatic narratives, the early modernist narrative's emphasis on 'memory, duration and expectation in human consciousness' is replaced by 'forms that deliberately make temporal progression difficult or impossible to conceive' (Heise 1997, 13). The novels of Samuel Beckett, Alain Robbe-Grillet and Julio Cortazar fragment time and narrative order, and increasingly resist recuperative readings attaching their disjunctive temporality to the representation of human subjectivity (as in early modernist literature) (64). Robbe-Grillet, for example, eschews character development and coherent plots in favour of looping or labyrinthine narrative structures and detailed descriptions of diegetic spaces. In such Robbe-Grillet novels as *Jealousy* (1957) and *In the Labyrinth* (1959), and more emphatically in later works such as *Project for a Revolution in New York* (1976), the past and the present are so tightly wound together that the distinction between them is erased. The reader is presented with multiple, contradictory versions of events, so that establishing a linear, causal flow of time is made impossible. Another type of non-linearity is offered by Julio Cortazar's *Hopscotch* (1963), which can be read in linear fashion, or in an alternative, non-linear order, suggested at the beginning of the book. Meanwhile, William Burroughs became notorious for introducing non-linearity into the composition of such novels as *The Ticket That Exploded* (1962) and *Nova Express* (1964), splicing together disparate pieces of text to create what he called 'cut-ups'. As Paul Ricoeur comments, these late modernist narrative techniques are 'aimed at shattering the very experience of time' (1984–8, 2:81). Time appears to splinter or bifurcate endlessly, independently of character psychology. As Heise points out, these novels do away at times even with the notion of character and hence with 'human experience as the central organizing parameter of narrative' (1997, 7).[9]

A key text in this regard is Jorge Luis Borges's short story 'The Garden of Forking Paths' (first published in 1941), in which Borges sets up a murder-mystery plot with a variety of possible permutations. This story anticipates the bifurcating temporality of Robbe-Grillet and Cortazar, and has provided the conceptual model for computer-based experiments with multilinear narrative. Indirectly, it is also the model for forking-path modular narratives such as *Run Lola Run* (Tom Tykwer, 1998) and *Groundhog Day* (Harold Ramis, 1993). However, while Borges's story posits an infinitely splintering narrative temporality, these contemporary films limit their disjunctive impact, either by restricting the number of narrative forks (*Run Lola Run*) or by restricting the setting and number of narrative agents (*Groundhog Day*). Yet the sense of a challenge to temporal unity is something retained even by the most formally conservative of these films. Anachronic modular narratives may also evoke a splintering of time, but this is often still anchored in character memory or imagination (as in *Eternal Sunshine of the Spotless Mind*). Other modular narratives, including *21 Grams*, do not appeal directly to memory to justify their disjunctive form. These films, however, tend to allow and encourage viewers to salvage a coherent account of events from the narrative fragments. To this extent, I would suggest that the experiments of late modernist writers (and Alain Robbe-Grillet in particular) constitute a kind of outer limit in terms of schismatic form. This sense of schism persists even in contemporary modular narratives, but is generally leavened by a countering impulse towards sense and order.

Accordingly, I suggest that these contemporary films form part of a modular tendency that was already emergent in late modernist and postmodernist literature. Amongst post-1960s literary examples, there is an increasing tendency towards modular order as opposed to schism. Italo Calvino's work, for example, explores the combinatorial potential of narrative elements. In *The Castle of Crossed Destinies* (1973), a series of tarot cards are arranged and interpreted in different ways, giving rise to a number of different narratives. Calvino's *Invisible Cities* (1972) ties together its chapters by the loosest of narrative threads, as Marco Polo lists and describes at length the fantastical cities he has visited. Each description details the design and social conventions of a city, but does not chart a narrative progression of any significance. Arguably, *Invisible Cities* is a database of descriptions rather than a narrative of any conventional sort. This weakening of temporal succession anticipates (and goes beyond) the disjunctive temporality of contemporary modular narratives, yet it is not purely schismatic. Similarly, Georges Perec's 1978 novel *Life: A User's Manual* describes a frozen moment in the lives of the inhabitants of a Parisian apartment building. The spatial, atemporal movement from room to room is leavened by a retelling of the histories of these characters and the possessions that clutter their dwellings. Here, an analytic perspective on time (framed by the conceit of the diegetic space as a jigsaw puzzle and the persistent cataloguing of household items) is mitigated by the narrative accretions of the building. The novel, based upon a single frozen moment in the present, becomes a paradoxical affirmation of narrative memory.

The late modernist cinema of the 1960s and 70s constitutes a more direct antecedent to the contemporary modular narrative. Here, the schismatic tendency is not as pronounced as in the literature of the period. Rather, one is more likely to observe an intertwining of subjective and schismatic modes. The precursor to the contemporary modular narrative is not so much the self-reflexive games of such French New Wave directors as Jean-Luc Godard, but more the contemporaneous 'New Cinema' of Alain Resnais, in which the mutations of narrative form are much more closely aligned with the literary modernism of Alain Robbe-Grillet. Robbe-Grillet and Resnais collaborated on *Last Year at Marienbad* (1961), which, like Robbe-Grillet's novels, presents a number of contradictory versions of events. In the film, a couple staying at an opulent hotel disagree over the status of their past relationship, and we see many different accounts of it. The narrative moves fluidly between present and past, and by the end of the film it is impossible to establish a definitive description of the fabula. In this way, *Last Year at Marienbad*'s narrative shape mirrors the schismatic form of late modernist literature. Yet the film retains an emphasis on memory that connects it to the subjective mode of Robbe-Grillet's *Jealousy* rather than the total rejection of psychology in such later Robbe-Grillet novels as *Project for a Revolution in New York* (1976). Although this was a fertile period for narrative experimentation in the cinema, it can be argued that the most prominent modernist filmmakers often stopped short of the narrative extremes of the 'new novel' and its exponents (although Robbe-Grillet himself went on to make a number of formally radical films during this time).

As Maureen Turim notes, the revival of modernist flashback techniques during the 1960s (echoing the experiments of 1920s European and Japanese films) was 'nourished in part by its concern with a relationship between narration and the unconscious on one hand and the ludic play of structure on the other' (225). Memory and the imagination are important concerns in such prominent modernist flashback films as *Hiroshima mon amour* (Alain Resnais, 1959), *8$\frac{1}{2}$* (Federico Fellini, 1963) and *Wild Strawberries* (Ingmar Bergman, 1957). The fluid movement between temporal modes creates a powerful sense of subjective time. Yet in recent modular narratives such as *21 Grams* and *Irreversible*, neither memory nor history can, strictly speaking, be identified as *direct* motivations for the temporal shifts. In this respect, they are related to the more ludic tendency of *Céline and Julie Go Boating* (Jacques Rivette, 1974), in which two young women try to reconstruct the events they witnessed in a house where one of them worked as a housekeeper. Eventually, the melodramatic plot takes the form of a film cut into fragments, in which Céline and Julie take turns playing the role of housekeeper. They attempt to reconstruct the plot from these fragments, which play over

and over in increasingly ordered configurations.[10] Despite this movement towards order, the film's self-reflexive narration is much more
playful and disruptive than that of its modular descendents, which may
break linear flow but tend to preserve diegetic wholeness.

By the close of the 1970s the heyday of art cinema's non-linear narrative experiments was coming to an end. As Maureen Turim notes, films
in the 1980s were more conservative in their use of flashback, treating it
mainly as a device for filling in narrative gaps (1989, 7). 'Modernist'
flashback techniques were adopted in limited form by Hollywood cinema, in such films as *Dressed to Kill* (Brian de Palma, 1980) and *An Officer
and a Gentleman* (Taylor Hackford, 1982), and in international films
addressing politics and history such as *Missing* (Costa-Gavras, 1981),
Marianne and Juliane (Margarethe von Trotta, 1981) and *Breaker Morant*
(Bruce Beresford, 1980). A less restricted use of modernist techniques can
be identified in Nicolas Roeg's *Bad Timing* (1980), in which the troubled
relationship between Alex and Milena, two American expatriates in
Vienna, is told via an elaborate flashback-flashforward structure. The
beginning stages of their relationship, for example, are intercut with
Milena's drug overdose and subsequent operation. The disjunctive back-
and-forth narrational aesthetic is maintained throughout the film, creating uncertainty over the order of events and the motivation of the
characters. Roeg uses this structure to create confronting juxtapositions:
most notably, by intercutting Alex and Milena's lovemaking with her
apparent death throes, giving the sex act a distinctly necrophilic cast.
Bad Timing is an atypical case within the 1980s cinema, but provides a
bridge of sorts between the 1960s modernism of Resnais and Bergman,
and the modular narratives of contemporary cinema. In particular, *Bad
Timing*'s jumbled narrative structure closely resembles that of *21 Grams*,
in which the fragmented structure juxtaposes the beginnings and aftermath of violent, traumatic events while providing an analogue for the
troubled relationships of the characters. One key difference, however, is
that *21 Grams* synthesizes three interconnected plotlines, while *Bad
Timing* focusses only on one. More significantly, *Bad Timing* places
emphasis upon temporal schism and uses its structure to critique Alex's
moral failings. *21 Grams*, by contrast, orients itself towards the moral
redemption of its characters and the recuperation of narrative order.

Postmodern culture: between schism and modularity

This trajectory from schism towards modularity is also evident in popular genres. Cinematic modular narratives can be connected, for example,

to the omnipresence of television from the second half of the twentieth century. Arguably, television institutes a formal regime built upon discontinuity, via commercial breaks and channel-hopping. The television-specific genre of the music video thrives upon the formal exploration of discontinuity. Yet television ameliorates these disjunctive effects by incorporating narrative and stylistic forms to traverse and connect separate elements. For example, the flow of the music links together the disparate images of the music video. In addition, television has adapted the narrative forms of the series and the serial to its own uses. The series tells a different self-contained story with each episode, although maintaining key characters, locations and situations. The serial, on the other hand, tells a continually unfolding story from week to week, that may also consist of multiple plotlines. The key example of the serial form is the soap opera. In the soap opera, individual narrative threads may work towards a closure of sorts, but this is never final. Therefore, audiences already familiar with televisual narratives are well-equipped for negotiating the complexities of modular cinema.[11] Yet it must also be emphasized that television and cinema, although interrelated, have developed along different lines. For the most part, audiences still expect a film to tell a single story. Most do so in a fashion that might be described as classical. In this context, modular narratives stand out as atypical cases.

Certain cinematic movements may have explored alternative narrative modes during the 1960s, but for popular cinema it was business as usual on the narrative front. The story of twentieth-century cinema, when placed in the context of the rethinking of temporal organization in literature and philosophy, is the story of narrative's remarkable persistence. However, the discourse of schism has not been absent from popular cinema itself, and has been particularly evident within the genre of science fiction. Scott Bukatman, building upon the work of Vivian Sobchack, argues that contemporary science fiction films and media texts narrate 'the dissolution of the very ontological structures that we usually take for granted' (1993, 10).[12] For Bukatman, electronic mediation as it is represented in science fiction confirms and enacts the end of both centred subjectivity and traditional narrativity. Similarly, Giuliana Bruno posits *Blade Runner* (Ridley Scott, 1982) as a metaphor for the postmodern condition described by Fredric Jameson, as it dramatizes the temporal and historical disorientation associated with the technologized postmodern world (Bruno 1987). The artificial memories of the 'replicants' in *Blade Runner* and their dependence upon photographs as a marker of identity embody 'the lost dream of continuity' in postmodern times (193). In this case, schism is not represented syntagmatically through the narrative structure.[13] It is, rather, communicated via the plight of the characters and the dense *mise-en-scène*, which crams together styles and motifs associated with a panoply of locations and historical times.

As with modernist literature and cinema, it is possible to detect in such popular genres a growing emphasis upon modularity. Witness, for example, the representation of spatial modularity in such contemporary science fiction films as *The Matrix* (Wachowski brothers, 1999) and *Cube* (Vincenzo Natali, 1997). In the former, the main character Neo discovers that he has been living not in the 'real world' but in a virtual projection. In order to navigate this world, Neo has his mind 'loaded' with different programs enabling him with new skills such as prowess in martial arts. The subject itself therefore becomes modular, receptive to technological upgrades that are simply added on. In *Cube*, a group of strangers find themselves in a maze-like structure consisting of almost identical cube-shaped rooms. Navigating the maze involves finding out whether or not a given room contains a lethal trap. The structure of the maze is modular: it appears to have no boundaries, and the configuration of the rooms constantly changes, so that the characters unexpectedly find themselves in rooms they have already visited. Modular narratives, then, enact this type of spatial arrangement on the level of temporal ordering.

While the experiments of the literary and cinematic late modernists peaked in the 1960s and moved to the margins in the 1970s, popular cinema and television continued to convey temporally coherent narratives, and also found ways of domesticating the schismatic tendencies of postmodern culture. For Jim Collins, the 1970s and 80s mark a transitional phase in which modernism's 'shock of the new' was giving way to postmodernism's 'shock of excess' (1995, 5). Yet Collins also suggests that contemporary culture was already moving beyond the radical postmodern decentring described by theorists such as Jameson and Baudrillard:

> The architecture, interior design, television programs, films and novels produced in the late eighties and early nineties reflect another transformation – when the shock of excess gives way to its domestication, when the *array* of signs becomes the basis for new forms of art and entertainment that harness the possibilities of semiotic excess.

(5)

The crisis of subjectivity brought on by the multiplication of media and representations (particularly visual ones) finds its solution in the creation of new structures or 'architectures' that can tame excess and subject it to rational or affective organization. These architectures, I suggest, are commensurate with a modular approach that regards schismatic forms not simply as crises but as opportunities for connecting and reconfiguring cultural materials.

Jim Collins's 'architectures of excess' also point towards the subject of the next section: the rise of digital culture and technology and the increased ability of individuals to control and manipulate temporal representations. Nonetheless, concerns regarding temporal schism, while tamed in part, did not disappear entirely from the cultural domain. Indeed, the changes to spatial and temporal experience offered by new technologies have to some extent revived these concerns, as I discuss in subsequent chapters. Nor have 'early' modernism's obsessions with memory, history, contingency and simultaneity (in short, with the *representation* of time) been erased in the postmodern era.[14] Describing the contextual importance of modular narratives therefore involves a dual project of establishing continuities and disjunctures between present and past aesthetic practices, while thinking beyond the idea of a definitive postmodern 'rupture'. What is particularly noteworthy about the past decade and a half is that it marks the point at which disjunctive narrative strategies have fully entered *popular* cinema. Even the use of modular structures in contemporary 'art cinema' must be viewed against the backdrop of their popular acceptance. Related to this change is the growing influence of digital culture upon all aspects of contemporary life, including our sense of time.

Digital culture, database and narrative

Modular narratives abut upon concerns regarding the role of narrative in the era of digital culture. Neither these concerns nor digital culture itself emerge out of a vacuum. Rather, they are closely related to the modernist and postmodernist approaches to time. Indeed, I would suggest that digital culture in its present form constitutes a development *within* cultural postmodernism rather than a departure from it. Digitality, according to Charlie Gere, is a cultural marker, which extends beyond technology, defining and encompassing 'the ways of thinking and doing that are embodied within that technology, and which make its development possible. These include abstraction, codification, self-regulation, virtualization and programming' (2002, 13).[15]

David Nye (1997) aligns computerization more explicitly with cultural postmodernism, and identifies three distinct phases of computerization.[16] The first phase, covering the post-war period up until the late 1970s, involved the institutional (governmental and industrial) adoption of computers. The second involved the miniaturization and decentralization of computer technology, and the spread of the personal computer. The third and current phase, beginning in the early 1990s, corresponds to the rapid emergence of the Internet (Nye 1997, 161). Nye explicitly counters Jean-François Lyotard's earlier, pessimistic account of computerization's contribution to the 'postmodern condition'. For Lyotard, computerization legitimizes certain power structures and types of knowledge (science and law, in particular) by means of 'data storage and accessibility, and the operativity of information' (1984, 47). In this way, power and knowledge are centralized, systematized and placed beyond the reach of individual subjects. Yet Nye points out that Lyotard's argument fails to anticipate the way that computers, in the second phase, would shed their authoritarian connotations and take on positive associations with democracy, education and economic growth (1997, 164). Although Nye's argument here is sound, he overstates the democratizing potential of computers (168) and brushes aside the negative effects of phase two computerization: 'If there was less privacy than before', he blithely asserts, 'this condition was universal' (166). To synthesize, I suggest that the decentralization of computer technologies has allowed for a domestication of their apparent threat, but also produced newer concerns regarding privacy, ethics and the integrity of temporal and spatial experience. Accordingly, modular narratives correspond to the third phase of the computerized postmodern. Their domestication of schism is qualified by renewed concerns regarding the representation of time.

Indeed, the rise of digital culture coincides with a further rethinking of temporality, which extends that described by analysts of the modern and postmodern. In an echo of postmodern theory, Charlie Gere suggests that developments in science, media and capital produce a dematerialization of physical space and an acceleration effect which challenges our ability to respond to events (2002, 11), while Manuel Castells argues that 'time is erased in the new communication system when past, present, and future can be programmed to interact with each other in the same message' (2000, 406). Castells' argument here resonates with the warnings of such postmodern theorists as Jameson (1991), Baudrillard (1983) and Harvey (1990). The parallel with Jameson's ideas becomes more evident when Castells proclaims that, in contrast to classical social theories, which privilege time over space, 'space organizes time in the network society' (407). Yet I want to suggest that the story of digital culture's impact upon temporality cannot simply be described in terms of the annihilation of time. Digitality provides a threat to temporal organization in the same way that industrialization did in the modern era; however, it is also the case that digital culture offers the means of rearticulating time, investing it with meaning and making it assimilable to human experience. In this way, the analytic perspective on time is domesticated and reconciled with traditional modes of temporal organization, including narrative.

This sense that digital mediation both threatens time and promises to liberate it is implied by debates over narrative's place in new media forms. Literary hypertext emerged in the 1980s and early 1990s as a response to the new narrative opportunities offered by computers. Rejecting the teleology and linearity of traditional narratives, hypertext theorists describe a new model for storytelling, in which stories are created from discrete blocks of text (or *lexias*). These lexias are connected in a computer via hyperlinks; readers may navigate a multitude of different paths through the lexias, producing radically different reading experiences and narrative outcomes.[17] George Landow suggests that hypertext enacts the type of intertextual play and indeterminacy described by poststructuralist theorists such as Jacques Derrida and Roland Barthes (Landow 1997, 33).[18] Hypertext, in other words, makes literal the linking operations that already exist within and among all types of texts. However, Landow goes on to admit that the more interesting examples of hypertext may increasingly be poetic rather than narrative in form (215). To this extent, hypertext literature often adapts the schismatic narrative techniques of the late modernist writers. Hypertext, no less than the contradictory plots of Alain Robbe-Grillet, challenges narrative's grounding in temporal coherence and legibility. At the same time, it appears to liberate time from the shackles of linear narrative.

This question of digital media's suitability as a vehicle for narrative is an undeveloped thread in Landow's argument, but it is addressed more directly by Janet Murray and Lev Manovich. Murray argues that the twentieth century has seen the development of the '*multiform story*', a term referring to 'a written or dramatic narrative that presents a single situation or plotline in multiple versions, versions that would be mutually exclusive in our ordinary experience' (1998, 30). Cinematic examples of the multiform story cited by Murray include the 'multiple alternate realities' (37) of *Groundhog Day* (Harold Ramis, 1993) and the contrasting points of view in Akira Kurosawa's *Rashomon* (1950). These types of narratives encourage an active role on the part of readers/viewers, fore-grounding the presence of the storyteller 'and inviting us to second-guess the choices he or she has made' (37). Yet for Murray, the multiform story has found its ideal vehicle in interactive stories and games. Murray distinguishes between two types of electronic narrative environments: 'the solvable maze and the tangled rhizome' (130). The former, associated with games, has a mythic, heroic dimension. The latter, associated with literary hypertext, is anti-heroic and resists resolution (132). Murray's vision is for a narrational form somewhere between these two extremes, 'in stories that are goal driven enough to guide navigation but open-ended enough to allow free exploration and that display a satisfying dramatic structure no matter how the interactor chooses to traverse the space' (134–5). Although Murray's dream of uniting open-ended interactivity with well-rounded literary structure often seems like wishful thinking, her discussion of narrative possibilities demonstrates the way in which digital narratives offer both the threat of schism and the consolations of modularity.

Lev Manovich, by contrast, sees in contemporary culture a conflict between database and narrative. Whereas narrative 'creates a cause-and-effect trajectory of seemingly unordered items (events)', the data-base 'represents the world as a list of items, and it refuses to order this list' (Manovich 2001b, 225). He argues that while the novel and cinema affirm narrative as the key cultural form, in the computer era, narrative's role has been usurped by the database (218). Cinema is a particularly divided art form in this respect, for it 'already exists right at the intersection between database and narrative' (237). In other words, the process of editing a film usually involves creating a narrative, out of a database of shots and sequences. Critically, however, Manovich asserts that the database's spatial, acausal arrangement undermines both temporality and narrative.[19] In the age of the computer, then, narrative itself is threatened by the analytic perspective on time. This 'conflict' between database and narrative is confronted by every filmmaker, although Manovich argues that very few do so with any self-reflexivity, citing Peter Greenaway as an exception (237–8). Yet contemporary modular narratives, by fashioning stories out of an array of discrete pieces, refer directly or indirectly to the modularity of new media described by Manovich.[20] Indeed, the narrative form of these films itself 'remediates' the digitally enabled chapter structure of DVDs, to use the term coined by Bolter and Grusin for 'the representation of one medium in another' (1999, 45). As Sean Cubitt notes, the database form also inflects filmmaking in other ways, given that it is 'intrinsic to

Hollywood market research, scriptwriting, and editing' (2004, 237). He sees in contemporary modular narratives such as *Memento*, *12 Monkeys* and *Pulp Fiction* the triumph of the 'pattern-making impulse' over genuine narrativity, and by extension, time and history (239, 243). Ultimately, the effect of these techniques is 'to make the narrative, like the diegesis, spatial' (239).

Although Manovich and Cubitt correctly identify the ascendency of an analytic perspective on time, they misstate its significance in two respects. First of all, the notion of spatialization (grounded in Henri Bergson's concerns about the rationalization of temporal experience, and reaffirmed by postmodern theorists such as Fredric Jameson) is in some respects a misleading metaphor, because it fails to acknowledge contemporary culture's changing spatial dynamics, and opposes space and time in reductive ways. Secondly, it fails to acknowledge that narratives *in general* have a spatial dimension. In this regard, Mikhail Bakhtin's notion of the 'chronotope' is helpful: the '*chronotope* (literally, "time space")' refers to 'the intrinsic connectedness of temporal and spatial relationships that are artistically expressed in literature'. In the chronotope, 'Time, as it were, thickens, takes on flesh, becomes artistically visible; likewise, space becomes charged and responsive to the movements of time, plot and history' (1981, 84). Furthermore, Marsha Kinder challenges Manovich's opposition of database and narrative, seeing them as complementary rather than conflictual; they are 'two sides of the same process, which is usually hidden from view' (2001, 82).[21] In films such as *Pulp Fiction*, Kinder sees the paradigm (the database of choices) extended into syntagmatic form. *Pulp Fiction* therefore marks for Kinder the extension of avant-garde practices (espoused by filmmakers such as Bunuel, Greenaway, Marker and Ruiz) into the mainstream. Although Kinder's argument for the interdependence of database and narrative is convincing (the dislocations of the database provide a rich source of narrative innovations), she does not fully acknowledge that the relationship between the two can be articulated in degrees. The films of Greenaway and Ruiz, for example, have demonstrably weaker narratives than any classical film, because their structure undermines the temporal and causal connections upon which narrative depends. I suggest, then, that database and narrative are complementary, but that one has the potential to dominate the other. Database aesthetics may, furthermore, be used to create schismatic or modular temporal structures. Indeed, one of the most interesting aspects of contemporary modular narratives is the way that they combine a database structure with conventional storytelling devices.

Tales about modular time

Contemporary complex narratives display a tendency towards modular temporality. Yet there is no definitive rupture, in this respect, between modern and postmodern, or analogue and post-digital. Rather, the temporality of contemporary complex narratives can best be understood as an interplay between subjective, schismatic and modular modes, in which the modular mode has assumed greater prominence than before. In comparison with early modernist texts, modular narratives offer a more analytic conception of time. Yet they are also distinct from the schismatic temporality described by Ursula Heise (1997). Whereas certain late modernist writers deal with the disintegration of temporal experience, modular narratives tend also to perform (to varying degrees) a recuperation of the temporal. They emphasize not only fragmentation but also the making of narrative links. In this way, contemporary cinematic modular narratives can be situated along an axis between schism and modularity. If the postmodern era (as described by Fredric Jameson) offered the fragmentation of time via the juxtapositions of media culture, the digital era is distinguished by the extended ability of subjects to actively navigate and order time (or, rather, representations of time). Similarly, time in contemporary complex narratives is subject to fragmentation, but the resources are usually provided for audiences (and sometimes characters) to reconstruct temporal order and continuity, salvaging both time and narrative.

The connection between complex narrative structures and digitality has been made explicit in speculative analyses by Dana Polan and Slavoj Zizek, separately addressing two prominent examples from the 1990s, *Pulp Fiction* and *Lost Highway*. Polan notes the parallels between computer hypertext and *Pulp Fiction*'s deployment of its diegetic spaces, narrative segments and pop-culture references; together, these constitute a 'shifting universe based on disjunction, substitution, fragmentation' (2000, 35). These formal games, however, can be processed by those accustomed to the informational architecture of cyberspace: 'If you understand mouse-clicks and web-links and hypertext, you're in the same structural mindset as *Pulp Fiction*, with its disjunctions, its loops of narrative, its dramatic shifts of tone and image' (36). Similarly, Slavoj Zizek suggests a parallel between hypertext and the 'coexistence of multiple fantasmatic narratives' in *Lost Highway* (2000, 36). Zizek invokes Janet Murray's notion of the 'violence hub' narrative to describe the way that Lynch's film explores psychological trauma without, on the one hand, resolving itself into a linear maze structure (as in adventure games), or refusing closure on the other (as in experimental 'rhizomatic' hypertexts) (38). For Zizek, *Lost Highway* (like Altman's *Short Cuts* and a number of Kieślowski's films) foreshadows digital textuality in much the same way that the novels of Charles Dickens and Emily Brontë foreshadowed such cinematic techniques as flashbacks, cross-cutting and close-ups (39–40). However, although these hypertextual metaphors illuminate the complex narratives of *Pulp Fiction* and *Lost Highway*, the differences between the two films are equally instructive.

In fact, I suggest that these films embody the hypertrophy of the analytic perspective on time, pushed in two distinct directions. Specifically, *Lost Highway* veers towards schism, while *Pulp Fiction* is built upon a modular framework. In this way, these films suggest that modularity and schism are not opposites; rather, they are obverse sides of the same tendency. In *Lost Highway*, the schismatic is also imbued with a subjective dimension. The eruption of a parallel narrative world in the film appears to stem from the psychological breakdown of the main character, Fred Madison, who has been accused of murdering his wife. Midway through the film Fred is abruptly transformed into another character, Pete Dayton. Pete starts a relationship with a mobster's mistress closely resembling Fred's wife (Patricia Arquette plays both roles), and ends up murdering the mobster. Critical discourse on the film has tended towards psychoanalytic interpretations, in which Pete acts as a fantasmatic projection compensating for Fred's thwarted desires: at the end of the film, the wife/mistress character disappears altogether, and Pete becomes Fred once more, tormented by his psychological breakdown (see Zizek 2000 and McGowan 2000). However, Fred's loss of psychological control is paralleled by a loss of narrative coherence that strains the limits of such recuperative psychological readings. In other words, the psychoanalytic interpretation is utterly plausible, but it must be noted that many viewers experience the film as a collision of incommensurable worlds. Lynch's film is certainly not impervious to psychological readings (in contrast with Robbe-Grillet's later novels, for example), but it challenges its viewers to produce such readings retrospectively and with a high degree of cognitive reflexivity. *Pulp Fiction* also figures the loss of control as both a diegetic and narrational element. It is no accident, for example, that Vincent Vega, the character who creates the most conspicuous mess in the film by accidentally shooting a young man, is shot after being caught out sitting on the toilet. He dies because he lacks control and restraint, unlike his partner Jules. On the narrational level, audiences are similarly challenged to keep control over the film's multiple narrative threads and temporal shifts.

Yet in *Pulp Fiction*, the potential for schism is domesticated. Unlike *Lost Highway*, it does not connect its non-linear structure to character psychology, and rewards the attentive viewer with a secure vantage point overlooking the entire narrative action.

A number of recent complex narratives display a combination of subjective, schismatic and modular temporal modes. Some tie their narrational permutations to the 'psychological' state of characters who are eventually revealed to be dead. This group includes *The Jacket, The Butterfly Effect, Donnie Darko, Waking Life, Jacob's Ladder, 12 Monkeys, Open Your Eyes* and *Mulholland Drive*. These films depict not simply psychological crises but also the crisis of the subject itself. Unlike *Sunset Boulevard* (Billy Wilder, 1950), which frames its narrative as the recollections of a dead man, these films associate such post-mortem subjectivity with a disruption of diegetic coherence. In these films, the ludic dimension of the narration undermines exclusively psychoanalytic readings. As if to illustrate this point, the character of the psychiatrist in *Open Your Eyes* is ultimately revealed to be a projection associated with a technologically based memory fabrication process undergone by the protagonist. Here, the sci-fi premise trumps any purely psychological explanation for the complexity of the narration; analysis vies with psychoanalysis. Such films are closely related to the ironic perspective on subjectivity in such films as *Fight Club, Primer* and *Being John Malkovich* (Spike Jonze, 1999). In *Primer*, a homemade machine allows its protagonists to go back and forth in time, but multiplies them with each voyage. Eventually, one of the characters decides to destroy another copy of himself. In *Malkovich*, the titular actor's consciousness is invaded via a tunnel found behind a filing cabinet, a detail that serves to invest subjectivity with a sense of bureaucratic banality. In these films, which offer a recombination of science fiction and *noir* tropes and techniques, subjectivity becomes conditional, and the abrupt time shifts function both as memory and anti-memory.

In this way, these films bring a degree of instability to what Murray Smith refers to as our 'imaginative engagement' with the characters (1995, 75). Smith suggests that there are three main levels of engagement. The first of these is *recognition*: we identify characters within the films we are watching, and generally speaking, associate them with a particular physical form. Beyond this, our relationship with characters is shaped by *alignment* and *allegiance*. The first refers to the extent to which we share in the experiences and knowledge of the characters; the second refers to our assessment of the characters' attributes and moral qualities (Smith 1995, 75). Certain avant-garde or modernist filmmakers, argues Smith, have challenged recognition by undermining the elements of identifiable characters, in particular physical and psychological consistency. Such films, one might suggest, tend to present subjectivities rather than characters. Modular narratives, in many cases, play upon the unstable boundaries of this distinction between character and subjectivity.

They do so by destabilizing what Smith refers to as *alignment*. In many cases, we are presented with temporal shifts or loops that are explicable neither as memory nor as parallel worlds. In such films as *Mulholland Drive, Donnie Darko, Waking Life, Fight Club* and *The Jacket*, we are often uncertain as to the ontological status of the characters' experiences. What we are aligned with is either the projection of the protagonist's subjectivity out into the world, or a world that operates as if it is subjective. In such films, alignment becomes the direct object of our cognitive activities, as we reflect directly upon the unstable relationship between what we are experiencing and what the characters are experiencing. Time is central to this reflection, as in many cases we are presented with hallucinations, parallel realities and false memories. Despite the sophistication of his argument, however, Smith does not deal explicitly with flashback or other types of temporal articulation. Here, I suggest, lies an important area of character engagement, one that is closely entwined with processes of recollection (for both viewers and characters). In Chapter 4, I dwell in particular on memory, because it is the psychological movement most explicitly called up by the time-shifts of the anachronic narrative. It is where the alignment between the formal articulation of time and the diegetic articulation of subjectivity comes into sharpest focus.

Although the films I have discussed above combine subjective, schismatic and modular temporal modes, their ludic foregrounding of narration invites viewers to take on an analytic perspective: their tendency is thus towards the modular. This modular tendency finds clearest expression, I argue, amongst the group of films I go on to discuss in subsequent chapters. The anachronic modular narratives *Memento, 21 Grams* and *Irreversible* invoke modular temporality by presenting time as readily divisible into discrete segments, which can then by implication be arranged in a variety of ways. Forking-path narratives, including *Run Lola Run* and *Groundhog Day*, split time into clearly defined threads, but also allow for a connective relationship between these threads. Episodic narratives may invoke modular time by emphasizing abstraction or repetition. In all cases, the emphasis is not only on the disjunctures between different times and temporalities, but also on the modular connections that allow audiences and characters to traverse these disjunctures.

If these narratives recall modernist and digital techniques simultaneously, then it must be emphasized that the roots of digital culture are themselves modern, stemming from the rise of capitalism and industrialization (Gere 2002). At the same time, the emergence of modular narratives within mainstream and independent cinema reveals a resurgent interest in questions of time, memory and contingency that is most reminiscent of early literary modernism and late cinematic modernism. These types of narratives often emerge at moments in which our sense of temporality is undergoing a shift. Digital culture and technology are to some extent catalysts for such a shift, although they also provide tools for domesticating and ordering temporal experience. In this context, modular narratives may constitute both a resistance to modular temporality and an embrace of it. Furthermore, these films affirm that narrative is still a crucial way of articulating human time. Although some of these films may appear anti-narrative in orientation, most of them conform to, or actively endorse, the requirements of narrative. In some cases, narrative is reinforced, in others displaced, but maintained in a reduced form.

Modular narratives explore the intersections between different forms of temporality, including narrative time, technological time and mnemonic time. The question of linearity is often assumed to separate narrative form from the structure of the database. In the most immediate sense, this is true: the database allows access from multiple points. Yet despite this non-linearity, most digital media forms present us at least with chunks of linearity (in the form of mp3s, DVD chapters and news articles). Furthermore, although a traditional narrative is linear in the literal sense, non-linear movements (flashbacks and other time shifts) are part of the armoury of classical narrative. The relationship between digital temporality and narrative temporality is therefore highly complex. The interaction of different temporal modes allows for modular narratives to explore a number of issues that abut on the temporal. Thus, these 'tales about time' focus upon such issues as narrative, chance and determinism, the body and mortality, memory and identity, technology and mediation and space and globalization.

3
Projecting the Future: Order, Chaos and Modularity

A number of modular narratives display, as a central stylistic and thematic concern, a fraught relationship between contingency and narrative order. These films invite viewers to question whether the events they depict are predetermined or contingent. Episodic modular narratives such as *13 Conversations About One Thing* (Jill Sprecher, 2001) may invoke contingency by linking ostensibly separate characters and events, or determinism by organizing the narrative along non-temporal lines. In the case of forking-path narratives such as *Run Lola Run* (Tom Tykwer, 1998), we are invited to think about alternative narrative possibilities, and the chance events that produce them. Anachronic modular narratives directly raise the question of determinism by making endings precede beginnings. In anachronic narratives such as *Pulp Fiction* (Quentin Tarantino, 1994) and *Amores Perros* (Alejandro González Iñárritu, 2000), contingency functions as a narrative engine, alternately presenting the characters with the threat of violence and opportunities for success or human contact. The non-linear narrative structure allows for a heightened examination of causes, effects and coincidences.

Arguably, all narratives involve the accommodation of both contingency and necessity. However, given that narratives in general depend upon the separation of present, past and future, they tend to conceal the strong element of determinism in their construction, thereby preserving the narrative future as a realm of possibility. Therefore, tales that rearrange chronological order so as to offer the ending of the story at the beginning are usually flirting with determinism. Such films confront a crisis in the conception of the future, which is threatened by reification. Conversely, contingency often plays an important diegetic role within modular narratives, via stories that hinge upon chance events.

In *Pulp Fiction,* a number of narrative threads are complicated or resolved by arbitrary events. For example, Butch, a boxer who has just enraged his boss Marcellus Wallace by refusing to lose a fight, accidentally encounters Marcellus crossing the street. This chance meeting, and the ensuing chase, leads to another arbitrary episode, as Butch and Marcellus are both captured by a group of urban hillbillies. Crucially, however, these random events lead to Butch saving Marcellus from the depraved attentions of their captors, thereby securing a truce of sorts with him. In this way, Butch is first threatened and then saved by contingency. On the one hand, the temporal juxtapositions within these narratives invite us to question the extent to which events are determined in advance. On the other, contingency asserts itself both as diegetic force and as structural principle: modular narratives mimic contingency itself by leaping between narrative segments in apparently arbitrary or unpredictable ways. This tendency finds particularly strong expression in two contemporary examples: *21 Grams* and *Irreversible* (Gaspar Noé, 2002).

In *21 Grams* and *Irreversible,* determinism and contingency are taken to narrative and stylistic extremes. Both films give away the ending of the film at the beginning, and both begin in strikingly chaotic fashion. In *21 Grams,* this is achieved through the extreme fragmentation of the narrative, while in *Irreversible,* disorientation is manifested in dizzying camera movements. These films also go further than most other modular narratives in highlighting the relationship between death and narrative closure, and weighing up the comparative value of 'human time'. In each case, violence and trauma seem to permeate the fragmented narrative structure, and the film itself becomes a study of causes and effects. While *21 Grams* is a 'Hollywood independent' film (distributed by Focus Features, a subsidiary of Universal Studios), directed and written by expatriate Mexicans, *Irreversible* is a French film directed by an expatriate Argentinean. Although these films come from different industrial contexts, both articulate a particularly complex and intense relationship among narrative, order and contingency.

In the stark and minimal narrative of *Irreversible,* a young woman named Alex is raped and beaten, after which her boyfriend Marcus embarks on a quest for revenge, followed reluctantly by Alex's ex-boyfriend Pierre. However, the narrative recounts these events as a series of segments, arranged in reverse chronological order. Towards the beginning of the film, we see Marcus and Pierre storming through a gay nightclub in search of Alex's rapist. A violent confrontation ensues, resulting in

Pierre killing a man who has attacked Marcus. Next we see the 'preceding' segment, following Pierre and Marcus as they find their way to the nightclub. Marcus is determined to track down Alex's rapist, while Pierre tries to convince him to give up this violent quest. Progressing backwards in time, we witness Alex's rape, followed by a party attended earlier in the evening by Alex, Pierre and Marcus. Next we see the three friends on their way to the party, followed by a scene that shows Alex and Pierre together in their apartment earlier that day. Finally, we see Alex taking a home pregnancy test (result: positive), and reading a book in the sun. Like *Memento*, *Irreversible* takes the form of a series of segments, arranged in reverse linear order. Unlike *Memento*, *Irreversible* does not further complicate the narrative structure by interpolating extra, temporally indeterminate, scenes. Instead, temporally discontinuous segments are linked largely via camera movements that provide the illusion of spatial contiguity – either by so blurring the shot that the transition is made invisible, or by making the transition on a common visual element, for example, a light. This technique creates a disorienting sense of time – as if going back in time involved leaping or slipping from one thread of a spiral to another.

While *Irreversible* displays a reversed linear narrative structure, *21 Grams* employs a radically *non*-linear, associative structure to tell its story. In *21 Grams*, three apparently disparate tales turn out be inextricably linked. In one, wife and mother Cristina is recovering from the death of her husband and two daughters in a road accident. In another, Jack, an ex-convict, battles with guilt – he is the driver of the truck that killed Cristina's family. In the third, Paul, a mathematician, seeks to find out who donated the heart for his transplant operation (it turns out to have been Cristina's husband). Despite the film's chaotic and disjunctive opening, a sense of narrative clarity gradually emerges, and we realize that these three characters are headed towards a dramatic and violent shared conclusion. As discussed in Chapter 1, the structure of the film is one of the most radical displayed by any Hollywood film (of either the mainstream or semi-independent variety). *21 Grams* opens with a bewildering array of scenes, darting backwards and forwards in time to offer a series of narrative segments from before and after the accident. As the film goes on, this temporal oscillation between past, present and future stabilizes, so that all the connections are eventually resolved. Nonetheless, *21 Grams* departs from the rules of classical Hollywood cinema to an extent that is still rare in the current context.

Modernity, postmodernity and contingency

This self-conscious representation of time has much in common with modernist literature (both the early modernism of Proust and Woolf, and the late modernism of Cortazar and Robbe-Grillet) and modernist cinema. The emergence of these tales about time can be linked to the standardization of time demanded by modern industrialization. Examples included the introduction of punch-cards in factories, the attempt to orchestrate workers' physical movements, the introduction of railway timetables and the establishment of a globally synchronized measure of time. Contingency was to be kept to a minimum by these systems. Conversely, resistance to industrialization was often based upon the *appeal* of contingency, stemming from 'its resistance to systematicity, in its promise of unpredictability and idiosyncrasy' (Doane 2002, 225). Prominent modernist artists created works that placed value upon aspects of time that escaped rationalization: chance, indeterminacy and flow. The rambling narratives of James Joyce's *Ulysses* (1922) and Virginia Woolf's *Mrs. Dalloway* (1925) can be seen in this context. In this respect, the modernist writers and artists shared to some extent the ideals of French philosopher Henri Bergson, who complained that industrialization standardized and spatialized time, which in reality consists of an indivisible flow (Kern 1983, 25–6).

In relation to these contradictory tendencies towards rationalization and contingency, cinema occupied an ambivalent ground. As a product of the mechanical age, cinema itself was inextricably linked with the rationalization of time (it standardized movement by capturing it in a finite number of frames per second), and also with attempts to represent time. Yet the camera, by automatically recording whatever was in front of it, presented images teeming with random details, and thereby reproduced contingency. As Mary Ann Doane puts it, 'Cinema comprises simultaneously the rationalization of time and an homage to contingency' (2002, 32).[1] Whereas cinema itself proved a significant arena for the working-through of notions regarding contingency and determinism, cinematic modular narratives enact this working-through on the level of narrative form.

However, Mary Ann Doane suggests that such formal games with narrative time are, in most cases, directed towards a recuperation of linear time. Diegetic temporality may contradict the 'linear, irreversible, "mechanical"' unfolding of cinematic time (the time of the camera and projector), in the form of flashbacks, for example (Doane 2002, 30).

However, the flashback itself consists of a segment of irreversible, linear time, and thereby affirms the forward movement of cinematic time (131). For Doane, the flashback reinforces classical cinema's domestication of contingency: the time of classical cinema 'consistently reaffirms the plausibility, the probability, the irreversibility, and the fundamental recognizability of "real time"' (139). This raises questions regarding the use of *non*-classical narrative or temporal structures. Do the temporal disjunctures of modular narratives subvert the rational, linear temporality of classical cinema? Doane seems to suggest that this is not the case, even in a film like *Memento*, which displays an apparently radical structure. Apart from *Memento*'s opening sequence, in which the images unfold in reverse, Doane points out that the rest of the film consists of chunks of forward-moving time: 'the fragmentation and reordering of time in this film is supported by a basic irreversibility of movement' (252, n. 49). Here, however, Doane links linearity, irreversibility and determinism too closely. Narrative itself is not simply the triumph of order over contingency. Rather, it consists of a negotiation between the contingent and the predetermined.

Chaos theorists Ilya Prigogine and Isabelle Stengers (whose book *Order Out of Chaos* first appeared in English in 1984) suggest that such a negotiation is possible. Chaos theory is a field involving the study of complex systems, which emerged in the wake of scientific developments (such as non-linear dynamics, irreversible thermodynamics and meteorology) that questioned the tenets of classical science. In contrast to classical physics, which represented physical processes as *deterministic and reversible* (affirming the static notion of time that Henri Bergson and many literary modernists were so intent on resisting), Prigogine and Stengers suggest that *irreversible and chaotic* processes are the rule rather than the exception. The contingent operations of chaotic systems confirm the irreversibility of time itself, because processes involving entropy cannot run in reverse without overcoming overwhelming statistical improbability, or what Prigogine and Stengers refer to as an 'infinite entropy barrier' (1984, 278). However, deterministic and reversible systems can emerge from within these chaotic processes (292). Indeed, as Katherine Hayles puts it, Prigogine and Stengers see chaos as '*that which makes order possible*' (1990, 100). The static 'Being' of Newtonian physics is thus reconciled with the temporal 'Becoming' of irreversible thermodynamics (Prigogine and Stengers 1984, 310). Although Prigogine and Stengers are addressing questions of time and not narrative, there are narrative implications in their argument. The underlying confirmation of linear time that Mary Ann Doane detects in cinematic modular narratives such as *Memento* is actually upheld by Prigogine and Stengers. They insist that 'Time flows in a single direction, from past to future. We cannot manipulate time, we cannot travel back to the past' (277). Here, irreversibility is tied not to mechanistic determinism, but to the workings of contingency. The interplay between linear and non-linear time in films such as *Memento* and *21 Grams* therefore parallels chaos theory's articulation of determinism and chaos, reversibility and irreversibility.[2]

These questions of chaos and order, contingency and determinism, did not disappear from the cultural domain with the passing of the modern era.[3] The concern with the domestication and liberation of time lives on in contemporary techno-culture: on the one hand, the digital era embraces the ability to archive material in digital formats; on the other, it betrays the fear that this archival process will reify experience. In this respect, as Mary Ann Doane has argued, the contemporary era constitutes an echo of the modern, rather than a rupture with it (2002, 29). In this sense, contemporary modular narratives look back to cinema's earliest attempts to grapple with the representation of time, and forward to the modular forms and complex temporal dynamics of new media. In redeploying modular structures, these films offer the opportunity to consider how such structures shape and reflect our temporal experience.

For Sean Cubitt, modular narratives betray a distinctly deterministic turn in contemporary cinema. In his book *The Cinema Effect* (2004), Cubitt argues that the task of the characters in these modular narratives is not to effect change, but to come to terms with their destiny (239). A kind of fake contingency appears in the form of coincidences, which, according to Cubitt, are nothing more than a send-up of the classical working through of cause and effect (249).[4] Furthermore, modular narratives 'only appear to be narrative. In fact they are the result of one of many possible rifles through a database of narrative events whose coincidence is more structural or even architectural than temporal' (237).[5] For Cubitt, the incorporation of a database aesthetic into Hollywood narratives spatializes narrative, turning temporal becoming into spatialized Being (239).

As narrative theorist Paul Ricoeur has remarked, this type of 'spatialization' argument depends upon the conflation of real time and chronological time. The reordering of time, Ricoeur points out, is in fact the starting point of any narrative. Moreover,

> the struggle against the linear representation of time does not necessarily have as its sole outcome the turning of narrative into

'logic', but rather may deepen its temporality. Chronology – or chronography – does not have just one contrary, the a-chronology of laws or models. Its true contrary is temporality itself.

(Ricoeur 1984–8, 2:30)

This assertion complicates the relationship between narrative, on the one hand, and the contingency-determinism dialectic, on the other. Narrative has an episodic dimension, drawing it 'in the direction of the linear representation of time' (67), yet it also has a configurational dimension, which makes of the events a meaningful whole, defines these events in relation to an ending and, via the repetition and recollection of the story, provides an alternative to linear time, encouraging us to 'read time backwards' (68). Thus, *Memento*'s non-linear plot does not drain the film of its temporality; rather, it encourages the audience to explore the narrative's configurational dimension, reading the past in the present and vice versa. Similarly, *21 Grams* and *Irreversible* set up complex relationships between their episodic and configurational dimensions, exploring the relationships among narrative, order and disorder via stories that pivot upon violent chance events.

Anachrony and contingency: *Irreversible* and *21 Grams*

The narrative structure of *Irreversible* is, on many levels, highly schematic. The episodes are ordered in a reverse chronological, but linear, sequence. Furthermore, the film is built on a series of binary oppositions. The violent, masculine, narrative thrust of the first half of the movie (in which Marcus leads Pierre on a violent quest) eventually gives way to the relatively calm and unstructured 'feminine' scenes (featuring Alex on her own at the end). Even more bluntly, *Irreversible* sets up an opposition between the anal and the vaginal (Brottman and Sterritt 2004, 39). The gay nightclub itself is known as 'Rectum', and the cinematographic techniques in the early scenes (dim lighting and corkscrewing camera movements) seem designed to approximate a journey inside the large intestine. This is of course a kind of pre-emptive joke regarding the narrative's backwards structure – it is a film that goes up its own arse, as it were – but it also connects this hyper-masculine space to the rape itself, which is, we are explicitly informed, anal.[6] The end of the film (or the beginning of the story) counters this with the news that Alex is pregnant. The idyllic, peaceful conclusion of the film appears to cast this information (and by extension, the reproductive function) in an appealing light. When, in a scene near the end of the film, Marcus suggests the idea of anal sex to Alex, the connection with the violence that will follow (and which we have already witnessed) is obvious.

Paralleling these schematic progressions is another, more literary model. The film is in effect a reversed apocalyptic narrative: it commences with the Book of Revelations (the hellish world of Rectum), and ends with Genesis (the conception of Alex's child, as well as the scene in which Marcus and Alex awaken together, a naked and innocent Adam and Eve). In witnessing the shocking events that link these two extremes, audiences may perhaps feel they are expected to turn into pillars of salt. In any case, it should be clear at this point that there are ample opportunities to find the film's conceptual structure either unintentionally amusing or outright objectionable. Indeed, the most objectionable feature of this film is undoubtedly its presentation of homosexuality, with the ludicrous yet apparently serious suggestion that a gay nightclub is the closest one can get to Hell on Earth. However, I am going to suggest despite these caveats that it is worth persevering with this film in investigating questions of contingency and determinism.

The narrative structure would appear, to some degree at least, to confirm the argument that Cubitt makes regarding Hollywood modular narratives. This is a story where the ending is already a given. The actions

Figure 3.1   Irreversible. Studio Canal+/The Kobal Collection

of the characters, subsequently shown, can do nothing to change the outcome. Furthermore, the overlay of schematic oppositions, combined with the intimations of Apocalypse and Eden at the beginning and end of the film, seem to further restrict the narrative to a recounting of necessary events. This impression is borne out by the director's gloomy pronouncements on destiny: 'We are not only predestined but destiny writes itself ... Time exists only in our reptilian perception' (Noé 2002). Yet I would argue that both Noé and Cubitt's assertions offer an insufficient account of the film's contradictory aesthetic project, which also includes a significant emphasis on the contingent.

Most directly, contingency is embodied in the unhappy accidents that befall the characters, particularly Alex's rape (which depends upon a chance encounter between Alex and her attacker) but also the killing that it provokes. When Marcus confronts some men in the nightclub, he is attacked and Pierre reacts savagely, hitting Marcus's attacker with a fire extinguisher. Pierre, who has been a determined pacifist until this point and has tried to dissuade Marcus from seeking revenge, loses control and kills the man. In the meantime, le Ténia, the rapist himself, watches on as someone else bears the brunt of the vengeance meant for him. Both Pierre and his victim, then, suffer as a result of a chain of chance events.

This sense of randomness is mimicked by the film's hectic, swirling visual style. As Marcus and Pierre descend into the nightclub, the camera swings around unpredictably, showing flashes of the location and characters but denying the audience a clear sense of orientation. Both characters and viewers are submitted to a contingent visual field, in which causal and spatial relations are rendered unpredictable and chaotic. Later in the film, this unsteady camerawork calms down, and a different kind of diegetic and stylistic contingency emerges instead in the loose, apparently improvised scenes featuring first the three friends and then Marcus and Alex alone. These scenes are shot in single takes, emphasizing duration and temporal flow.

The first part of the film, then, has a strong (albeit reversed) narrative momentum, driven by Marcus's vengeful rage, but it is a momentum that spins out into chaos and disorder. The will to act, to shape time with one's actions, leads to violence and death. The second half of the film, by contrast, moves increasingly towards scenes with little narrative content. The final scene shows Alex lying in a park, reading a novel in the sun. Here, non-narrative drift is a utopian movement, associated with fertility and possibility. The film thereby succeeds in creating a sense of time that flows in two directions – one in the direction of narrative momentum, determinism and death, the other in the direction of drift, contingency and life.

Memory loss is inscribed into the film: the scenes preceding the rape and murder are shown last, and are therefore allowed to ameliorate the horror we have already witnessed. As the last half of the film unfolds, the memory of the traumatic events in the middle of the film has faded somewhat, displaced by memories of more pleasant, chronologically prior moments. This sense that the retrieval of a utopian, contingent personal time is possible, even in the face of death and determinism, is what rescues the film from outright nihilism. At the same time, we cannot help but be reminded that this is not 'real time' – the rearrangement of temporality at the narrative level can never rescue the chronological story's descent into violence.

In this way, the merciful memory loss of the second half of the film is marked specifically as a human articulation of time. Irreversible time is affirmed by the film, not only by the reversed linear structure, but also by the treatment of individual scenes, which are presented as shot-sequences. The lack of edits reinforces temporal flow, not least of all in the rape scene, making the event in question into a test of endurance for characters and audience alike. The separation of human, experienced time from 'real' time is carried over into an ironic (if rather arch) quotation from Kubrick's *2001* (1968), represented by a poster on the wall of Alex and Marcus's bedroom. In *2001*, the minimal narrative structure extends beyond human history in two directions, beginning with a tableau of pre-human apes and ending with the visualization of a post-human future. In the film's enigmatic ending, however, a gigantic human foetus floats in space, appearing as a kind of speculative projection of humanity into the future. Although uncertainty surrounds this representation of the future, the image of the foetus carries connotations of optimism and possibility. *Irreversible*, too, concludes with a pregnancy; crucially, however, it is already doomed.

In addition, *Irreversible* mirrors *2001*'s progression from animal savagery to reflective peace. Of course, in the case of *Irreversible*, we know that the spectacle of Alex reading her book will eventually be followed by Marcus and Pierre's violent actions. Rather than evolving towards a higher consciousness, the characters in *Irreversible* are headed towards regression and brutality. This realignment of order is paralleled by the way that *Irreversible* reimagines the circular motifs of *2001*. In Kubrick's film, the circular shapes of the space station, planets and amniotic sphere are animated by graceful movements. As the space station spins around, the characters can walk right around the cylindrical interior, even when apparently upside down. In Noé's film, the circular movement is embodied in the violent spiralling action of the camera. Being upside down is at least a graphical feature of this world, but it is a chaotic, rather than a graceful, aspect. The end of the film returns to the circular motif in the form of a lawn sprinkler: as Alex reads on the grass, the camera draws closer to the sprinkler, then begins to spin itself, spiralling up to show the sky. The sprinkler, an icon of domestic bliss, is transformed into an agent of disorientation as the camera becomes subject once again to its spinning action. Within this peaceful setting, then, lurks an emblem of the chaotic spiralling action of the opening scenes.

The conclusion of the film extends its direct treatment of time further by replacing the final image of the sky with an intensifying flickering effect. The film then ends with the words 'Time destroys everything' emblazoned across the screen, in a rather heavy-handed gesture. The flicker effect, however, is significant, because it makes direct reference to cinematic time, and its basis in a series of still images separated by a spinning shutter. In other words, it refers to that irreversible and mechanical temporality of the apparatus mentioned by Mary Ann Doane, that temporality against which Bergson and many modernist figures were reacting. Despite its radical temporal structure, the film emphasizes linear temporality in the unfolding of its narrative as well as in its very title. Nonetheless, the film's narrative has placed emphasis on chance events, and has embedded contingency in the workings of its narrative and visual style. By playing irreversible time in reverse order, the film sets up a dialectic between two temporalities – the cinematic temporality of the story, and the modular temporality of the plot. This complex arrangement allows for a recuperation of contingent time (the database form allows us to return to an idyllic past moment unafflicted by violence), as well as a recognition of its limits.

Like *Irreversible*, *21 Grams* displays a strikingly segmented plot, and revolves around violent events that resonate with notions of chance and necessity. The central chance event in the narrative is the death of Cristina's husband Michael and their two daughters, because it links Cristina to the driver of the truck that killed them (Jack) and to the man who receives Michael's heart (Paul). The theme of contingency is also addressed in other ways. For example, Paul, having researched the identity of the heart donor, develops an attraction to Cristina. As they eat lunch together, Paul invokes chaos theory to describe the accident of their meeting. Yet Cristina remains unaware that their encounter was effectively pre-determined rather than accidental, as it was orchestrated in advance by Paul.

Contingency and determinism are also entwined in the film's concern with conception and pregnancy. Paul's partner Mary is having trouble conceiving a child, and both of them undergo fertility tests. Aware that Paul is dying, Mary wants to bear his child. As their relationship begins to disintegrate, Mary raises Paul's ire by admitting to having had an abortion in the past. Finally, as they separate, she vows to keep a sample of his semen. Yet it is Cristina who discovers she is pregnant at the end of the film, presumably with Paul's child. Mary's difficulty in conceiving, and Cristina's surprise pregnancy, illustrate that the beginnings of life are as subject to chance as the endings. At the same time, pregnancy determines the shape of subsequent events, projecting the moment of birth into the future. In *Irreversible*, Alex's discovery that she is pregnant also unites chance and fate. The fullness and potentiality of this conception of time, however, will later be interrupted by violence. *21 Grams*, by contrast, allows crushed potentialities (in particular, the deaths of Cristina's children) to be balanced out by a new pregnancy (which may prove viable despite being jeopardized by Cristina's drug use).

Time marks itself on the body in other ways, allowing the audience to reconstruct the progression of the story. In *Irreversible*, the scene in which Marcus and Pierre see a horribly disfigured Alex wheeled into an ambulance on a stretcher serves as evidence that what will come later has already passed. Similarly, in *21 Grams*, Jack's attempt to carve a crucifix tattoo out of his arm provides graphic proof of his progression from evangelist to unbeliever, and Paul's physical sickness, bloody bullet wound and surgery scars allow us to recognize, eventually, the temporal order of his scenes. The body functions as an index of time (as in *Memento*, in which the main character tattoos a series of numbered notes on his body throughout the course of the film), reminding us of the effects of contingent events, but also of the inescapable fate of the characters.

The degree of overt determinism one perceives in a film like *21 Grams* depends very much on how one deals with the question of temporal perspective. On the one hand, the fact that we are given information regarding the story's culminating events at the very beginning of the film seems to imply that the future is determined in advance. At the same time, the main characters in the film are all shown reflecting upon the meaning of their *past* experiences. Indeed, this film is all about reconciling oneself with what has gone before, as it concerns characters driven by emotions oriented towards the past, namely grief, guilt and gratitude. In this sense, the film is closely aligned with traditional literary narratives, which make use of the past tense, telling the tale of what has gone *before*. In cinematic narratives, which lack a clearly marked system of tenses, the question of temporal perspective is harder to answer directly, a task made virtually impossible by *21 Grams*. The opening of the film, in particular, does not clearly distinguish between events from the past and those from the future, and a clear framing narrative is never established. The lack of a clearly grounded temporal perspective places events in an indeterminate time between the past and the future, making it difficult to claim that the events depicted are simply determined in advance, narratively speaking. The undecidability of this question closely relates to the contingency-determinism dialectic that runs through the film.

In contrast to *Irreversible*'s reversed linear structure, the temporal logic of *21 Grams* is less transparent, as the plot leaps backwards and forwards in time abruptly. A great many of the temporal leaps appear not to be directly motivated by narrative content, and some function via an associative logic. Thus, the scene in which Jack tells his employer at the golf club that he has renounced a life of crime and is now 'clean' is followed by a scene in which Cristina washes the clothes of her dead children. The emotions of guilt and grief are connected in this way by the motif of cleansing. This points forward to the connection that will be established between the two characters (Jack is responsible for the death of Cristina's family), and to the cleansing process that will see Jack overcome his guilt and Cristina come to terms with her grief. Similarly, Paul and Mary's visit to a fertility expert is juxtaposed with Cristina's arrival at the hospital (where she will learn about the fate of her family), thereby connecting the contingencies of conception with those of death. This associative logic invokes memory, yet it is not a type of memory grounded in any character's point of view. The film cannot be described in terms of psychologically motivated flashbacks. Instead, temporal connections occur via a logic of chaos and order that lies beyond the awareness of the characters themselves. Arguably, this achieves a narrative effect that mimics the contingent, unpredictable form of chaotic systems. In this context, establishing cause and effect becomes difficult, and events seem to proceed independently of any human power to intervene.

Yet as the film progresses, relations between characters and events are clarified, and the narrative stabilizes itself, domesticating the contingent elements of the story and bestowing meaning upon them. In part, this growing sense of stability is achieved by conventional narrative techniques. For, although much of the story's culminating events are shown at the beginning, key narrative details are withheld until the end of the film. For example, we know within the first few minutes that Cristina, Jack and Paul will encounter each other, and that Paul will be wounded.

However, the fact that Paul has shot himself to protect Jack from Cristina's attack is not revealed until the very end of the film. This contrasts markedly with *Irreversible*, in which the violent, climactic scenes are shown in their entirety at the beginning and in the middle of the film, without any omissions (each unfolds as a long take).

The dialectic between contingency and determinism emerges not only in the narrative structure and key events, but also in the characters' own reflections on these events. Jack is an instructor for a Christian youth-group, and his truck bears the word 'Faith' in large letters (in a heavy irony, this is the truck that will claim Cristina's family). Early on in the film, he tells one of his students that God 'knows when a hair on your head moves'. In prison after confessing to the hit-and-run incident, however, Jack comes to question his faith – if it was really an accident, he tells his friend Reverend John, then why must he ask for Jesus' mercy? Just as Jack finds his deterministic, faith-based philosophy inadequate to account for the operations of chance, Paul (who is a mathematician) invokes chaos theory directly in a conversation with Cristina. He tells her of his interest in fractals, graphic shapes that are formed out of chaotic systems. In this way, the film makes reference to two competing models of time, one theological (Jack), the other chaotic (Paul). This dialectic is a key thematic element in a number of modular narratives. For example, in *Pulp Fiction* hired hit men Jules and Vincent debate whether God was responsible for saving them from being shot by a nervous young man (the Bible-quoting Jules claims divine intervention, while Vincent insists that it was luck). *13 Conversations About One Thing* features a physics lecturer teaching his students the basics of chaos theory (including the notions of entropy and irreversibility), but also makes overt references to gypsies' curses, Milton's *Paradise Lost* and the concept of Fortune. This invocation of theological, mystical and scientific models is not designed to resolve metaphysical questions. Rather, it serves to underline the thematic negotiation between contingency and determinism in these films.

In *21 Grams*, this thematic thread comes to an ambiguous resolution. At the end of the film, Cristina is determined to kill Jack as a way of avenging the death of her family. Paul, however, shoots himself in order to interrupt Cristina's attack. Cristina and Jack then work together to get Paul to a local medical centre. Paul's selfless act allows Cristina to move beyond vengeance and come to terms with her grief, and allows Jack to return to his family (he has left them because he feels unworthy of fatherhood). Paul's subsequent death comes to appear as redemptive. In one sense, he can be viewed as a Christ-like figure, who has given up his life to save others and atone for their sins. Yet from another per-spective, the redemption of the characters is simply the by-product of the contingent events that brought them together in the first place. Order and meaning thus emerge from the contingent moments that make life a fertile ground of possibility. Indeed, the title of Prigogine and Stengers's book, *Order Out of Chaos*, could almost function as a subtitle or a logline for the film, which builds a pattern of relationships out of disjunctures, invoking chaos theory directly (through Paul's com-ments) and indirectly (through its narrative form). Ultimately, contin-gency is seen not only as a threat; importantly, it also bears the promise of community, bringing Cristina, Jack and Paul together and allowing for their ultimate redemption.

Narrative, mortality and meaning: order out of chaos

Although I have argued that *Irreversible* and *21 Grams* recuperate con-tingency in the face of determinism, this reading is complicated by the fact that both films have a parallel attachment to order and narrative meaning. Indeed, these films explicitly connect the question of contin-gency and determinism to that of human mortality and meaning. This connection is innate in many modular narratives, but few address it so directly. In this respect, these films intersect with the modern discourse regarding death as a site of contingency. Remarking upon early cinema's fascination with the depiction of death, Mary Ann Doane suggests that 'Death and the contingent have something in common insofar as both are often situated as that which is unassimilable to meaning' (2002, 145). The same connection among death, contingency and meaning is evident in modern literary narrative. In his landmark 1967 book *The Sense of an Ending*, Frank Kermode argues that modern narratives displace the traditional notion of the End (grounded in the biblical notion of apoc-alypse, with its concomitant fusion of death and meaning) from the future to the present (6).[7] For example, James Joyce's *Ulysses* describes a day in the life of the city of Dublin (and of the characters of Leopold Bloom and Stephen Dedalus), a day full of contingent events that appear to resist the ordering function of a unified plot. Rather than working towards a narrative culmination, *Ulysses* places narrative order into a state of crisis, albeit 'a crisis ironically treated' (113).

Despite this eruption of the contingent, claims Kermode, we still 'measure and order time with our fictions' (63), and expect from them meaningful resolutions. This process is figured as a negotiation between two temporal orders: *chronos* and *kairos*. Drawing upon the work of theologians Cullinan and Marsh, Kermode defines the two terms as follows: '*chronos* is "passing time" or "waiting time" – that which, according to Revelation, "shall be no more" – and *kairos* is the season, a point in time filled with significance, charged with a meaning derived from its relation to the end' (47). *Ulysses*, although placing greater emphasis upon the passing, contingent time of *chronos*, still recuperates meaning and order via the human time of *kairos*. The novel invites us to find value in the random events of the day, and to develop an understanding of the characters via their actions and their internal monologues.

A similar relationship among contingency, mortality and order is described by Janet Murray, who uses the term 'violence hub' to refer to narratives that place a violent incident 'at the center of a web of narratives that explore it from multiple points of view' (1998, 135). Although Murray is most interested in attaching the term to hypertext and new media works, the violence hub model is evident in such films as *Rashomon* (Akira Kurosawa, 1950), *Pulp Fiction* and *Amores Perros*, as well as the films discussed here. What connects them together is a sense of the confrontation between contingency and order, with the violent event representing an eruption of the contingent that the surrounding narrative may, to varying degrees, attempt to explain or resolve. We might suggest, then, that the 'violence hub' narratives described by Murray, and the modular narratives under discussion here, displace death from the ending to the beginning or middle of the narrative; they make death immanent rather than imminent. According to Murray, the violence hub structure answers a problem within interactive games and stories: a refusal of closure that amounts to 'a refusal to face mortality' (175). For Murray, the violence hub is the answer to a contemporary narrative problem regarding contingency and determinism. Writing about computer-based, interactive fiction that uses the labyrinth as a structural model, she suggests that there are two extremes: 'the overdetermined form of the single-path maze adventure', and the 'underdetermined form of rhizome fiction' (in which associative exploration is privileged over narrative structure). Both of these forms, she argues, 'work against the interactor's pleasure in navigation' (134). In short, the former is too deterministic and the latter too contingent. The violence hub, without offering a single solution, nonetheless combines narrative clarity with meaningful plots. The variety of narrative perspectives preserves the complexity of the situation, but also permits audiences to work towards a 'deepening' of their understanding of the violent events (136).

Catherine Russell explicitly contests Kermode's (and, by extension, Murray's) argument in her 1995 book *Narrative Mortality: Death, Closure, and New Wave Cinemas.* In the films of a number of 'new wave' film-makers (Lang, Wenders, Oshima, Godard, Altman), Russell finds a challenge to the customary union between death and closure, a challenge she dubs 'narrative mortality' (2). Narrative mortality also questions other features associated with traditional narrative such as determinism and teleological temporality (2, 21), the conflation of history and identity (3), unified subjectivity and the primacy of the heterosexual couple (6). For example, Jean-Luc Godard's *Pierrot le fou* (1965) concludes with the titular character's suicide, a gesture virtually devoid of affect and narrative meaning. It sheds no light upon Pierrot's psychology or his aborted relationship with his girlfriend Marianne, and serves in no way to unify the film's digressive and disjointed plot. The film ends with a shot of the sky, indicating, for Russell, the impossibility of representing eternity (209). This refusal of transcendent meaning is also a refusal of human time, of *kairos*. Accordingly, Russell rejects Kermode's insistence upon the necessity of form and meaning. In the films of Bresson, Antonioni, Ozu, Tati, Wenders, Hou and Akerman, Russell finds 'durational strategies of "waiting"' that imbue the mortality of human body with a corporeal, material quality *independent* of meaning and dramatic closure (21). Russell, in other words, finds in late modernist cinema an affirmation of pure contingency.

Both *21 Grams* and *Irreversible* literally separate death and closure via their inverted narrative structures: *Irreversible* places death at the beginning of the plot, while *21 Grams* makes it immanent by distributing mortal moments throughout the narrative. *Irreversible* further adheres to Russell's notion of narrative mortality by downplaying narrative content in certain scenes in favour of the waiting time of *chronos*, in particular during the languidly paced closing scenes. Like *Pierrot le Fou*, the film ends with a shot of the sky, gesturing towards the limits of human time and meaning. Yet *Irreversible* also places its segments of *chronos* within a highly articulated structure oriented towards *kairos*. The biblical undertones of the narrative, from its hellish beginning to its edenic ending, ensure that death, separated from the literal ending of the film, is nonetheless inescapably linked to meaning. Furthermore, the peace and affection shown in the final scenes are lent additional meaning and affective power by the violent events that precede them. The relationship with earlier narrative segments encourages us to parse these scenes for narrative meaning – to read the ending in the beginning, and vice versa. In this way, the database structure of both films creates ambiguity around the distinction between chaos and order, by aligning itself simultaneously with *chronos* and *kairos*. On the one hand, the sudden, apparently arbitrary temporal shifts in both films mimic the unpredictable, contingent events of their narratives. On the other, these temporal juxtapositions increasingly function as a manifestation of *kairos*, a configured time that frames and structures events in relation to meaning and closure. The database structure is outside human time (not directly connected to memory), but also articulates a sense of order and meaning.

This recuperation of unity and meaning places these films somewhere between early literary modernism and the later modernism of such authors as Alain Robbe-Grillet and Julio Cortazar. Ursula Heise suggests that while contingency in the modernist text is a vehicle for 'moments of epiphany and privileged insight', thereby creating temporal unity, within *late* modernist literature it 'disseminates and divides time' (1997, 58).[8] Rather than working in a speculative mode with regard to future events, late modernist novels use metafictional strategies as a way of 'reflecting on the interplay of determinism and indeterminacy, or causality and contingency in our temporal experience' (68). Although *21 Grams* and *Irreversible* also envision contingency in terms of narrative fragmentation, and frame it in relation to determinism, there is a sense in which contingency nonetheless becomes a unifying force, producing a sense of community (*21 Grams*) or reflective peace (*Irreversible*).

Both films depart further from Russell's criteria by linking the heterosexual couple to notions of narrative order. In *Irreversible*, the fall into chaos is paralleled and precipitated by the separation of Alex and Marcus. In contrast to the masculine violence at the nightclub, the couple itself appears as a utopian ideal. At the end of *21 Grams*, the reconstitution of Jack's nuclear family (husband, wife and two children) provides a sense of balance and recompense for the loss of Cristina's family. Most significantly, however, both films end with a direct appeal to meaning and mortality, and a weighing up of the value of human time. *21 Grams* effectively reunites death and closure at the end of the film. The final moments of the film show Paul's death in hospital, intercut with momentary segments from the rest of the narrative. Overlaying this montage is Paul's voiceover outlining his musings upon life and death: 'How much does life weigh?' he asks. Looking back from the moment of death (as apocalyptic narratives are framed in relation to the End), this agnostic query offers no transcendent answer, and invites us instead to find value in the contingencies that have redeemed the characters.

Irreversible also weighs up the value of human time. The rape scene is the fulcrum upon which the narrative rests, tipping one way towards the murderous opening scenes, and the other towards the peaceful conclusion. The backwards construction of the film invites us to weigh up the contemplative pleasures of the latter against the unredeemed horror of the former. In one sense, *Irreversible* answers Paul's question with a negative affirmation: human life weighs nothing. Leaving Alex's body behind, the camera ascends into space at the end, turning the waiting time of the final scenes into weightless time. But this is no heavenly ascent, and nor is it the post-human heightened consciousness of *2001*'s 'Stargate' sequence. Rather, this is a spiral into nothingness, concluded abruptly with the words 'Time Destroys Everything'. This phrase artificially reconnects death and closure, yet at the same time asserts the entropic power of contingency to wipe away both pleasure and pain. The film refuses to project beyond human time, affirming death as the unrepresentable sublime, as contingency that rejects all meaning. On the other hand, by concluding with the utopian pleasures of Alex's waiting time, *Irreversible* allows us to recuperate the value of human temporality, however ephemeral it might be.

In both films, then, the reconnecting of mortality and meaning acts as a paradoxical affirmation of the contingent. Contingency itself redeems human time and meaning by creating the conditions for positive human interactions and reflective peace. Yet it can just as easily set in train events with fatal consequences. The database structure of these films performs an ambiguous role in this connection, suggesting the chaotic workings of contingency, as well as providing order by contributing to the configurational dimension of the narrative. At the same time, the audience is invited to take a certain degree of pleasure in establishing order out of these chaotic narratives, in spite of the pain and violence depicted on screen. In these ways, both *21 Grams* and *Irreversible* stage a reconciliation of sorts between order and contingency. This reconciliation bears similarities with encounters between order and contingency in modernist literature, in early cinema and in the chaos theory of Ilya Prigogine and Isabelle Stengers. In the face of determinism, both of these films redeem the temporal dimension of experience via *chronos*, while revealing on the other hand an attachment to the ordered, human time of *kairos*. In the contingent they find both the threat of annihilation (car accidents and violent chance encounters) and the promise of rebirth (the 'happy accident' of pregnancy and the formation of a community out of erstwhile strangers). Ultimately, a sense of order emerges from these chaotic events, if only as a temporary effect.

Circularity, irreversibility and retrospection: *13 Conversations About One Thing*

Episodic modular narratives, like their anachronic counterparts, often set up a formal and diegetic negotiation between order and contingency. Certain episodic narratives make use of a non-narrative formal system which appears to dictate (or at least overlay) the organization of narrative elements. Those that use an abstract organizing principle in this way may invoke the contingency-determinism dialectic indirectly. Peter Greenaway's *Drowning by Numbers* (1988), for example, overlays its narrative with the numbers 1–100, which appear within the diegesis in various forms (on a sign, on a runner's singlet and so forth). This technique appears to satirize the film's underlying narrative structure, as if narrative were, like enumeration, simply another arbitrary system for organizing the contingent. Yet the anthology-style episodic narrative goes further in examining contingency. In its anthology form, the episodic modular narrative consists of a series of shorter tales which are apparently disconnected but often turn out to share the same diegetic space. Films in this vein such as *Mystery Train* (Jim Jarmusch, 1989) and *13 Conversations About One Thing* (Jill Sprecher, 2001) invoke the contingent by telling a series of apparently separate tales that nonetheless intersect in unpredictable ways.

13 Conversations About One Thing is particularly concerned with questions of fate and chance. It articulates these concerns via an unusual formal structure, in which the episodic turns out to be dovetailed with the anachronic. In this way, the connections among the characters are framed as intersecting paths not only in space but also in time. Like *21 Grams* and *Irreversible*, this film stages a thematic encounter between order and contingency. In this case, however, this encounter is framed in relation to episodic structure and to a thematic and aesthetic concern with circularity, which in turn is placed into productive tension with the notion of temporal irreversibility.

Indeed, the 'one thing' around which the conversations in this film all centre is arguably contingency itself. The film is broken up, as the title indicates, into 13 conversations, each of which is preceded by an intertitle quoting a section of the dialogue (for example, 'show me a happy man', and 'you look so serious'. These sections, then, function a little like chapters. Initially, these appear to be telling entirely separate stories, but as the film goes on, we revisit characters and situations, and discover the connections between the different narrative threads. In essence, this is a multithreaded narrative in the vein of *Short Cuts* (Robert Altman, 1993) that initially disavows its interconnectedness by breaking up its narrative into discrete pieces.

The various narrative sections follow four separate groups of characters. In one narrative thread, Troy, a young criminal lawyer, boasts to a stranger in a bar (Gene) about his latest professional victory. Later, after accidentally hitting a young woman (Beatrice) with his car, he leaves the scene of the accident and attempts to conceal what has happened. In a second thread, Walker, a physics professor, lectures his class on chaos theory, and carries on an affair with Helen, a professor of English. The third thread follows Beatrice, a housekeeper who is attracted to one of her clients, an architect. Walking home, she is run down by Troy's car. In the fourth thread, Gene (a manager for an insurance company, and the stranger that Troy met at the beginning) is annoyed by Wade Bowman, an irrepressibly buoyant employee, and conspires to have him dismissed. Despite this, Bowman retains his positive outlook.

Once these threads are established, the film works to knit them more closely together. Troy sells his BMW (the one he was driving when he ran over Beatrice) to Walker. Both Beatrice and Troy lose their positive outlook after the accident (crippled by guilt, Troy has even taken to cutting himself with a razor blade). Later, after discovering that the girl he ran over is still alive, Troy expresses a wish to make amends. Meanwhile, Beatrice, in an epiphanic moment, sees a man on the street smiling, and abandons her suicidal urges. The man is none other than Bowman himself. Bowman meets Gene and tells him about his new job, unaware that Gene, in a fit of guilt, had covertly arranged it for him. In a bar, Gene tells his colleague Dick that he has been 'downsized', and encounters the boastful Troy once more (in other words, we are revisiting the scene from the beginning of the film). Finally, on a subway train, Gene and Patricia (who do not know one another) exchange a smile.

This convoluted narrative plays a very deliberate game with time. Firstly, contingency is a structuring principle for the plot, as the various narrative threads are connected by the most tenuous filaments of chance. Walker's plot, for instance, appears connected to the others only by the fact that he buys Troy's car (although it is possible that the person who mugged him may have been Gene's son Ronnie). Beatrice is connected to Gene only by her brief encounter with Bowman, and Gene to Walker by the smile he exchanges with Patricia (Walker's wife). On examining these tenuous connections, however, it becomes clear that the film constructs an improbably tight network of chance. The carefully plotted encounters begin to take on the whiff of determinism, as it seems that these characters are united by fate. The film balances this tendency by leaving the connections open-ended. The improbable contingencies are never allowed to transform into outrageous coincidences, as the characters generally remain unaware of the connections.

At the same time, chance is actively foregrounded as a theme within the diegesis. Walker's lecture is an explanation of irreversibility, couched in terms familiar to any reader of Prigogine and Stengers' *Order Out of Chaos*. Walker explains that entropy, 'the movement of an isolated material system from one state of equilibrium to another', affirms the irreversibility of time, because 'it can never go back to the way it was'. In his own story, this observation reflects upon the ill-advised decisions that he will not be able to remedy later: leaving his wife, and turning away a student who later commits suicide. Chance and irreversibility are therefore the drivers of the story.

Conversely, the film is also thematically informed by a long-lived popular idea that emphasizes circularity, namely the wheel of fortune. From the beginning of Troy's obnoxious boasting at the beginning of the film, we are led to expect a reversal of fortune for this character. This notion is reinforced by the story Gene recounts to Troy, concerning a friend who suffered bad luck after winning a lottery. In accordance with this principle, Troy has his accident that very night. The wheel of fortune appears to shape and direct the outcomes for the other characters too: Beatrice cycles from optimism to despair and back to optimism again; Bowman's sunny outlook cannot save him from redundancy, but it carries him back to employment; Walker escapes domestic entrapment only to be returned to another type of entrapment; and Gene's confidence is diminished by his son's conduct and his feelings of guilt regarding Bowman. Characters who are at the top of the wheel move to the bottom, and vice versa. Conversations between characters emphasize this movement: 'show me a happy man', says Gene, 'and I'll show you an accident waiting to happen'. Here, the word happy retains a little of its archaic meaning: the notion of 'hap', or chance. We are reminded that contentment is merely a matter of chance. 'There's no reason', concludes Beatrice after her accident. Yet if chance is framed in terms of accidents and unhappiness, it also possesses the power to unite characters and bring happiness (as in *21 Grams*). Beatrice witnesses Bowman's smile by accident, and it leads to a positive change in her thinking.

Of course, the notion of the wheel of fortune also has roots in determinism, and this is affirmed by sense of inevitability to the reversals of fortune undergone by the characters. The penultimate scene reinforces the dialectic between contingency and determinism. Gene delivers to Troy the gypsy curse: 'may you get what you want, and want what you get'. We are aware that Troy will immediately suffer his reversal of fortune, so this scene asks us to imagine, at least, that the curse has taken effect. Following this, Dick comments to Gene that 'life only makes sense when we look at it backwards... too bad we gotta live it forwards'. This comment reinforces the role of contingency in determining the fates of the characters. In an affirmation of Frank Kermode's argument, only retrospective vision demonstrably offers the consolation of form, turning *chronos* into *kairos*. The circular form of the wheel of fortune is therefore a way of reconciling irreversible, contingent time with retrospective order and meaning.

Finally, circularity emerges in the film's narrative dynamics. Indeed, the culminating game of time played by this episodic narrative turns out to be an anachronic game. The second and penultimate scenes are, it transpires, variations on the same scene, in which Gene and Troy have their conversation regarding happiness and chance. The arrival of this revelation at the end of the film creates a temporal split in the preceding narrative. During the rest of the film, we have been given no clues that Troy's narrative thread and Gene's are not, in fact, contemporaneous. Effectively, the end of Gene's thread is the beginning of Troy's. We now realize that Gene had been speaking with the benefit of hindsight at the beginning, because this scene, in diegetic terms, comes *after* his manipulation of Bowman's fate and his own redundancy. The penultimate scene thus serves as a flashback in relation to Troy's story, but not in relation to Gene's. Like more overt anachronic modular narratives, *13 Conversations About One Thing* articulates temporal differences in ways that cannot be described purely in terms of flashback.

Furthermore, the film's episodic structure has served to conceal the temporal split between Gene's story and the others. Two distinct times have been interleaved as if they were parallel. Our discovery that this is not the case creates a fragmented, schismatic temporal model. Yet as with *21 Grams*, this fragmentation is mitigated by the contingencies that allow for human connections to be made. Unlike late modernism's affirmation of schism, these films recuperate narrative order via the mediating influence of database structure. In this way, schismatic temporality becomes interconnected, re-ordered modular temporality, and Dick's comment about life taking on order retrospectively resonates through the film's structure. For we have been looking at the characters all along with a kind of retrospective vision grounded in Gene's world-weary, but humanist, perspective. In addition, the circular structure of the narrative provides an artificial narrative analogue to the film's wheel of fortune motif. These formal games gesture towards a sense of order bordering on the deterministic, but like *Irreversible*, this film asserts that such order manifests itself only in retrospect. The characters in this film must resign themselves to living their lives forwards, or in other words, to the challenge and promise of contingency.

Remediation, games and the database: *Run Lola Run*

The motif of circularity takes on a more literal significance in forking-path narratives. Whereas anachronic narratives manipulate the *syuzhet* (plot) without indicating a fundamental disruption to the underlying *fabula* (story), forking-path narratives focus upon crucial events in the fabula, and the various outcomes that may result from (often very minor) differences in these events. Each iteration of the syuzhet corresponds, in other words, to a distinctly different version of the fabula. As in anachronic modular narratives, contingency is embodied in the chance events that help to shape the course of the narrative. However, the parallel worlds invoked by forking-path narratives provide a fundamental challenge to the notion of irreversible time. We are invited to parse each iteration of the syuzhet for differences, heightening our awareness of the mediating role of narrative. In this way, forking-path narratives query the relationship between representation and contingency. If all worlds are possible worlds, then the narrative outcomes within these worlds may be seen as predetermined. In this scenario, order is not retrospective but simultaneous; it is simply a matter of finding oneself in the right world.[9]

This section will focus upon a prominent example of the forking-path narrative: Tom Tykwer's *Run Lola Run* (1998). Other films that make use of this conceit include *Sliding Doors* (Peter Howitt, 1998), *Groundhog Day* (Harold Ramis, 1993), *Blind Chance* (Krzysztof Kieślowski, 1981) and *La double-vie de Véronique* (Krzysztof Kieślowski, 1991). More than any of these films, *Run Lola Run* can be said to display a digital aesthetic, in particular because its narrative structure directly invokes the database structure of new media and computer games. In addition, the film foregrounds mediation – not only the mediating role of narrative, but also the temporal mediation afforded by clock time and by different film and video formats.

As with the films already discussed in this chapter, contingency emerges as both threat and opportunity in *Run Lola Run*. The film follows three alternative paths, with the main character Lola trying in each case to acquire 100,000 Deutschmarks by noon in order to save her boyfriend

Manni, who owes the money to some underworld figures. With each iteration of the narrative, a small difference in timing leads to a wildly different outcome: the death of Lola (she is shot by the police), the death of Manni (he is run over by an ambulance) and with the final iteration, Lola's success. In the third iteration, Lola secures the needed funds by letting out a piercing scream that not only shatters the windows of a casino but also happens to determine a game of roulette in her favour. In this way, contingency provides both the threat of fatal consequences and the conditions for Lola's success.

The forking-path conceit is reinforced throughout the film. During the exposition, as Manni describes how he has lost the money to a tramp on the subway, he suggests a list of exotic destinations to which the tramp may have escaped. This list is accompanied by a rapid-fire series of postcard images corresponding to each of the destinations. Here, the diegesis momentarily becomes a catalogue of narrative possibilities – paths which *might* be taken by the character in question, but not necessarily (in fact, we later find out that the tramp remains in Berlin). This technique (a barrage of still images cataloguing potential outcomes) is repeated throughout the film, in amusing and inventive ways. As Lola bumps into various characters on her quest, we hear the sound of a camera flash, followed by a rapid series of photographs showing us what is to become of the character in question. In each iteration of the narrative, minor circumstantial changes appear to produce radically different outcomes for the characters in these 'flashforwards'. Thus, in three distinct flashforward sequences, a sour-faced woman that Lola bumps into variously steals a baby, wins the lottery and becomes a born-again Christian. A young man who offers to sell his bike to Lola variously meets and marries a young woman, dies of a drug overdose, and sells his bike to the tramp.

In a sense, these flashforwards, and the film's tripartite narrative, serve as a virtual illustration of chaos theory, bringing to mind the bifurcations in chaotic systems described by Prigogine and Stengers. Furthermore, the non-linear functions that characterize chaotic systems 'connote an often startling incongruity between cause and effect, so that a small cause can give rise to a large effect' (Hayles 1990, 11). As Prigogine and Stengers describe it, contingency is a stronger force at moments of bifurcation, 'while between bifurcations the deterministic aspects would become dominant' (Prigogine and Stengers 1984, 176). Similarly, a small initial change in Lola's narrative (jumping over the dog on the stairs) leads to a series of divergent and unpredictable outcomes. Lola's actions change the course of events at key moments, while at other times events seem to follow a pre-determined path. The film thus demonstrates what Prigogine and Stengers describe as 'a delicate interplay between chance and necessity, between fluctuations and deterministic laws' (176). Thus, irreversible time is manifest in the events that inexorably shape Lola's world.

At the same time, by presenting three parallel narrative segments, the film undermines irreversible time, suggesting that time can be played back and the course of events reversed or altered. This sense of reversible, deterministic time is heightened by the overt deployment of multiple layers of mediation. *Run Lola Run*, indeed, is a film that sets out to make its audience aware of formal considerations. J. David Bolter and Richard Grusin use 'hypermediacy' to refer to the way that certain media texts remind us of their status as mediations, often by multiplying 'the signs of mediation', or rupturing 'the illusion of realistic representation' (1999, 34). In *Run Lola Run*, this is accomplished through frequent switching among colour and black-and-white film, digital video footage, still photographs, postcards and 2-D animation (most notably, in the scene where Lola runs down the staircase of her apartment building). The immediate experiences of Lola and Manni are portrayed in 35mm colour; black-and-white footage is used for flashbacks and video for the characters associated with the bank. Hypermediacy is also to be found in the split-screen sequences in which Lola races to intercept Manni at the supermarket. In each case, Lola and Manni share the screen despite being in different locations, and the image of a ticking clock is eventually added as well. By consistently associating certain forms of mediation with certain events (for instance, animation for Lola's sprint down the stairs), the film seems to suggest that each narrative path consists of nothing more than a series of media clips. Lola may fail or succeed in reaching the bottom of the stairs in time, but she will always do so in the form of a cartoon character, viewed from the same perspective each time.

Temporal mediation is also foregrounded in the narrative set-up, which gives Lola precisely 20 minutes to achieve her goal. This emphasis on clock time is further enhanced by incorporating a ticking sound into the insistent beat of the film's techno soundtrack, and by showing a clock onscreen at crucial moments (in particular, in a split-screen image as Lola runs to stop Manni from holding up the shopping centre). *Run Lola Run* therefore presents a temporal world far removed from the modernist literary techniques of Joyce, Proust and Woolf, and the theories of Henri Bergson, all of which counterposed subjective time to official, 'clock' time. Here, all aspects of time are mediated technologically, and there is no serious attempt to represent Lola's psychological workings in order to excavate a deeper, personal temporality. Public time is inescapable. Yet time itself (both public and private) is also splintered by the film's narrative bifurcations, producing a schismatic time reminiscent of late modernist literature and cinema. The difference is that, in this case, modular structure allows for a recuperation of narrative sense and order. 'What a Difference a Day Makes', sings Dinah Washington as Lola and Manni escape the shopping centre in slow motion, reasserting temporal difference and overcoming both clock time and temporal schism, at least for a moment. Yet the foregrounding of clock time nonetheless frames contingent events in relation to rational, ordered time.

Temporal mediation extends to the film's remediation of other media forms. Jim Bizzochi has described the way that *Run Lola Run* remediates music videos (in its reliance on music and visual style, and the combination of 'immediate engagement with sustainability'), video games and computerized databases (Bizzochi 2005, 2). For Bizzochi, the remediation of database aesthetics is the film's most significant formal feature. Yet I would also emphasize the way that *Run Lola Run* invokes the database *via* its remediation of video games. The film's direct goal-driven exposition and tripartite structure (comprising two failed narratives followed by a successful one) is immediately reminiscent of the classic arcade-game set-up, where players have three 'lives' in order to achieve their mission. In *Run Lola Run*, Lola 'dies' or fails twice, with victory occurring on the third attempt. As in a computer game, Lola learns techniques during her unsuccessful attempts that allow her to complete the mission on the final pass. For example, she struggles with the safety catch on her gun in the first section, but operates it confidently the next time.

The film's most direct acknowledgements of videogames (and games in general) come at the beginning and end of the film. In the first scene, a man (who is later revealed to be a security guard at the bank where Lola's father works) appears from amongst a mob of people to declare that 'the ball is round; the game lasts ninety minutes'. He then kicks the ball high into the air, initiating the film's title sequence. The resolution of the film's central conflict also depends directly upon a game: Lola accumulates the money required to save Manni by playing roulette at the local casino. The roulette wheel, ball and clock on the casino's wall reiterate the circular motif established with the soccer ball at the opening of the film. This motif has been reinforced throughout the film with repeated shots of clocks and spirals. Spiral patterns appear in the animated opening of the film, in the hair of a woman depicted in a painting in the casino (a direct reference in turn to the main female character and spiral motif in Alfred Hitchcock's *Vertigo* [1958]), and in the staircase descended by an animated Lola at the beginning of each quest.[10] These stylistic gestures form part of another kind of game: the one that is being played with the audience's expectations, as we make connections among these motifs and among the small, but crucial, changes in each reiteration of the narrative. Although the narrative is not drawn directly from an existing computer game, it is one of the clearest examples of cinema mimicking the form of games.

In this respect, *Run Lola Run* is more vulnerable than *21 Grams* or *Irreversible* to Sean Cubitt's charge that modular narratives are essentially deterministic. According to Cubitt, such narratives unfold within closed worlds, revealing the diegesis as 'a knowledge base, its secrets resources to be picked up and used, like the energy and weapons in computer shoot-'em-ups' (2004, 240). It is certainly the case that the world of *Run Lola Run*, with its videogame references and structure, appears as a closed system, in which a finite number of objects, characters and scenarios are deployed in three variations. Here, the city itself functions as a database of characters, tools and situations. For Cubitt this type of diegetic environment is so fundamentally deterministic that it undermines narrative itself. Modular narratives therefore 'only appear to be narrative. In fact they are the result of one of many possible rifles through a database of narrative events whose coincidence is more structural or even architectural than temporal' (238). Yet games and narratives are not as mutually opposed as this argument would suggest. In video games, as Marie-Laure Ryan points out, players perform actions which could later be recounted as dramatic plots (although this is generally not the main focus of players during gameplay). In this way, games 'embody a virtualized, or potential dramatic narrativity', regardless of whether the 'plot' of the game is actually recounted (2001). Furthermore, Cubitt's argument overlooks the extent to which narratives *in general* are constituted from a database of possible characters and events. The idea that modular narratives are an affirmation of 'personal destiny' (239) might equally be applied to a great many conventional narratives.

Moreover, *Run Lola Run*'s forking-path structure is not directly opposed to the operations of narrative. Whereas computer games offer the potential for numerous iterations of the 'story', this film makes these iterations finite, and yokes them to cinematic three-act structure. The observation of rules is central to the film's structural games. On the one hand, *Run Lola Run* gestures self-consciously to the rules of computer games, while on the other demonstrating the way that these rules can fit within the framework of narrative. In doing so, the film revisits the negotiation between the contingent and the pre-determined from a ludic perspective, refiguring narrative itself as a kind of game. The remediation of computer game tropes serves as a way of bringing contingency into a narrative context.

While games function according to a predetermined set of rules, they proceed according to the unfolding of contingent events. *Run Lola Run* invokes this ludic contingency by remediating games, both of skill (soccer and videogames) and of chance (roulette). Notably, Lola's defining narrative act is to use her 'superpower' – her glass-shattering scream – in order to turn the roulette game in her favour. A game of chance is suddenly transformed into a game of skill. In one sense contingency is overcome, but only, it must be noted, in the most perversely ironic way. There is no indication that Lola is able to alter the outcome of the game with any precision. Rather, her actions add another layer of contingency to the game, and this is what allows for the happy resolution of the plot. Similarly, contingency manifests itself both in the accident that takes Manni's life, and the encounter with the tramp that allows him to retrieve the money.

Rather than doing away with contingency, *Run Lola Run* places contingency in the context of digital mediation and database aesthetics, while reflecting upon the contemporary viability of narrative form. In this way, the film connects to an existing literary tradition of forking-path narratives. Addressing the temporal games of Robbe-Grillet and other authors of experimental literature, Ursula Heise comments that 'the insistent play on the almost same without any psychological motivation introduces a strong element of contingency into narrative' (1997, 58). In making use of such a bifurcating narrative model, argues Heise, such writers aimed at making contingency narratable. Contingency in the late modern novel is 'made narratable not by its conversion into teleological form, as in the nineteenth-century novel, or by its recuperation through the human mind, as in the high-modernist novel, but through its displacement from the future to the present and past' (67). In a similar fashion, *Run Lola Run*'s games with narrative are directed towards making contingency narratable. Although such fictions can be criticized for avoiding the task of envisioning the future (paralleling Cubitt's criticism of modular narratives), their value, as Heise suggests, lies in the way that they reflect upon the interplay between causality and contingency (68).

Run Lola Run offers a (fanciful and highly artificial) 'solution' to the temporal problems articulated by late modernist literature and literary

hypertext. Rather than fusing together its disjunctive array of temporalities, the film simply allows its protagonist to navigate among this array.
It also facilitates reflection upon the workings of narratives in general.
As Edward Branigan argues, any fiction plays host to a number of
'alternative plots and failed stories whose suppressed realization is the
condition for what is seen to be more safely offered in the explicit text'
(2002, 110). In this sense, there is great value to be found in what is
'nearly true' in any fiction: the 'ghostly' unrealized futures that underlie
the completed narrative (111). By extension, forking-path plots, by drawing explicit attention to a few of these alternatives, elevate contingency
rather than neutralize it: 'a forking-path plot makes explicit the causal
hypothetical, "What if?" that is present but is generally implicit in
conventional narratives' (2002, 110).[11]

One apparent difference between forking-path and anachronic narratives is in their treatment of mortality. Narrative endings and death are
very obviously connected in *Run Lola Run*, as the first two unsuccessful
iterations of the plot end with the deaths of Lola and Manni, respectively. These deaths, separated from the conclusion of the film, recall
Frank Kermode's assertion that the End (apocalypse and death) is immanent rather than simply imminent in contemporary fiction (1967, 6).
Yet whereas *21 Grams* and *Irreversible* saturate their anachronic narrative
structure with a concomitant mood of violence and doom, *Run Lola Run*
is upbeat by comparison. The post-mortem revival of each of the main
characters diminishes the dramatic and thematic weight of mortality in
the film. In this regard the film is certainly vulnerable to Janet Murray's
charge that contemporary non-linear narratives and games exhibit a
denial of closure that is also 'a refusal to face mortality' (1998, 175).

Significantly, however, *Run Lola Run* departs from computer game
structure by following up each death with a conversation between Lola
and Manni. In each case the image is saturated with red, separating it
visually from the rest of the film. These scenes are not situated temporally, and the fact that each follows on from the death of one of the
characters gives the segments an atemporal quality, as if the characters
are in some kind of afterworld. Yet rather than simply disavowing the
deaths of the protagonists, the film uses the conversation scenes, in
which they discuss their love for one another, as a way of investing the
deaths with emotional weight and meaning. Not only do these scenes
reaffirm the connection between death and meaning, they also reinforce
the traditional centrality of the heterosexual couple in narrative fiction.
Like its anachronic counterparts, *Run Lola Run* is far from Catherine
Russell's description of the separation of death and meaning in late

modernist cinema (1995, 2). The affirmation of contingency in *Run Lola Run*, as in anachronic modular narratives, is qualified by a reconciliation with narrative order and meaning.

The films discussed in this chapter present narrative time according to a number of different models that depart from the linear. In these films, time becomes variously a spiral, a circle, a series of bifurcating paths or a heap of fragments. These temporal models have divergent implications. On the one hand they suggest contingency by proceeding according to a logic of chaos, or by juxtaposing divergent narrative possibilities. On the other, they invoke determinism by foregrounding mediation, replaying narrative events and allowing endings to precede beginnings. In these films, there is a concern with preserving narrative time both from determinism and from disorder. Modular narrative form mediates between these two poles. The preservation of contingency in these films is distinct from the early modernists' valorization of contingency in the form of individual psychology, as well as from the late modernists' embrace of pure schism, although it draws a little from both. The relative commercial success of recent modular narratives suggests that this discourse of contingency and order has well and truly emerged into the popular sphere. On the one hand, the ubiquity of digital media has allowed audiences to grapple with the database aesthetics of modular narratives, and to make sense of them. On the other, this ubiquity invites a renewal of public anxieties regarding the representation of time and the viability of traditional narrative forms.

4

Navigating Memory: Temporal Anchoring and the Modular Subject

Intersecting with contemporary cinema's treatment of contingency and temporal experience is a discourse regarding memory and forgetting. This discourse has its roots in the persistent anxiety (from ancient times to the present day) that technology erodes the capacity for recollection. Indeed, the connection between memory and narrative extends as far back as the origins of storytelling itself. Prior to the written word, cultures depended upon the memory of their storytellers for the retention and transmission of both fictional and historical narratives. For the Ancient Greeks, memory techniques were an essential aspect of rhetoric, and the preservation of memory a significant concern. With the emergence of new forms of mediation throughout the modern and postmodern eras, anxieties regarding both the erasure and reification of memory have been substantially renewed. The struggle to remember is a central concern of a great many recent films, a trend which shows no signs of abating.[1] Modular narratives are particularly marked examples of this trend, as the temporal shifts within the narrative are often linked directly to the action of mnemonic recall. Modular narratives are part of a literary-filmic tradition concerned with the representation of memory, and also participate in a fraught discourse questioning representation's threat to memory.

Even when not directly concerned with representing character memory, anachronic modular narratives address memory via their very narrative structure. This effect is often produced through the multiplication of narrative gaps and redundancies. In *21 Grams*, for example, abrupt time shifts at the beginning of the film appear to disrupt the exposition. The first few scenes show Cristina and Paul lying in bed together, Cristina's husband and kids walking along the street, Cristina in drug rehabilitation and Jack exhorting a young man to believe in Jesus. We are not offered the diegetic information that would allow us to properly identify these characters or their significance to the narrative. *21 Grams* offers us a dramatically disrupted exposition, setting up an abnormally large number of narrative 'gaps' to be filled by the subsequent scenes. In this way, the film deliberately challenges our ability to retain narrative information, and to organize diegetic temporality in meaningful ways. As the film progresses, we are able to piece together the context for these initial scenes. Yet by foregrounding narrative gaps, *21 Grams* draws attention to the memory processes involved in making sense of a narrative, and invests these with a heightened urgency. Thus, temporal organization becomes a potential source of anxiety for viewers. In *Irreversible*, the reversed linear structure is easier to grasp than the scrambled order of *21 Grams*, yet audience memory is still addressed and foregrounded. In this case, each segment ends almost arbitrarily and is superseded by an 'earlier' scene. Again, abnormally emphasized narrational gaps confront the spectator with the task of deciphering the film's temporal code. At the same time, we are made distinctly aware that the violent events of the beginning and the middle of the film are in the diegetic future rather than the past, and thus of the disparity between the characters' knowledge of events and our 'memory' of what befalls them.

Forking-path narratives also address memory directly, firstly by invoking the audience's memory of parallel narrative threads. These stories derive their particular effect from an interplay between repetition and difference, inviting audiences to recall previous narrative iterations and observe the changes in subsequent iterations. In some cases, forking-path narratives may raise the issue of memory within the diegesis, showing us characters who consciously experience the narrative bifurcations. For example, *Groundhog Day* (Harold Ramis, 1993) tells the story of Phil, a misanthropic weatherman who is forced to live the same day over and over until he becomes worthy of the affections of his producer, Rita. Phil is eventually able to predict the events that shape his day, and alters his behaviour to create different outcomes. In this situation, the protagonist remembers everything that his fellow characters forget. Phil moves through a kind of memory-world that enables him to orient himself. Yet this is also a problem for Phil, who wants to overcome repetition and establish an ongoing romance with Rita. In this sense, the resolution of the romantic narrative depends upon the domestication of 'excess' memory. Although *Groundhog Day* does not set out to represent memory itself, the film establishes a dialectic between memory and forgetting, and stakes the narrative upon the resolution of this dialectic.

Anachronic modular narratives, however, are the ones most closely concerned with memory, because flashbacks are conventionally used as a representation of human psychological processes. This connection is particularly noticeable in films concerned with psychological crisis and the failure of memory (exemplified by the amnesia plots of classic *film noir* and the time-shifting narratives of science fiction). *Memento* (Christopher Nolan, 2000), and *Eternal Sunshine of the Spotless Mind* (Michel Gondry, 2004), both examples of the memory problem film as anachronic modular narrative, set up a particularly complex relationship between memory (specifically, *mediated* memory) and narrative, in which forgetting plays a central and ambiguous role. The films discussed here represent a kind of synthesis of earlier generic traditions: *Memento* is a neo-*noir* that takes the flashback structure of noir to new extremes; *Eternal Sunshine*, on the other hand, is a romantic comedy that also invokes postmodern science fiction by exploring the connections between subjectivity and technology. In representing the thematics of memory directly in their syntagmatic structures, both films are closely related to late-modernist 1960s French cinema, particularly the narrative and temporal experiments of Alain Resnais (including *Last Year at Marienbad*, 1961). What these films share, articulated via their convoluted narrative structures, is an ambivalence towards memory, despite the apparent attempts at retrieval on the part of the main characters. In one sense at least, memory becomes a problem to be surmounted in order for narrative sense and order to be established (the fact that this is never achieved in *Last Year at Marienbad* marks it out from the current crop of modular narratives). Indeed, in each case forgetting becomes the necessary precondition for experience (sometimes at great cost to the other characters, as in *Memento*). In both of these films, memory becomes externalized, through technological means or otherwise, and transformed into a navigable archive. The traversal of this archive provides the characters (and potentially audiences) with opportunities for pleasure and control, but also provokes anxieties regarding forgetting and the loss of identity.

Memory and mediation: *Eternal Sunshine of the Spotless Mind*

Eternal Sunshine of the Spotless Mind tells the tale of Joel and Clementine, an eccentric couple whose relationship founders, leading Clementine to have the whole messy business erased from her mind, courtesy of a mysterious company called Lacuna Inc. Learning that this has happened,

Joel too undergoes the procedure, but deciding part way through that he does not want to forget Clementine, he frantically attempts to foil the erasure process from within his own mind. Although Joel ultimately fails in this attempt, he and Clementine are later reunited and given a second chance. The film uses a database aesthetic to show the anxiety attached to discontinuity and the loss of memory in an era of digital mediation. At the same time, it echoes modernism's attachment to discontinuity, both as a pragmatic way of overcoming the past, and as a way of intensifying memories through the threat of their destruction. The film's database structure sets up a complex, fluctuating relationship between anchored and floating time, which reflects in turn upon memory and forgetting, and the articulation of (structured) work and (unstructured) play time. A comparison with Alain Resnais's *Je t'aime, je t'aime* (1968) will illustrate the extent to which Gondry's film both revisits and renovates the modernist treatment of time. In particular, both films reveal a desire to be free of order, and to retain it; to break the grip of the past upon the present, and to reinforce it. In *Eternal Sunshine*, however, the relationships between order and disorder, work and play, memory and forgetting, become increasingly ambiguous. The film's convoluted narrative structure moves away from memory, chronology and order, and towards them as well. The modernist affirmation of creative forgetting may still be present, but it is heavily qualified.

Eternal Sunshine highlights the intimate relationship between memory and mediation, a relationship that is not unique to the digital era but extends throughout the history of representation. Douwe Draaisma observes that artificial aids to memory have 'not only supported, relieved and occasionally replaced natural memory, but they have also shaped our views of remembering and forgetting', providing 'the terms and concepts with which we have reflected on our own memory' (2000, 3). Both Plato and Aristotle envisioned memory as a waxen tablet, upon which thoughts and impressions were inscribed, and from which they could also be erased (Yates 35–6).[2] Memory has also been imagined as 'an electrical trace, a cluster sparking on a network, a library made of eroding fabric, a mental theater with painted doors' (Klein 1997, 14). Among these memory metaphors, erasure is a recurring feature (14).[3] During the nineteenth century, the accelerating rate of technological development produced a host of new scientific metaphors for memory, from the daguerrotype and other early forms of photography, to colour photography and eventually cinematography (Draaisma 2000, 3). Yet photographic metaphors for memory began eventually to be abandoned by scientists, because they suggested 'a memory that forgets nothing, that contains a perfect, permanent record of our visual experience' (121). This analogy clearly failed to account for the shifting, unpredictable nature of memory. Coincident with these relatively immutable models for memory, and alongside the ongoing struggle to preserve memory, emerged a more ambivalent, strand of thinking, in which the loss of memory, rather than something to be simply mourned, came to be seen as a catalyst for new ideas and aesthetic experiences. As Norman Klein puts it in his book *The History of Forgetting*, the Romantics 'gloried in the ruins of memory' (1997, 304). This elevation of an 'exotic forgetfulness' extends into the modern, exemplified by Proust's evocation of the vulnerability and volatility of memory in *In Search of Lost Time* (1913–27), but also by popular horror tales such as *Dr Jekyll and Mr Hyde* (Robert Louis Stevenson, 1886). Meanwhile Freidrich Nietzsche complained of the modern hypertrophy of monumental, official history, and argued for creative forgetting as a cure (1983, 62).[4]

These notions of personal memory and romantic forgetfulness have been substantially reframed by postmodern theorists. Fredric Jameson argues, for instance, that postmodernism has largely cast aside modernism's intense interest in duration and personal memory, replacing it with an addiction to images and sensations unmoored from their historical context (1991, 16). This hypertrophy of mediation, driven essentially by the rise of market capitalism, has produced a radical loss of social, historical and cultural memory. Indeed, the reproduction and juxtaposition of unrelated styles and fashions has eroded our sense of history and temporal order, producing a schizophrenic experience of temporality (27).[5] Yet Andreas Huyssen, while observing that contemporary culture is afflicted by a loss of history (a technologically driven collective amnesia), argues that this is offset, particularly since the 1970s, by a 'memory boom of unprecedented proportions' (1995, 5). This memory boom encompasses the growth in architectural restoration and museum attendances, the popularity of nostalgia and retro fashions, the postmodern historical novel, the embrace of home video technology and the public focus on the ethno-political traumas of colonialism (Huyssen 2000, 24–5). For Huyssen, the memory boom is not simply another version of the empty pastiche described by Jameson. Instead, it represents an anchoring technique with which contemporary subjects can orient themselves. Huyssen turns to Nietzsche to contextualize the current status of memory. In contrast to Nietzsche's emphasis on the burden of monumental official history, which must be resisted through 'active forgetting', Huyssen points out that in our own times, culture and knowledge come to us in a more fragmentary and free-floating form (1995, 7). In this context, active *recollection* is what helps us to establish a more stable sense of temporality. Huyssen's notion of temporal anchoring illuminates the struggle to retain memory in modular narratives such as *Eternal Sunshine of the Spotless Mind* and *Memento*.

Eternal Sunshine of the Spotless Mind overflows with memory metaphors, both ancient and modern. First of all, Joel's fragile memory is echoed thematically by the rather literary metaphors of snow, sand, cracking ice and the crumbling house in which the lovers take shelter at the end of the film. Secondly, memory is figured as a kind of writing. Despite the fact that Joel's occupation remains a mystery, we do know that he is a writer, as he keeps a journal. The erasure of his memory is represented in the blank pages he finds in his diary. Clementine herself is a 'book slave' at Barnes and Noble, and in one scene we see the titles erasing themselves from the spines of the books. As Joel and Clementine lie upon the frozen surface of the Charles River, she challenges him to identify a constellation. Unable to, he inscribes one upon the heavens with a gesture ('a swoop, and a cross'). Both the ice and the sky lend themselves to games involving writing and erasure. After Joel and Clementine's treatment, a Lacuna employee, Patrick, takes Clementine back to the river, where the frozen surface acts as a blank slate for his acts of romantic plagiarism.

In its use of narrational techniques particular to the cinema, *Eternal Sunshine* invokes cinema itself as a memory metaphor. Cinematic metaphors came to dominate scientific thinking on memory at the turn of the twentieth century, and in comparison with photographic metaphors, were better able to incorporate the properties of change and movement. The cinematic metaphor was a long-lived one. Maureen Turim notes that following World War II, cinema was 'an operative metaphor for the brain's imaging capacity' embodied by modernist cinema's temporal articulations but also current within the broader cultural and scientific context (1989, 206). Throughout cinema's history, filmmakers have been conscious of the potential for representing memory cinematically, in particular through the device of the flashback. Turim comments that 'memory, in its psychoanalytic and philosophical dimensions, is one of the concepts inscribed in flashbacks' (2). Early experimental filmmakers from Europe and Japan used the flashback to portray associative mental processes (an approach that was to influence the modernist cinema of the 1960s), and it was also taken up by the German expressionists (and eventually, *film noir*) with a psychoanalytic emphasis (101). During the 1940s and early 1950s, the flashback was embraced by Hollywood, particularly in the genre of *film noir*. David Bordwell credits the contemporaneous popular influence of Freudian psychoanalysis with this shift (Bordwell, Staiger and Thompson 1985, 43). Within Hollywood cinema, the intensified use of the flashback often coincided with an attempt to represent psychological crisis. In the case of *Eternal Sunshine*, Joel's mnemonic slippages are themselves identified directly with the film's disjunctive flashback structure.

Finally, digital technology provides a way of envisioning memory in *Eternal Sunshine*. To some degree, this metaphor also parallels developments in scientific thinking. Following the dominance of cinematic metaphors for memory, in the period following World War II the computer began to take over as a leading metaphor, because it had the apparent ability to process symbols and meaning (Draaisma 2000, 231). In the 1970s computer metaphors became less popular, as they failed to account for human memory's use of intuition and supposition, its relative fallibility and the brain's ability to process many impulses simultaneously (160–1). Yet more recent theories such as connectionism, while ostensibly rejecting computer metaphors, often make use of computers to simulate neural networks (232). Thus, the computer metaphor has retained at least some of its explanatory power. Moreover, in our contemporary context, 'numerous "artificial" memories are available for what the eye and ear take in: cassette recorders, video, CDs, computer memories, holograms' (2). Among these modes of storage, recent digital technologies as well as older memory aids have become popular metaphors for memory. Increasingly, the tools we use to store and access archived materials are digital ones: from digital photographs stored on a computer hard drive, to mp3 playlists, to mobile phone address books. These mnemonic technologies have not entirely supplanted older forms: we still, of course, keep photographic prints, read books and write shopping lists. Rather, digital technology coexists with these existing technologies, and inflects the way that we think about stored information.

Eternal Sunshine foregrounds the technological mediation of memory. Lacuna's brain-scanning equipment, which targets and destroys unwanted memories, consists of a clunky headset connected to a slightly out-of-date laptop computer. The headset itself, constructed from wires and unwieldy pieces of metal, offers a mocking reminder of virtual reality technology of the 1990s. Instead of a futuristic, streamlined device, the headset resembles something salvaged from a scrap metal yard. There is a nostalgic aura attached to these apparently obsolete technologies that makes them a fitting analogue for the disappearing memories of the protagonists.[6] Yet the erasure of Joel's past is itself achieved with the aid of high technology. Consulting a computerized map of Joel's brain, the technicians zap the places where the memories are supposedly located; these show up on the computer screen, rather quaintly, as collections of coloured dots. Memories are not only representations; they are representations stored as data. In *Eternal Sunshine*, the digital mediation of time is also embodied by the overt use of special effects to represent the breakdown of memory – as when Joel's childhood home appears to 'morph' into a rundown building, people and objects suddenly disappear from the railway station and the spines of the books in Clementine's bookshop become blank. Technological mediation also makes itself felt in the disjunctive transitions between sections of Joel's past. During some of these transitions, a buzzing noise intrudes, reminding Joel (as well as the audience) that the temporal shifts are produced technologically. It is this digitally mediated process that ultimately determines the film's database structure. Although Joel eventually achieves a measure of control over his memories, deciding which to recall next or how to combine them, the sequence of memories is largely dictated by the digital erasure process. The process of recall and the process of erasure are yoked together by this process. Rather than the reminiscences of a free subject, the disjunctive structure reveals the workings of an all-pervasive digital memory, literalizing the 'high-tech amnesia' that Andreas Huyssen detects in contemporary society (1995, 5).

Eternal Sunshine of the Spotless Mind invites comparisons with the science-fiction novels of Philip K. Dick, and with 'postmodern' sci-fi films such as *Blade Runner* (Ridley Scott, 1982), *Total Recall* (Paul Verhoeven, 1990) and *Strange Days* (Kathryn Bigelow, 1995), all of which depict a future in which artificially implanted memory has become a reality. These films suggest that technological models of storage and retrieval are inseparable from the 'natural' phenomenon of human memory. Similarly, in *Eternal Sunshine*, memories are representations, and can be destroyed, manipulated or repurposed as representations. Arguably, however, this film presents an extension and a modification of the science fiction tradition by suggesting that such mnemonic mediation has become so ubiquitous that it is now virtually invisible and can be addressed without recourse to spectacular depictions of high technology. In *Eternal Sunshine of the Spotless Mind*, the digital process of memory erasure is so pervasive that its effects emerge on the level of narrative form, extending the digital memory-metaphor to the film's anachronic narrative structure. While other memory problem films (*Total Recall*, *Paycheck* [John Woo, 2003], *Johnny Mnemonic* [Robert Longo, 1995], *Dark City* [Alex Proyas, 1998]) use science-fictional tropes to address the mediation of human memory, modular narratives such as *Eternal Sunshine* extend this project by inscribing memory-loss and retrieval into the narrative structure itself.

In this respect, *Eternal Sunshine* reveals its kinship with European narrative experiments of the 1960s, particularly the films of Alain Resnais. Resnais's film *Last Year at Marienbad* (1961) is in some ways the quintessential memory problem film: it shows a series of mysterious encounters between a man and a woman, the former claiming a past relationship with the latter, who denies in turn that any such encounter took place. The narrative flows unpredictably from the present to the past and back again, to the point where a definitive version of events becomes impossible. As in *Eternal Sunshine*, the movements and failures of memory determine the shape of the story. The scrambled narrative structure, and the situation in which one character insists on memory while the other forgets, links this film to *Eternal Sunshine*. Yet there are even closer parallels in Resnais's less well-known film, *Je t'aime, je t'aime*. In this film, scientists send a man named Claude Ridder on a trip into his own past (like Joel, Claude is a frustrated writer and possesses a surname that suggests, in English, both exile and erasure). However, they are unable to bring him back, and he is shuttled between his memories in a highly disjunctive fashion. In particular, the story revisits his disintegrating relationship with an enigmatic woman named Catrine. It is unclear whether this film provided direct inspiration for *Eternal Sunshine*: screenwriter Charlie Kaufman downplays the connection to Resnais, while Gondry lists Resnais among his influences.[7] Nonetheless, the thematic and formal parallels are striking.

The key difference between the two films is that in Resnais's version neither the scientists nor the subject of their experiment have much control over mnemonic processes. Indeed, the experiment is a catastrophe: the scientists have 'lost' Claude in his own past, and he finds himself unable to return to the present. In *Eternal Sunshine*, by contrast, the scientists are able to pinpoint and eliminate individual memories in Joel's brain, and Joel discovers that he has some (limited) capacity to resist or control the erasure process. As a result, the narrative relations between associative and chronological order in the two films are quite different. Nonetheless, the mediating role of technology is central to the reworking of temporal order in both films. In *Je t'aime, je t'aime*, the operative metaphor is a filmic one. Maureen Turim comments that Resnais's film presents the past as 'a giant film archive ...; to relive a moment of the past means to arbitrarily start the image sequence at a certain point in this mass of accumulated film footage' (220). Certain actions are replayed, such as Claude walking backwards out of the sea, towards Catrine. Unlike *Eternal Sunshine* (and *Last Year at Marienbad*), *Je t'aime, je t'aime* portrays a past that is not directly altered by the process of recollection. Yet the film shows that the database structure of cinema, and its suitability for representing memory, was already an area for aesthetic investigation prior to the current dominance of digital technology, as recent work suggests (Manovich 2001b, 237; Kinder 2002a, 6).

Temporal anchoring meets temporal drift

Maureen Turim suggests that certain modernist films, including those of Resnais, not only represent memory, but also foreground fictional devices, a technique Turim frames in terms of knowledge and forgetting (190). For Turim, complex multiple, nested or disjunctive flashback structures 'can serve to self-consciously expose the mechanisms of filmic narration, the artifice through which time becomes an expressive element of narrative form' (16). Modernist flashback films are characterized by their 'concern with a relationship between narration and the unconscious on one hand and the ludic play of structure on the other' (225). Many modernist films are built around narratives showing 'The process of reassembling fragments as more complete memories' (209). These fragments are not, however, pieces of the truth, but are subject instead to a 'secondary elaboration, like the telling of a dream' (209). Memories in these films may even become blended with dreams or are distributed intersubjectively, foregrounding narrational processes and undermining conventional assumptions about the representation of memory. In conventional cinema, however, spectators can be made to 'forget' the formal workings of narrative via a process of naturalization, in which temporal structures are simply reflections of the psychological or physical activities of the characters. In these cases, the 'intellectual distance' that Turim labels a praiseworthy effect of modernist techniques is overwhelmed by its opposite: 'no emotional distance, extreme identification' (17). Here, Turim seems overly attached to a didactic spectatorship model, in which pleasure is to be avoided. Nonetheless, she is correct to suggest that classical narrative encourages audience identification and the illusion of immediacy, and therefore depends upon the 'forgetting' of mediation. In *Eternal Sunshine of the Spotless Mind*, elaborate temporal structures are used to reflect upon the fictive nature of memory, reminding us of the structuring role of narrative. Yet in contrast to Turim's model of distanciation, the disjunctive structure offers one of the key pleasures of the film, as we navigate and attempt to make sense of the details with which we are presented. Nonetheless,

Turim's model enables us to see how the relationship between flow and disruption in these films is also, at one level, a relationship between remembering and forgetting.

The narrative organization of memory is central to *Eternal Sunshine of the Spotless Mind* and *Je t'aime, je t'aime*. Yet each film operates according to distinct principles, which can be characterized in terms of temporal anchoring and temporal drift, respectively. Whereas the former refers to the work of recollection that relates the past to the present, the second describes the playful, unstructured interrelation of decontextualized temporalities. This dichotomy between work and play operates also on the diegetic level, as the characters try to escape the compartmentalized time of the workplace through the pursuit of leisure. In *Je t'aime, je t'aime*, Claude's recollections are split among leisure time with Catrine, time spent at work, and 'dead' time (waiting for trams, for example). His work time is characterized by repetition and boredom. At one point, he sits at his desk, amusing himself by telephoning the 'talking clock' and reflecting upon the succession of virtually identical three o'clocks that precede and follow the one he his currently experiencing. His time with Catrine is largely holiday time: rock-climbing in Provence, a trip to Glasgow and snorkelling in the Riviera. It is the last of these that provides the initial point of entry into Claude's past (the first image is of Claude under water), and it is the one that we return to the most often. It is also the most fragmented: Claude repeats several times the action of walking backwards out of the water towards Catrine, and each time the shots are played in non-chronological order. The free play of memory leads Claude to a contingent past moment undetermined by professional schedules. He is floating, both literally (in the water) and metaphorically (in time). Yet this temporal freedom also tilts towards chaos. Set adrift in his past, Claude cannot re-establish a connection with the present. As the film goes on, Claude cannot escape a return to the memories he would rather forget (indeed, his recent attempted suicide represents a failed attempt at forgetting). Claude blames himself for Catrine's death, which occurred as a result of a gas leak in their Glasgow hotel. The free play of achronological time leads him first to Catrine's death, and then to his own. Recalling his own suicide, Claude is launched out of the experiment. We see him lying on the ground in a number of places outside the scientific institute. In each location, he disappears. Finally, he lies on a stretcher within the institute, and it is unclear whether he will survive. The temporal drift of Claude's time-travel experiment produces a rift in temporal order that amounts to the breaking of a taboo, producing deadly consequences.

Joel is also intent upon escaping regimented time in *Eternal Sunshine*. After musing in voiceover about the commercialization of Valentine's Day, Joel decides to miss the train that will bring him to work on time, escaping to another train bound for Montauk. We never find out what Joel's job is; the film focusses upon his leisure time with Clementine, and also upon moments of play from his childhood. Yet for the other characters in the film, work time and play time become almost indistinguishable. Clementine's romances with Joel and Patrick take place during work-time at Barnes and Noble. Stan plays peekaboo with Mary at the Lacuna offices, and finds time to drink alcohol, smoke pot and have sex with Mary while working at Joel's apartment. Even Dr. Mierzwiak finds it difficult to separate work from leisure time, as he is awakened at home by Stan when Joel's erasure goes awry. It also becomes evident that Mierzwiak and Mary have previously been involved in a workplace romance. Whereas work time and play time are separate in *Je t'aime, je t'aime* (aside from one scene in which Claude imagines a young woman bathing in his office), in *Eternal Sunshine* they are inextricably linked, a connection enabled by the portability of modern technology.[8]

Play and forgetting are connected in *Eternal Sunshine*, and become fused in the film's narrative structure. The erasure process disarticulates time, sending Joel backwards into leisure time spent with Clementine. At the same time, Joel and Clementine engage in games of forgetting or death: Joel smears ketchup across his neck and lies on the floor, playing dead; Joel and Clementine place pillows over each other's faces, in a game of mock suffocation; Joel draws a picture of Clementine as a skeleton. While Claude blames himself for Catrine's death, Joel enacts Clementine's as a pleasurable game. As the erasure process goes on, Joel playfully combines memory and fiction, so that Clementine can accompany him into the past. As a child, she saves him from a cruel game that involves hitting a bird with a hammer. Together, they enjoy a bath in the sink, until forgetting literally sucks them under the water. Death, loss and forgetting underlie the film's temporal drift, but they are combined with pleasure. Indeed, *Eternal Sunshine* is an intensely romantic film. After all, it is the prospect of erasure that has lent a romantic, elegiac quality to Joel's memories in the first place. The sense of aporia, of not knowing where to begin, is not simply an obstacle to be overcome; rather, it allows for an intensity of experience and a pushing of past experience into the present.[9] Thus, this romantic comedy reveals a deeper link to earlier forms of romanticism, in which the ruins of memory evoke a heightened intensity of experience.

Yet *Eternal Sunshine* portrays a world in which play and non-linearity are at best equivocal solutions to the threat of rationalism. For the technologically produced forgetting in the film itself produces non-linearity. As Andreas Huyssen points out, creative forgetting is now an inadequate response in a context where culture is already affected by fragmentation and drift (1995, 7). The film's database structure offers freedom and temporal drift, but also threatens the characters with the triumph of rationalism. Accordingly, *Eternal Sunshine* displays an opposing tendency, towards temporal anchoring. After embarking on the memory erasure treatment, Joel decides that his memories of Clementine are too precious to be lost, and he attempts to resist the erasure. Attempting to retain memories of Clementine, Joel deliberately seeks out events from the past in which to take refuge. His approach can be described as a kind of digital mnemotechnics. In her classic study *The Art of Memory*, Frances Yates describes how the Romans took up the Greeks' discipline of mnemotechnics, which could enable an orator 'to deliver long speeches from memory with unfailing accuracy' (1966, 2). The art of memory involved imagining a series of places (*loci*), within which one could place the objects or concepts in need of being recalled. Using this architectural model, classical orators could remember lengthy speeches, strolling through the virtual space they had created and drawing upon the stored ideas and images (3). Upon the various *loci*, 'such as a house, an intercolumnar space, a corner, an arch, or the like', one could place the images, which are 'forms, marks or simulacra (*formae, notae, simulacra*) of what we wish to remember' (4). *Eternal Sunshine* invokes the art of memory by showing the ways that Joel attempts to anchor himself temporally by navigating among the virtual spaces of his memory.

Yet the film illustrates the limits of the mnemotechnic enterprise in the contemporary context, in which places become images, and images become places. Effectively, *Eternal Sunshine* portrays a psychological space in which the art of memory is rendered impossible through the technology of erasure, and also through memory's tendency to alter things as it recalls them. In one scene, Joel leaps out of his car to follow Clementine, who eludes his attempts to engage her in conversation. Turning back, he is surprised to discover his car at the opposite end of the block. Meanwhile, Clementine has suddenly reversed direction, and is walking back along the street, where Joel's car appears once again. In this way, the carefully structured space of mnemotechnics described by Frances Yates, with each item in its place, gives way to a fluid space and time in which memories abruptly distort or disappear.[10] Even a modification of the art of memory, in which Joel decides to store memories in 'places' or times where they don't belong, fails to halt the decay. Clementine (not Clementine herself, but a replica of her inside Joel's memory) encourages Joel to place his memories of her within other memories, so that the staff at Lacuna will be unable to erase her completely from his mind. For instance, in a sort of psychoanalytic parody, Joel conflates Clementine with a babysitter from his childhood, and is unsure whether to be attracted or repulsed by the view up her skirt. In *Eternal Sunshine*, the shuffling of images and places, places and images, produces a distorted technologically mediated mnemotechnics that defies spatio-temporal consistency. Confusing the distinction between places and images, Joel's mnemotechnic efforts show, in a sense, what happens when images begin to take over from *loci*.[11] These dislocations occur as a result of the erasure process, but are also willed by Joel himself, as in the above example.

Joel's manipulation of his memories proceeds according to an associative logic. Aristotle, notes Frances Yates, distinguished between two connected principles of recollection, one based upon association, the other upon order. In the first case, we remember through 'similarity, dissimilarity, contiguity'; in the second, we remember by recovering 'an order of events or impressions which will lead us to the object of our search' (Yates 1966, 24). The modular narrative, in its very form, demonstrates the relationship between these two principles of recollection. When Joel actively attempts to evade the erasure process, he actively exploits associative memory by conflating Clementine and his babysitter. Many of the transitions between memories are determined not by temporal or spatial order, but by relations of 'similarity, dissimilarity, contiguity'. In another scene, Joel and Clementine lie together on a frozen river. When Clementine disappears, Joel finds himself lying on another hard surface – a footpath. There is a dream logic to these transitions that brings together similar spaces and sensations. Both voluntary and involuntary memory are affected by this logic, which inflects Joel's memories with elements of fiction and fantasy. Few of the scenes appear as 'pure' memories. Instead, Joel traverses his own mnemonic landscape, simultaneously replaying and altering his memories en route.

It is possible to argue that Joel's technologically mediated journey through memory exemplifies the postmodern dominance of space over time (Cubitt 2004, 240; Jameson 1991, 16). After all, Joel's memories are accessed and destroyed via a spatial map of his brain. Yet we also see the way that the memories are altered in the act of recall. To remember is to repeat, but also to repeat differently, and therefore to reveal the workings of temporality. Joel's temporal anchoring deploys memory not simply as a direct representation of the past, but also as the combination and refiguration of elements of the past. Thus, a memory of Joel and Clementine sitting together on the sofa at home takes on fictional qualities as they shelter from the rain at the same time. In this way, even the schematized erasure process fails to completely determine the unfolding of Joel's recollections. Transitions between memories are not only associative, however, but are also shaped by a narrational logic based upon order. In one memory Joel walks from a bookstore where he has seen Clementine, straight into the living room of Rob and Carrie, to whom he has been describing the encounter. This transition is motivated by Joel's retelling of the events of the previous few days, and it establishes a clear relationship between the past (in which he visited Clementine in the bookstore) and the present (in which he tells his friends about it).

The film's narrative structure, then, is determined by an interplay between association and order. For the most part, the account of the failed relationship is told in reverse chronological order, while the Lacuna employees' activities are intercut in chronological order. The structure of the film, then, is not entirely non-linear, but consists of a complex interplay between linearity and non-linearity. Although Joel's journey through memory seems to unfold according to a free, associative model, there is an underlying linearity to its progress, a linearity determined by technological rather than human processes. The Lacuna erasure technique largely erases Joel's memories of Clementine in reverse chronological order. As he begins the brain-mapping process at Lacuna, the narrative leaps forward again to show Stan and Patrick at Joel's apartment as he undergoes the erasure, and there is some cross-cutting between the mapping and erasing scenes. After the extended series of scenes setting up Joel's decision to have his memories erased, the narrative then leaps back in time again. This time we see Joel and Clementine's last, unhappy, shared moments, as Joel accuses Clementine of infidelity and she treats him with contempt. From this point on, the film largely consists of successively earlier scenes of Joel and Clementine, as we trace the relationship back towards happier times. The legibility of this progression is aided by a seasonal logic. The end of the relationship is accompanied by winter scenes, while the lead-up to its demise occurs in autumn, and so forth.[12] This seasonal progression is accompanied by Clementine's changes in hair colour: from blue (winter), to red (autumn), tangerine (summer) and green (spring). These changes, in turn, help the audience to reconstruct the linear progression of the relationship.

Intercut with Joel's memories are the bumbling attempts of Patrick and Stan to clear out Joel's store of memories. These scenes are ordered chronologically. The reversed linearity of Joel and Clementine's scenes is complicated by the exigencies of the erasure process, and of memory itself. When Joel visits Clementine at the bookstore where she works, he is still holding the chopsticks from the Chinese restaurant (a scene which we have just witnessed, but which actually comes later in the story, chronologically speaking). In fact, as the film unfolds, Joel's memories are increasingly inflected by fiction and fantasy, as in the scene where Joel and Clementine find themselves lying in bed on a snowy beach. Joel also inserts his memory of Clementine into scenes from his childhood, temporarily nudging the erasure process off its linear path. Ultimately, however, Joel is led back to the beginning of his relationship – to the beach party where he met Clementine for the first time. Thus, the main progression of the narrative is from the misery of Joel and Clementine's break up, to the hope of their initial romance. This progression is charted via a database logic that is reminiscent of the reversed linearity of *Memento* (Christopher Nolan, 2000). As Joel's memories become increasingly chaotic and blended, the linearity of causal narrative begins to assert itself. At the mid-point of the film, having rediscovered pleasant memories of his relationship with Clementine, Joel decides he wants to halt the erasure. 'I want to call it off!' he yells. At this point in the film, Joel takes a more active role, and becomes an agent of change: recalling memories at will, reacting to events in the outside world (in particular, to Patrick's confession that he has been courting Clementine) and running from the erasure as if from a materially present threat. Joel's internal temporality becomes implicitly aligned with the 'real' time of the Lacuna technicians. As the technicians become intoxicated on alcohol and pot, Joel's mind sharpens, and he becomes attuned to the workings of time. In this case, narrative depends not simply on the retention of memories. In fact, it is created through the traversal, re-ordering and even destruction of memory. The space-time of digital mnemotechnics is revealed as unstable; it is an environment in which temporal anchoring may depend equally upon remembering and forgetting. Although *Eternal Sunshine* is far from classical narrative in its deployment of non-linear structures of temporality, it has not dispensed with narrative. The film is supported by a hidden narrative framework, one that re-establishes temporal and causal relations and dramatizes the process of temporal anchoring in the face of a past made unstable through digital mediation.

Here, the main emphasis is not so much on reconstituting narrative as it is on retaining the memories in Joel's database of experiences.

Yet ultimately, Joel's attempt to reconstitute his memories has a narrative purpose: it is a way of re-enacting (and re-activating) the love story involving Clementine and himself. Ultimately, it is a reconciliation between remembering and forgetting that resolves Joel and Clementine's problems, and allows for the observance of the rules of romantic comedy. At the end, Joel and Clementine have had the unpleasant memories of their relationship erased, allowing them to begin again. Like so many other couples in romantic comedies, Joel and Clementine forget their apparent differences in order to be together. It is the erasure itself that enables the resolution of the narrative. Yet technology in the film also facilitates memory – Joel and Clementine learn of the failure of their past relationship via audiotapes sent to them by a disgruntled worker from Lacuna. Armed with this artificial memory of their failed relationship, Joel and Clementine are granted the opportunity to start over, but with a sense of the compromises this may involve. In this way, the narrative of *Eternal Sunshine* mediates between the two poles of remembering and forgetting.

Eternal Sunshine of the Spotless Mind thus combines the contemporary affirmation of memory and temporal anchoring with the modernist attachment to temporal drift and forgetting. In relation to this, the film's database structure is ambiguous because it appears on the one hand to unmoor the past from the present, and on the other to offer a rearticulation of their relationship. It is both memory and anti-memory. In the film, time appears to move in two directions. One involves journeying into the past on a mission of retrieval. The other charts this mission in the present, and shows the victory, through forgetting, of the present over the past. In this way, the film moves simultaneously towards memory, and towards forgetting; towards work, and towards play; towards chronological narrative, and away from it. The temporal anchoring of the subject is accomplished by the retention of memory, but also depends upon an acceptance of forgetting.

The detective and the database: *Memento*

Memento (Christopher Nolan, 2000) is similarly concerned with temporal anchoring in relation to forgetting, and with the technological externalization of memory. Yet this film is quite distinct from *Eternal Sunshine* in other ways. Here, the romantic drift of Gondry's film is replaced by a more insistent focus upon narrative order, and *Eternal Sunshine*'s movement towards memory is supplanted by a movement towards forgetting – along with a progressive revelation of forgetting's role in constituting narrative. In *Memento*, we witness the predicament

Figure 4.1 Eternal Sunshine of the Spotless Mind. Focus Features/The Kobal Collection/David Lee

of Leonard, an insurance adjuster who has been injured and can no longer retain short-term memories beyond a 15-minute time-span. Leonard's sole concern is tracking down the man who raped and murdered his wife, and also robbed Leonard's memory with a blow to the head. The story is told in reverse chronological order, in a series of short episodes, to parallel Leonard's disjunctive temporal experience. Thus, the plot works in the opposite manner to a conventional narrative structure. Instead of waiting to see what will happen *next*, our attention and anticipation are drawn towards the mystery of what has *already* happened. Yet Leonard lacks the chronological perspective granted to the audience. During each episode, Leonard is forced to re-orient himself, learn the names of people he has already met and figure out what has been happening. Leonard takes photographs and tattoos notes on his body in order to make sense of his world. Although he occupies a disjointed temporal universe, Leonard actively works to remember and contextualize events and people, and relies upon his long-term memory to motivate his actions in the present.

Like *Eternal Sunshine of the Spotless Mind*, *Memento* embeds the representation of memory processes not only in its temporal structure but also in metaphors for memory, often in the form of memory-aids. In *Memento*, these memory-aids include tattoos (Leonard has notes inscribed all over his body), Polaroid photographs (with handwritten captions, which are often subject to revision) and other items (including, for example, a bar coaster). In contrast with *Eternal Sunshine*, high-tech mnemonic technologies are conspicuously absent. By drawing upon memory-aids that seem 'primitive' in the contemporary context, the film lends a sense of obsolescence and unreliability to Leonard's meticulous system. The externalization of memory is made particularly literal in the image of Leonard's body as a writing-surface. The murders and assaults that punctuate the film emphasize the fragility of this body, and thus highlight the contingent nature of the memories inscribed upon it. Just as Leonard reads his own body in order to make sense of the past, the film itself becomes a 'body' marked with mnemonic traces, which the audience is invited to decipher.

Each segment of continuous time in *Memento* marks the limits of Leonard's attenuated memory-span. Yet the film's depiction of memory is not that of the classical flashback. Normally, a narrative film establishes a linear, 'first' narrative from which the flashbacks depart. Initially, one might assume that the black-and-white scenes provide the initial temporality, in relation to which the colour 'flashbacks' are staged. Yet as it turns out, the black-and-white scenes all precede the colour scenes in diegetic terms. Thus, *Memento* undermines the premise of the flashback, which normally depends upon a clear relationship between a recalled past moment, and a subjectivity that does the recalling. Furthermore, rather than depicting Leonard's memories, the colour scenes (apart from

Figure 4.2   Memento. Summit Entertainment/The Kobal Collection

some brief flashbacks to the time before Leonard's memory loss) show us what he will be *unable* to remember from the present. Just as Leonard has assembled a database of materials and must create a coherent narrative from this material, the audience is asked to construct a narrative from a database of segments.

Despite its modular structure, *Memento* is not a truly alinear film. This is because the main segments of narrative follow the irreversible forward motion of classical narrative cinema. Furthermore, these segments are arranged in linear fashion – backwards, but still linear. In addition, intercut with these segments is an ongoing chronologically ordered scene, shot in black and white, showing Leonard in his motel room. The film thus consists of two narrative lines, one (in colour) proceeding backwards in a series of temporal leaps; the other (in black and white) proceeding forwards chronologically. This structure, although very complex, is in fact defined by its splicing together of two linearities, rather than by a radically non-linear structure. Furthermore, the linearity of the film's structure allows for the revelation of plot to occur in a more-or-less conventional way. As we progress backwards and forwards in time, we learn more about Leonard's condition, and about the actions and motivations of his acquaintances. Underlying *Memento*'s confusing temporality is a precisely articulated narrative structure.

In the final section of the film, the two temporalities overlap and move forward together: in black and white, we follow Leonard out of his motel and into a series of events in which he will kill Jimmy Grantz, a drug dealer whom Leonard wrongly identifies as the murderer. As Leonard develops a Polaroid image of Jimmy's corpse, the image shifts from black and white to colour. Minutes later Leonard will acquire an analogous sense of definition, as he realizes that Jimmy was not the man he sought after all. This is a moment of clarification for the viewers as well, because it confirms that the black-and-white footage predates the colour footage. In moving backwards through time, we have been moving inexorably closer to a rendezvous with the black-and-white sequences.

Despite its emphasis on external mediation, the film has clearly not dispensed with memory and character psychology. Like *Eternal Sunshine*, *Memento* displays a concern with temporal anchoring. Leonard's need to remember and avenge his wife's death, and his desperate attempt to retain present information, parallel the postmodern subject's need 'to live in extended structures of temporality, however they may be organized' (Huyssen 1995, 9). In Leonard's case, this extended temporal structure is emphatically organized as a narrative.

In a scene mid-way through the film, Leonard confronts this issue. The scene is a flashback, in which Leonard's wife re-reads a well-thumbed book. In an indirect reference to the film's own structure, Leonard comments: 'I thought the pleasure of a book was finding out what happens next'. Here, Leonard asserts the primacy of linear narrative in his view of the world. It is no coincidence, then, that Leonard later burns this book. It is a reminder of the potential for narrative to fall prey to non-narrative ordering. It is also the book that his wife reads as he gives her her insulin injections, which are the real cause of her death. It therefore has the potential to undermine the straightforward revenge narrative Leonard is creating for himself. Leonard's quest for narrative order is paralleled by the audience's journey through the film. For the audience, the repetition of the beginning of one segment in the ending of another is a way of making sense of the narrative. Yet in this case, repetition is domesticated and put to a narrative use. As the film unfolds, one is more and more able to make sense of the film's temporal ordering. In this sense, temporal anchoring is also closely linked to narrative for the audience.

Both *Eternal Sunshine* and *Memento* invoke the art of memory by showing the ways that the characters attempt to anchor themselves temporally by finding their bearings spatially. In *Memento*, Leonard must constantly establish the details of his physical location in order to plot his progress. He places photographs of locales and people onto a wall-chart in order to map the relations among them. Written notes are appended to the images in order to contextualize them. Leonard also connects photos to locations, holding up his photograph of the Discount Inn to match it up with the actual site. Leonard's mnemotechnic approach can be contrasted with that of Joel in *Eternal Sunshine*, in terms of Aristotle's two connected principles of recollection, one based upon association, the other upon order (Yates 1966, 24). While Joel's attempts to evade mnemonic erasure clearly partake of the former approach, Leonard seeks to establish 'an order of events or impressions' in order to achieve his goals. This model of recollection is consistent with the narrative. At certain moments, associative memory plays a role, as when Leonard hires a prostitute to stand in for his wife. Here, however, Leonard is taking advantage of associative memory in order to deceive himself by creating a scene which would appear to him not as a memory but as a present experience, however fleeting. Leonard also exploits associative memory in repressing his past. We eventually discover that Leonard's wife, tormented by his memory condition, has set up a test. She asks him to administer her insulin several times over, aware that if his disorder is genuine he will supply her with a fatal dose, which is exactly what happens. It would appear that this memory is not completely wiped out from Leonard's mind, as he has displaced his story onto a former client with a similar disorder, named Sammy Jankis. Any memories associated with the death of Leonard's wife are therefore transferred by association to Sammy. Associative memory is subordinated to ordered, narrative memory.

Unfortunately for Leonard, much of his time is spent in places with few distinguishing characteristics, a fact that complicates his mnemonic efforts: from featureless motel rooms to generic bars and industrial areas, he inhabits a landscape without identity. This is an environment characterized by 'non-places'. According to the anthropologist Marc Augé, a non-place is 'a space which cannot be defined as relational, or historical, or concerned with identity' (1995, 77–8). Non-places are spaces of transit (such as airports, supermarkets, hospitals and motels) which demand proof of identity (a ticket, a credit card) in return for the subject's anonymity (102), 'the passive joys of identity-loss, and the more active pleasure of role-playing' (103). These pleasures are offset, at least for Leonard, by his own crisis of identity and memory. The non-place is, in a sense, hostile to narrative. It proceeds 'as if there were no history other than the last forty-eight hours of news' (104). Indeed, if one says of narratives that they 'take place', then the non-place introduces a kind of spatio-temporal confusion. In *Memento*, the manager of the motel takes advantage of this fact, renting Leonard two virtually identical motel rooms in the knowledge that Leonard will neither remember the repetition nor recognize any difference between the rooms. Mnemotechnics is rendered impossible in this context. In this sense, non-places have the potential to create 'non-times' as well. Temporal indeterminacy is highlighted further by the technological features of Leonard's world. There are no mobile phones, digital cameras, CD players or the like, despite the fact that the film was made in 2000. Other than the vehicles in the film, which include recent models, there are very few clues as to when the film is set. This adds to the mood of temporal dislocation.

The spatial progress of the art of memory is largely displaced onto Leonard's own body, where the tattoos serve as images to be discovered in the movement of reading, and reincorporated into Leonard's personal narrative. In relation to this, the film's final moment serves as a brilliant summary of Leonard's mnemonic quest. Leonard notices a tattoo parlour and brings his car to a screeching halt outside. In voiceover, he asks, 'Now, where was I?' This not only captures a sense of Leonard's temporal forgetting (and by extension, his loss of identity); it also reinforces the importance of spatial orientation to his memory system. In this simple phrase, a question about time and identity is framed as a question about location. Of course, at the very end of the film's syuzhet (plot), we are deposited at the beginning of the fabula (story). Leonard's arrival at the tattoo parlour heralds the beginning of his mnemotechnic itinerary. As we shall see, however, this itinerary has turned out to be not only one of reading and remembering, but also one of writing and forgetting. Here, Leonard begins in earnest to inscribe his spatial environment (his body and his surroundings) with the clues that will later provide the basis for his narrative.

In the absence of spatio-temporal cues, Leonard's narrative takes the form of a detective investigation. 'Facts, not memories', Leonard claims in voiceover, are the basis for plotting past events. Seeking to overcome the instability of memory, Leonard establishes a false distinction between memory and evidence, and builds a methodology around it. By taking on the role of investigator, Leonard synthesizes two strands of *film noir*: one concerned with memory and amnesia, and the other drawing upon detective fiction. In effect, he conducts an investigation into his *own* past.[13] The former strand is exemplified by such films as *The Killers* (Robert Siodmak, 1946) and *Out of the Past* (Jacques Tourneur, 1947), which employ complex flashback structures in order to show how events from the past influence those in the present, and by amnesia films such as *Somewhere in the Night* (Joseph L. Mankiewicz, 1946). Leonard exemplifies the *noir* heroes described by Paul Schrader, who 'dread to look ahead, but instead try to survive by the day, and if successful at that, they retreat into the past' (1996, 58). *Memento* carries other reminders of classic *noir*. For example, Natalie, the waitress that Leonard meets, serves as the film's *femme fatale*. Although initially appearing sympathetic, it later (or earlier) turns out that she is taking advantage of Leonard's disability in order to have him carry out a 'hit' on an associate (Jimmy Grantz). The environment that Leonard inhabits is also typical of the *noir* film: it is an urban location, populated by a network of criminals and corrupt cops, and characterized by cheap motels, empty lots and seedy bars.

In its narrative structure, *Memento* both parallels and exceeds classic *noir*. J.P. Telotte notes that *films noirs* are concerned with the status of narration, a concern that emerges in their use of the voiceover/ flashback pattern. The narrator's voice motivates what we see, gesturing simultaneously towards the mind that narrates and organizes the past, and towards the narrated world itself, which 'is already possessed and shaped by the world of language and implicitly capable of exerting its own possessive power' (Telotte 1989, 41). There is thus a note of determinism in the world of the *film noir*, in which the protagonist 'longs to possess and order the confusing pattern of his existence but who invariably finds himself possessed and determined by all manner of forces' (40–1). This intertwining of memory and narration creates a kind of '*mise en abime*, wherein narrative and character seem to become infinite mirror images of each other' (42). These features of classic *noir* are repeated in *Memento*, in which Leonard's struggle to make sense of the past and present are both thwarted and determined by the world around him. Yet although *Memento* makes use of voiceover and flashback, it crucially separates them. Leonard's monologue regarding his memory problem is delivered during the black-and-white scenes, and is often directed towards an anonymous interlocutor via telephone. Temporal transitions, however, seem abrupt and arbitrary, and are not bridged by any contextualizing voiceover. Telotte notes that films such as *The Killers* juxtapose subjective accounts of the past (15), and that *Sunset Boulevard* (Billy Wilder, 1950) is narrated by a corpse (42). However, Leonard's database of lost memories is formally distinct from the psychological grounding of even the most complex of *noir* flashback structures.

Leonard's investigative quest connects him to a tradition of literary and cinematic detective-figures. He proceeds like any good detective, with a firm endorsement of empirical research. Memory, he concludes, is unreliable: 'facts, not memories, that's how you investigate'. This system of epistemological faith allows Leonard to invest in the clues left for him, by himself or by others. Like the character of Reardon in *The Killers*, he is an insurance adjuster, a profession that deals, as does *film noir* itself, with the interplay between chance and probability. Yet Leonard's use of photographs also highlights the connection with earlier forms of detective fiction. Notes Robert Ray, the emergence of detective fiction (the first example being Edgar Allen Poe's 'The Murders in the Rue Morgue' in 1841) coincided with the growth of photography, and was, in effect, 'an antidote to photography' (2001, 21). Whereas photographs were full of contingent details that threatened to undermine meaning, detective fiction 'offered to make the world, and particularly the urban scene, more legible' (21). At the same time, detective fiction's mode of looking was itself comparable to photography: Sir Arthur Conan Doyle's character Sherlock Holmes 'depends upon a photographic way of seeing that, like rack focus, redirects the gaze from foreground to background, and, like a pan, from center to margin' (22).

Similarly, Leonard's system literally depends upon photography, and upon a rational methodology for organizing his photographs and assigning them meaning. As in detective fiction, meaning for Leonard is specifically attached to the notion of legibility: Leonard's handwritten captions make his images legible. Similarly, Leonard's body functions as another mysterious, contingent image (the outer surface of his identity crisis), which also must be made legible through inscription. In this way, Leonard's quest appears quite distinct from the narratives of *21 Grams* and *Irreversible*, in which contingent events resonate not simply with threat but also with the promise of open-endedness and possibility. Leonard, by contrast, is intent on domesticating contingency, which continually threatens to overwhelm his narrative of identity.

Memento counters this tendency by maintaining a certain distance from classic detective fiction. For one, the film shows us the slippages that are possible within Leonard's system. A number of times in the film, we see Leonard scribbling out a note, and replacing it with a new comment. Furthermore, Leonard's system is extremely susceptible to manipulation. For instance, he annotates a photograph of Natalie with the comment that she is sympathetic. He is unaware that she has insulted his wife in order to provoke an assault, convinced him that the bruises were inflicted by Jimmy, and dispatched him to kill Jimmy. The disjuncture between Leonard's note regarding Natalie and her actual behaviour highlights the inability of Leonard's memory system to carry stable and meaningful information, and its susceptibility to manipulation. Indeed, the photograph of Natalie seems to emphasize its own limits: it shows Natalie in the doorway, backlit almost to the point of silhouetting her face. The lack of visual clarity is matched by a concomitant lack of semiotic clarity – the image's final meaning is contingent and slippery, subject to manipulation and misuse, its truth-status suspect at best. This epistemological instability is reminiscent of what James Naremore dubs the 'philosophical noir' of Michelangelo Antonioni's *Blowup* (1966) (1998, 203).[14] In Antonioni's film, a nonchalant fashion photographer becomes embroiled in a murder mystery after taking photographs of a couple in a park. Examining the photographs, he believes he sees evidence of a dead body. Blowing up the photographs, however, amplifies the mystery without aiding clarity. Finally, he begins to suspect that his imagination is responsible for the evidence – the 'body' was really a pile of leaves. *Blowup* invokes a noirish mystery, then deliberately departs from the genre. As in classic detective fiction, investigation and narrativization are linked to optical technologies. *Blowup*'s prototypical visual movement is the zoom-in, an optical technique which finds its parallel in the increasingly cloudy narrative, as the grain of the story overwhelms the protagonist's ability to make clear sense of it. In this way, the single photographic frame provides the ground for an epistemological investigation, in which it is revealed that narratives are constructed rather than discovered.

Pragmatic forgetting and the modular subject

Memento comes to a similar conclusion as *Blowup*, but also connects its epistemological concerns to ontological questions of being and identity. In this respect, it is closely aligned with science fiction films since the 1980s, many of which portray characters with artificially erased or augmented memories. In this sense, *Memento* is really a post-science fiction example of neo-*noir*. It recalls, in a more oblique way than *Eternal Sunshine*, the artificially altered memories of the characters in *Blade Runner*, *Total Recall* and *Strange Days*. These films raise questions regarding the relationship between subjectivity and postmodern image culture. In *Blade Runner*, which blends science fiction with the tropes of *film noir*, the evidential status of photographs is central to the narrative. In the film, a detective named Deckard is charged with tracking down and killing a group of renegade artificial beings known as replicants (who have been implanted with artificial memories). In one memorable scene, Deckard scans a photograph for clues regarding an escaped replicant. Using voice commands, he can direct the display equipment to show him areas of the image in detail. Where *Blowup*'s prototypical technique is the zoom-in, *Blade Runner* uses scanning as a way to extract high-resolution information from the image. Through the spatial manipulation of the image, temporal relations are created, resulting in a narrative. Photographs are also important for the replicants themselves. For the replicant named Rachael, photographs of her 'mother' enable her to invest emotion and identity in her implanted memories. For Giuliana Bruno, the replicants emblematize the fragmentation and historicism of postmodern culture itself and are analogous to Jameson's schizophrenic postmodern subject (1987, 189). Like schizophrenics, the replicants live only in the present, lacking both a remembered past and a conceivable future (189). While the replicants base their quest for origins and identity on photographs, this obsession with photography is in fact a 'phenomenological seduction', because it is treated as the proof of the real, erasing the boundary between signifier and referent (192). In one sense, Bruno's critique applies very directly to Leonard, who deliberately collapses the distinction between memories and photographs. Yet although mediated memory is clearly central to *Blade Runner* and postmodern culture in general, Bruno's analysis fails to properly acknowledge the ability of subjects to orient themselves within postmodern culture, a limitation that applies equally to Jameson's analysis.[15]

For Alison Landsberg, postmodern culture marks the moment, not of a simple bifurcation of reality and representation, but rather of a renewed fascination with experience (Landsberg 1995, 178). The value of memories, she argues, lies less in their ability to validate the past than in their utility for 'organizing the present and constructing strategies with which one might imagine a liveable future' (176). Thus, rather than conflating representation (the photograph) and reality, *Blade Runner* suggests just the opposite: the photograph of Rachael and her 'mother' effectively proves nothing about her past, but it matches her implanted memories. Thus, it 'helps her to produce her own narrative. While it fails to authenticate her past, it does authenticate her present' (185).

Landsberg's model of prosthetic memory provides another avenue of approach to *Memento*'s treatment of memory and identity. Leonard, despite his memory disorder, makes use of his memory of past events in order to create a coherent narrative. Rather than drifting helplessly through a detemporalized world, Leonard actively *retemporalizes* his experiences, giving them a temporal order and thereby endowing himself with a history and an identity. In this sense, he is a modular rather than a schizophrenic subject. *Memento* extends science fiction's examination of prosthetic memory, distributing its concerns regarding order and narrative into its very narrative structure. Similarly, Landsberg's argument can be extended to deal with contemporary digital technology, which allows for the fluid exercise of information storage and retrieval, and has become, in a relatively short time, an indispensable part of modern life. Landsberg does, however, warn that 'memories cannot be counted on to provide narratives of self-continuity' and that memories can overwrite each other, leading to breakthrough memories and a palimpsestic model of identity (1995, 187). Digital media, in its role as prosthetic memory, is also more volatile and subject to 'forgetting' than prior technologies such as print or celluloid. Accordingly, contemporary modular narratives dealing with memory seem equally concerned with the issue of forgetting, and with the possibilities for organizing and articulating memory in the context of excessive mediation.

In *Memento*, it becomes apparent that it is forgetting and false recollection that allow Leonard to overcome the limitations of his mnemotechnic system. Ultimately, we discover that Leonard himself has been tampering with his database of clues, to serve his own ends. After discovering that he has killed the wrong man (Jimmy Grantz) in attempting to avenge his wife's death, Leonard burns the photograph showing the man's corpse. This act erases the crime not only from the photograph but also from his memory – in a sense, it *is* his memory. We also learn, at the end of the film, that Teddy, who may or may not be a police officer and/or Leonard's friend, has already given Leonard a copy of the police file on the case, but that Leonard has removed certain pages, because they give a version of events that contradicts his simple narrative of vengeance. Teddy's final account explains the following facts that differ from Leonard's account: Leonard's wife did not die following the assault; she had difficulty coping with Leonard's memory condition; she tested Leonard out by having him administer her insulin injection repeatedly; failing to remember that he had already completed the task, he effectively medicated her to death; Teddy was the policeman assigned to investigate the original assault; and he took pity on Leonard and helped him to track down and kill the 'real' John G. In altering the police files supplied by Teddy, Leonard has wilfully deleted this account of events. Leonard also burns items that belonged to his wife (a hairbrush, teddy bear, a book and a clock). Associated with this act of forgetting is an act of false recollection: he hires a hooker to pretend to be his wife and re-enact the pre-dawn moments preceding her 'death'. In this sense, memory and forgetting are not opposites but two sides of the same coin. As Norman Klein comments regarding the pragmatics of recollection, *'In order to remember, something must be forgotten'* (1997, 13). At one point, Leonard recalls his wife in terms that invoke both memory and forgetting: 'close your eyes and remember her'. This line foreshadows Leonard's key determining action in the film: the creation of false memories through erasure.

Finally, Leonard takes the morally reprehensible step of framing Teddy for the imaginary murder of his wife. Unwilling to accept Teddy's account as the final word on the matter, he appends a note to Teddy's photograph: 'don't believe his lies'. He then takes a note of Teddy's car licence plate, with the intention of having it tattooed on his body. This will become a key piece of evidence in tracking down the 'killer'. Of course, Leonard is aware that he will later forget how he has produced this distortion but will remember the clue that results from it. This is the act that will later (or earlier) lead to Leonard taking Teddy's life, in the honest belief that he is killing his wife's murderer. Thus, Leonard embraces forgetting as a way of constructing a clear narrative for himself. In the process, Leonard gives a temporal order to his experiences and endows himself with a history and an identity. The chilling conclusion of the film reveals the hidden alliance between narrative and forgetting, made possible in this case by the externalization of memory. There are, then, two types of forgetting in Leonard's system: one based upon ordinary repression (Leonard chooses not to remember injecting his wife with insulin), and one based upon the outright elimination of memory (Leonard burns the photo of Jimmy Grantz's dead body).

In a sense, our own comprehension of the narrative also depends upon forgetting. Given that we are largely restricted to Leonard's own knowledge of events within each segment, we are subject to unreliable and suspect information. As we progress through the film, we are forced to discard possible versions of the past. For example, at the end of the film, we 'write over' Leonard's account of his wife's murder, in favour of the version proposed by Teddy. On one level, this is a feature of any detective story, in which various suspects and motives are considered and then discounted. The process of forgetting allows us to navigate through the confusing web of events, producing a definitive version. Yet the forgetting is not absolute: like a palimpsest, our memory of the film includes traces of those earlier drafts. Leonard, too, finds that the past resists his attempts to erase it entirely, in the form of mementoes, records and the memories of other characters such as Teddy.

Finally, however, the structure of the film highlights a kind of subjective bifurcation. The audience moves through a memory-world that is progressively less identified with Leonard's subjectivity. As Leonard's progress in the film moves away from memory and towards forgetting, the audience accumulates details that allow for meaningful connections to be made between the past and the present. Just as the audience moves towards temporal anchoring, Leonard sets himself adrift from the past. In this respect, *Memento* is the opposite of *Eternal Sunshine*. Joel begins by submitting to memory erasure, and then decides to rescue the past. Leonard, as he is presented in *Memento*'s reversed chronology, 'progresses' from temporal anchoring towards erasure. Furthermore, the characters exemplify two different attitudes towards the past: while Joel eventually decides that the past must be affirmed for its own sake, Leonard values the past only for what it offers him in the present.[16] By separating audience memory and character memory, the film offers a critical perspective on Leonard's forgetting.

Memento also sets up, like *Irreversible*, a bi-directional relationship between contingency and determinism. Here, this relationship is mediated by memory itself. In *Memento*, the main progression (associated with Leonard's subjectivity) is towards narrative order and causality, and away from temporal drift. Ultimately, it is also towards determinism: not necessarily ontological determinism, but certainly epistemological determinism. Leonard's actions at the end of the film pre-determine the general course of the narrative, including the fate of Teddy. This determinism is underwritten by forgetting. At the same time, the audience is offered a cumulative diegetic memory that progressively reveals the workings of contingency. Among other things, we are witness to the arbitrary events that lead to Leonard choosing Teddy as his victim. In this way, we see how control over memory affects events in the future, producing both foreseen and unforeseen consequences. The epistemological focus of the detective plot thus opens anew upon the ontological, as Leonard decides what kind of world to create for himself by deciding what to remember.[17] Early in the film, Leonard sets out the epistemological basis upon which his investigation is built. Given the impermanence of his memories, he is driven to depend upon visual clues in particular, a fact which leads him to state a key article of faith: 'the world doesn't disappear when I close my eyes'. Yet this is exactly the effect that Leonard achieves in his tactical deployment of forgetting. Replaying identifiably postmodern themes of identity and order in a database form, *Memento* displays the possibilities and the ethical dangers of modular subjectivity.[18]

Memory, mediation and the 'time-image'

In representing memory syntagmatically, *Memento* and *Eternal Sunshine of the Spotless Mind* both intersect with and depart from modernist cinema's representation of time. Another way of highlighting this distinction is to consider the extent to which Gilles Deleuze's theory of the 'time-image' describes the temporality of the modular narrative. Deleuze demarcates a boundary between the 'movement-image' of classical cinema and the 'time-image' native to cinema but not fully acknowledged until the post-war innovations of European filmmakers (1986, 1989). Where the movement image grounds temporal structure in the assumed physical and psychological motivations of the characters, the time-image exists for itself, following a durational rhythm that is not determined precisely by diegetic actions. *Eternal Sunshine* and *Memento*, in their investigation of temporalities that extend beyond their characters' ability to orient themselves, both relate to Deleuze's time-image. Yet the closeness of this relation is qualified by the films' grounding in the classical tradition of the movement-image – the characters are motivated to explore and domesticate their disorienting worlds, a narrative quest reinforced by continuity editing and the psychology of conventional narrative cinema.[19]

Deleuze's approach to cinema has sometimes seemed wilfully exclusive, as in *Cinema 2* (1989) he deals with what seems like only a small number of mainly European, high modernist films and filmmakers. Nonetheless, his description of the alternative temporal modes available to modernist filmmakers sheds light upon temporality in *Eternal Sunshine* and *Memento*. One of the most elegantly puzzling notions he puts forward is the distinction between 'peaks of past' and 'sheets of present', a distinction which emerges in his discussion of *Last Year at Marienbad* (1961) and its writer and director, Alain Robbe-Grillet and Alain Resnais. Robbe-Grillet's literary fiction and filmmaking is characterized by peaks of present, in which past, present and future coexist in the same moment, creating confusion and contradictions: 'there is *a present of the future, a present of the present and a present of the past,* all implicated in the event, rolled up in the event, and thus simultaneous and inexplicable' (100). In Resnais' work, by contrast, past, present and future are still separable. Yet in this case it is layers of *past* that coexist, causing confusion. In terms of memory, this layering of the past moves beyond a strict correspondence with the psychology of individual characters, and takes the form of 'a memory which overflows the conditions of psychology, memory for two, memory for several, memory-world, memory-ages of the world' (119). These two approaches to time are merged in *Last Year at Marienbad*. Deleuze frames this encounter in relation to the two main characters, a man who insists that a liaison occurred the year before, and a woman who disavows any memory of it:

> If *Last Year at Marienbad* could be divided, the man X might be said to be closer to Resnais, and the woman A closer to Robbe-Grillet. The man basically tries to envelop the woman with continuous sheets of which the present is the narrowest, like the advance of a wave, whilst the woman, at times wary, at times stiff, at times almost convinced, jumps from one bloc to another, continually crossing an abyss between two points, two simultaneous presents.
>
> (104)

Here, the encounter between sheets of past and peaks of present might also be reframed more directly in mnemonic terms. For the sheets of past surely present us with an excess of memory, while the abrupt leaps between peaks of present produce a series of lacunae – the absence of memory. *Last Year at Marienbad* presents an encounter between a character with too much memory, and a character with not enough: he wants to remember, and she wants to forget.

Deleuze's distinction is helpful in highlighting the similarities and differences between *Memento* and *Eternal Sunshine of the Spotless Mind*. Leonard's temporal world in the former film is characterized by the Augustinian temporality of Robbe-Grillet, in which past, present and future coexist in the present, producing anxiety through their inseparability. *Eternal Sunshine*, on the other hand, depicts a present that is lapped by waves or sheets of past, as Joel's memories surface during his treatment. Like X in *Last Year at Marienbad*, Joel is turned away by a woman who appears to crave less memory (to the point where she undergoes an artificial process to achieve this). As we follow events from Joel's perspective, Clementine abruptly appears and disappears in scene after scene, memory after memory. This abruptness is enhanced by her changes in temperament (which appear to alter as often and as drastically as her hair colour). Furthermore, the overall progression of the two films is contrasting. In *Eternal Sunshine*, Joel and Clementine move away from their use of forgetting as an anaesthetic, and towards an embrace of memory. In *Memento*, the progression of the film brings with it the realization that Leonard's initial quest for memory is underwritten and circumscribed by his choice of forgetting. While Joel and Clementine affirm the importance of the past in their experience of the present, Leonard has decided that the present is all that matters. His Augustinian notion of time presents a past of the present, a present of the present and a future of the present. Constructing his identity around this present-based temporality, he decides he has little use for a past that exists independently of it.

Deleuze's approach to thinking about temporal articulation in modernist cinema illuminates the possibility of different models of time coexisting among or within films. For Deleuze, there is a 'bifurcation' of time, a splitting and coexistence of the actual and the virtual, in such films as $8 \frac{1}{2}$ (Federico Fellini, 1963) and *Last Year at Marienbad*. For Deleuze, the comparative inadequacy of the classical cinema flashback lies in its attachment to an external (for example psychological) motivation, which confirms a linear model of time and therefore reinforces the determinism of linear narrative (48). Deleuze therefore reserves particular praise for filmmakers who go beyond the linear treatment of time and memory. He privileges Alain Resnais's films for the way that they parallel the temporal operations of the human brain, and their avoidance of direct or definitive representations of memory and the past. Resnais's treatment of memory brings forth not only 'recollection, but equally forgetting, false recollection, imagination, planning, judgement ...' (124). Here, Deleuze makes a distinction between the past in itself and its embodiment in a 'recollection' image. 'Pure recollection' (the past in itself) does not have simply one recollection-image pertaining to it (123). This recalls Henri Bergson's insistence that memories represented in images must therefore be distinguished from 'pure' memory: 'To *picture* is not to *remember*' (Bergson 1988, 135).

Yet *Memento* and *Eternal Sunshine* both present us with memory-worlds in which memory and fantasy are tied up with technological mediation – from the low technology of photographs and personal items to the high technology of digital scanning. In *Eternal Sunshine*, this sense of time as mediated is intensified by the overt use of special effects to represent the breakdown of memory – as when Joel's childhood home appears to 'morph' into a rundown building. In these films, memory is de-natured and displaced into external memory aids. False recollection and fantasy are not only problems of memory, but also of representational and archival error or misuse. *Memento* and *Eternal Sunshine*, by showing the impact of technological mediation on memory processes, describe a situation in which to picture is indeed to remember. The problem of mediation therefore haunts any attempt to apply Deleuze's ideas on cinema directly to these modular narratives. *Last Year at Marienbad* offers us a confusing model of time that eludes narrative domestication, is not a literal representation of memory and is not conspicuously mediated by anything other than fantasy and reminiscence. Yet in *Memento*, the segments of the past that are presented to us are recalled as definitive versions – it is only our knowledge of what else has happened that remains to be filled in. Both *Memento* and *Eternal Sunshine* also incorporate 'classical' flashbacks *within* the modular structure. In *Memento*, for example, Leonard's memories of the attack on his wife are presented as conventional flashbacks. In *Eternal Sunshine*, memories are more malleable. In this case, we are watching memories of the past that are contaminated with other memories, dreams and false recollection. In this sense, the film is an example of Deleuze's cinema of the brain. Yet these memories are also inseparable from technological mediation, and are susceptible to control and manipulation.

Deleuze largely avoids treating this question of mediation directly.[20] For Deleuze, cinema is not, or should not be, a *representation* of time. Rather, modernist cinema presents us with time in itself, in the form of the time-image. In contrast to Deleuze's emphasis on the 'immediacy of time', notes Dudley Andrew, Paul Ricoeur 'insists that time is unthinkable except as mediated' (Andrew 2000, 44). For Ricoeur, it is narrative that mediates our understanding of the temporal in a way that makes it assimilable to human experience. Whereas Deleuze values the radical uncertainty offered by Resnais and Robbe-Grillet (either undecidable alternatives or indistinguishable times), both of the modular narratives discussed here eventually recuperate a sense of order. The fraught question at the heart of both *Memento* and *Eternal Sunshine* is to what extent these films draw upon narrative as the solution to resolving the aporias of mediated time. The answer lies somewhere between Deleuze's model of time unmoored and Ricoeur's anchoring of the temporal in narrative. *Eternal Sunshine* explores the territory between temporal drift and temporal anchoring, while *Memento* suggests the contemporary relevance of narrative in the era of the database. Neither films issue an unqualified endorsement of narrative order, but both assert the importance of temporal anchoring in relation to mediated memory. Narrative appears as one, highly crucial, form of temporal mediation that helps to anchor the characters and the audience.

Both *Eternal Sunshine of the Spotless Mind* and *Memento* revolve around the struggle of their protagonists to establish a stable past for themselves in the face of excessive mediation. The space-time of digital mnemotechnics is revealed as unstable; it is an environment in which temporal anchoring may depend equally upon remembering and forgetting. In both cases, a solution is found by taking advantage of the process of mediation to alter or rewrite memory. The negotiation between memory and forgetting thus becomes the narrative and thematic centre of each film. Like the characters in *Last Year at Marienbad*, Leonard's and Joel's grasp on the relationship between present and past may equally be threatened by an excess or an insufficiency of memory. Here, the temporal anchoring of the subject is accomplished by the retention of memory, but also depends upon an acceptance (willing or otherwise) of the loss of memory. In *Memento*, Leonard follows a trajectory from remembering towards forgetting, while Joel in *Eternal Sunshine* proceeds from forgetting towards remembering. The former film examines the informational and epistemological implications of modular subjectivity, while the latter explores its affective dimension. Both revisit the modern and postmodern discourse of temporality, and renovate it for the contemporary digital context. In these modular narratives, the externalization and manipulation of memory function as a source of both order and forgetting, of pleasure and of crisis.

5
Articulating History: Archival Aesthetics and the National Narrative

Anachronic modular narratives, which go beyond the clear temporal hierarchy of conventional flashback structures, most conspicuously treat the past in relation to memory rather than history. Although such films as *Memento* and *Eternal Sunshine of the Spotless Mind* display an archival aesthetic, the juxtapositions of past and present are linked to the unpredictable movements of personal memory. Yet two other films, *Ararat* (Atom Egoyan, 2002) and *Russian Ark* (Aleksandr Sokurov, 2002) show that history itself is also a potential focus for the database aesthetic. These films not only question the assumption that history is simply a linear narrative; they also undermine the very distinction between memory and history, suggesting that history may be just as capricious and subject to revision. Accordingly, *Ararat* and *Russian Ark* display marked thematic and formal overlaps with the memory problem films discussed in the previous chapter. In these films, history, no less than memory, operates along the border between narrative and archive. As with the memory problem films, temporal structure and the conception of identity are closely connected. Here, however, modularity extends beyond the individual and becomes a feature of national identity. Again, mnemotechnics is a tool in the remembering process, but it is a tool that has its limits. Ultimately, a negotiation of sorts between memory and forgetting becomes the solution to the relationship between the past and the present. While each of these films questions the narrative underpinnings of identity, neither dispenses with it altogether. Rather, temporal anchoring and the reassertion of identity are given a qualified affirmation.

In *Ararat*, a variety of times, fictional and historical characters and locations are juxtaposed in a tale revolving around genocide and the representation of history. Edward, an Armenian film director, is shooting a film in Canada depicting the slaughter of Armenians by the Turkish army in 1915. In Edward's film (also called *Ararat*), actor Martin Harcourt plays Clarence Ussher, an American missionary who witnessed the atrocities. Preceding and during the filming, Edward and his screenwriter Reuben consult with Ani, an Armenian–Canadian who is an expert on the works of exiled Armenian painter Arshile Gorky. As Ani prepares to attend the film's Canadian premiere, her son Raffi is held up at customs. Raffi is returning from a trip to Turkey in which he videoed the landscape where the massacre took place. He also has with him a number of film cans, which he refuses to open because they contain, he claims, exposed film. David, a customs officer on the verge of retirement, is not prepared to allow uninspected film cans through on his watch. His suspicions are later confirmed when he finds that the film cans are full of drugs. However, despite discovering that Raffi's initial story was a lie, David nevertheless takes pity and allows him to leave. His compassionate urge extends finally to his gay son, who is in a relationship with Ali, an actor in the film. This complex web of situations and times is edited together in such a way that no single storyline is granted primary status. One might argue that Raffi and David's negotiation at the airport performs such a role, and that everything else in the film is a flashback in relation to it. Yet such a relationship is far from clear, particularly in the film's early stages. We see Raffi in other scenes that predate these ones diegetically, yet they are not marked as anterior. Also, it is not until the last 15 minutes of the film that we realize that the film's premiere coincides with Raffi's arrival at the airport. Like other modular narratives, *Ararat* fosters a sense of instability around temporal relations.

Russian Ark also fosters this sense of instability, via a much less disjunctive aesthetic approach. Indeed, promotional materials for the film make much of the fact that the film was shot in a single take, without cuts.[1] The camera, moving fluidly on a Steadicam mount, takes us on a guided tour through the rooms of St. Petersburg's Hermitage (Ermitzah), the Tsars' opulent winter palace, which is now a museum. Our guide is the Marquise de Custine, a real historical figure and writer of travelogues during the nineteenth century. Custine addresses his often acerbic remarks to the camera, where a figure we never see acts as his interlocutor. This figure, in spite of his virtual invisibility, is nonetheless identified as Russian, and might be seen as a kind of avatar for Sokurov, the film's director. Despite Custine's historical specificity, he is able to guide us and the camera through several centuries of Russian history, and he finds, much to his surprise, that he is able to speak Russian. The film's historical reach extends from the era of Peter the Great (in the early eighteenth Century) to the pre-revolutionary days of Nicholas II, with a few brief excursions into more recent moments, including the siege of Leningrad in World War II, and the present day. We become quiet observers to a range of recreated historical scenes, as Custine takes us on a tour of the Hermitage's paintings and sculptures. It might be objected that *Russian Ark* is not a true modular narrative. After all, the film's long-take aesthetic is very different from the discrete segmentation of *Memento, 21 Grams* or even *Irreversible* (which makes extensive use of long takes, but deploys them in temporally distinct scenes). In its insistent, uninterrupted movement through the space of the Hermitage, the mobile camera of *Russian Ark* implies a linear model of time. *Russian Ark*'s durational approach, however, is offset by the segmentation of history into distinct pieces. In this case, the pieces are accessed in the spatial movement from room to room inside the Hermitage. The continuity of the film's spatial movement is contrasted by the abrupt temporal movements from an indeterminate present into moments from the elapsed past. Like these other films, *Russian Ark* is a tale about time, deploying temporal transitions in ways that lie outside conventional narrative logic.

History, modernity and modularity

In their direct focus upon history, *Ararat* and *Russian Ark* are atypical cases within the current crop of modular narratives. In most cases, anachronic narrative structures examine the temporal experiences of individuals or small communities – from the memory-loss of *Memento* to the contingent intersections of *21 Grams* – but avoid broader historical questions. Yet history and narrative anachrony do have a shared cinematic and literary past. For early modernists, the subject of history stimulated a certain ambivalence. Stephen Kern notes a marked resistance in modern literature and philosophy to the notion of official, linear history (1983, 34). Freidrich Nietzsche argued for forgetting as a cure to the hypertrophy of monumental history (1983, 62), while James Joyce's narrative techniques (which explored simultaneity, and used interior monologues to link the past and future in a 'temporally thickened' present) served as an 'affirmation of the present as the only real location of experience' (Kern 1983, 86). This sense of schism intensified in the work of later modernist writers such as Samuel Beckett. While the historical past still constituted a 'source of order' for earlier modernists such as Pound, Yeats, Eliot and Joyce, the later modernists saw it is 'that which ought to be ignored' (Kermode 1967, 115). Yet modernist thought was not uniformly oriented towards forgetting the past. Walter Benjamin's writings, for example, emphasized the retrieval of neglected historical moments. In arguing for historical materialism, he asserted the importance of the present to history, and fostered the sense of history as a work-in-progress: 'History is the subject of a structure whose site is not homogeneous, empty time, but time filled by the presence of the now' (Benjamin 1968b, 263). In Benjamin's work, one finds not the rejection of history *per se*, but rather a notion of historical examination that favours non-linearity and disjuncture, seeking to 'brush history against the grain' (259).

A similar perspective on history is evident in the late modernist European cinema of the 1960s. Maureen Turim, writing about the cinematic flashback, argues that cinema generally approaches history via a 'subjective focalization', which narrates history through the individual (17). Turim is critical of such films because they 'create history as an essentially individual and emotional experience', imply a sense of inevitability regarding historical events, retreat to essentialist ideology in order to escape their own cyclical fatalism and are often overly didactic (17). Although Turim overstates the negative aspects of subjective focalization, she is correct in highlighting modernist cinema's examination of the shape of history. While certain modernist films abstract themselves from politics and history, others such as *Tout va bien* (Jean-Luc Godard, 1972) and *Night and Fog in Japan* (Nagisa Oshima, 1960) 'complicate the portrayal of the past beyond a fictive individual's psychology' (237), while third-world films such as *Memories of Underdevelopment* (Tomás Gutiérrez Alea, 1968) and *The Green Wall* (Armando Robles Godoy, 1970) use their flashback structures to 'provide a constructive alternative view of historical memory' (243). By drawing attention to their flashback structures, these films are able to question historical assumptions and narrational processes (18). Later films, according to Turim, have tended to fall back on generic uses of flashback, thereby allowing traditional narratives of national identity to take root, untempered by the appropriate critical distance (236). Examples include *Marianne and Juliane* (Margarethe von Trotta, 1981) and *Breaker Morant* (Bruce Beresford, 1980). In Hollywood cinema, Turim finds films that borrow modernist techniques without addressing 'historical positioning' or adopting the 'critical eye of modernist flashback structure' (242). Ultimately, Turim turns towards avant-garde cinema for the next innovations in flashback form (246). However, her rather pessimistic overview, published in 1989, does not address the wave of modular narratives that emerged in the early to mid-1990s within mainstream and independent cinema.

Certain prominent flashback films of the 1990s, however, would seem to confirm Turim's analysis. In Oliver Stone's *JFK* (1991), for example, an intensive flashback structure links the Kennedy assassination with preceding and subsequent events, and with investigator Jim Garrison's attempts to unravel the truth about these events. Temporal digressions consist of fictional scenes and archival footage, but also of scenes shot in black and white that mimic the look of the latter. At times, Garrison's investigation produces a multilevel flashback structure. For example, when Jim reads the Warren Commission's report into the assassination, we see a flashback of the Commission hearing testimony, which in turn spawns a black-and-white flashback motivated by a witness's testimony. At the end of this section, we see Jim waking up in his bed, as if from a dream. At another point, we see conflicting accounts of Lee Harvey Oswald's actions on the day of the assassination, accompanied by Jim's voiceover.

Despite the complexity of these flashback structures, *JFK* is not a modular narrative: the story is firmly anchored in Jim's investigation, which proceeds in chronological order and serves as the 'first narrative' for the rest of the film. At the same time, the film's archival sensibility fosters an awareness of the constructedness of history. Robert Burgoyne convincingly argues that the film's use of fragmentation and collage techniques 'expresses the fracturing of historical identity, the breaking apart of a once unified national text' (114). American history and, by extension, American identity are deconstructed in the juxtaposition of conflicting accounts and representations of Kennedy's assassination. Nevertheless, writes Burgoyne, 'the film seems to be split between its modernist form and its desire to reconstitute or recover a seamless national text' (119).[2] In other words, Jim Garrison's quest re-establishes truth and justice and, significantly, reconnects them to a resuscitated image of American national identity. Despite its questioning of the American national narrative, *JFK* is therefore open to Turim's charge that Hollywood flashback films recuperate identity by overcoming modernist disjunctures.

Modular narratives are no less vulnerable to such charges, a point taken up by Sean Cubitt in *The Cinema Effect* (2004). Concerning himself largely with Hollywood or semi-independent American modular narratives, Cubitt complains that they forsake history. This argument recalls Fredric Jameson's lament for the 'weakening of historicity' in cultural postmodernism (1991, 6).[3] Like Jameson, Cubitt suggests a spatial dominant in contemporary culture: the 'spatialized' structures of these films reveal the desire for 'a circumscribed perfection removed from history and thence from dialectical process' (2004, 243). His criticisms of contemporary modular narratives are very similar to those Turim levels at Hollywood's use of 'modernist' flashback structures in the 1980s. Just as Turim finds the flashback used to aid identification rather than critical distance, Cubitt argues that these contemporary films promote 'identification with fictional worlds' that exclude history (236). This argument, however, is in my view based in a false reading of the modular narrative's textual operations. For example, while *Memento* does not directly address broader historical questions, its critique of the process of writing narratives has historiographical implications. As I suggested in the Chapter 4, modular narratives are very concerned indeed with the value of the past to the present, and enact processes of temporal anchoring in affirming this relationship.

If modular narratives are more focussed upon memory than history, this may be seen as part of an existing (and hardly novel) tendency within popular culture. Nonetheless, Cubitt's account, by restricting itself to Hollywood and 'Hollywood independent' films, leaves aside those modular narratives that do confront historical questions, however obliquely. The South Korean film *Peppermint Candy* (Lee Chang-dong, 2000), for example, tells the story of one ordinary man against the backdrop of 20 years of Korean history. Despite the fact that the narrative follows a single protagonist, the film avoids fusing national and personal histories into a transcendent progression. Rather, the film serves to some extent as a broader commentary on history's impact on individuals, and as a subtle critique of the tendency to conflate history and progress. In the film, Kim Youngho, a middle-aged businessman, commits suicide at a school reunion in 1999. The film then proceeds to go back in time in increments, via a series of seven narrative segments, to a school trip to the same riverside spot 20 years before. Progressing backwards, we learn of Kim's immediate financial woes and failed marriage, his job in the corrupt and violent police force during the 1980s, his truncated love affair with Yun Sunim (whom he meets on her deathbed not long before his suicide) and his accidental shooting of a young student while on duty with the Korean military.

Peppermint Candy is a tale of lost innocence and lost opportunities, not only for Kim Youngho but also in relation to Korean history itself. The film uses the plight of its hapless protagonist to question South Korea's prosperous present, focussing not only on the merciless underside of its capitalist economy, but also on the state corruption and military brutality that form parts of its recent past. The film itself functions as an act of historical (fictional) memory, resisting the tendency to forget the past, and re-examining the lost opportunities for alternative actions and outcomes. Kim's suicide is preceded (in the story) by a scene in which he deliberately exposes the film inside a camera Yun Sunim had returned to him. Both of these acts are acts of forgetting, something the film's narrative structure resists by insisting upon the unearthing of the past. If the recurrent images of railway tracks (played in reverse) suggest Kim's predetermined fate, the dramatic scenes in between are full of chances for better or more ethical behaviour. The relationship with Yun Sunim, which is snuffed out by Kim's blunders and his entanglement in state corruption and violence, serves as a parallel for South Korea's missed historical opportunities. By grounding itself in political and social history, *Peppermint Candy* suggests that memory and history are mutually illuminating. In a similar, if less comprehensive, way, *Jacob's Ladder* (Adrian Lyne, 1990) links its modular structure to the turbulent history of the Vietnam War. A young Vietnam veteran suffers from a series of strange visions that intertwine with reality, to the point where the two become indistinguishable. Finally, we realize that he has died, and we have been witness to the final convulsions of his memory and imagination, possibly triggered by government-sponsored experiments. The individual's tortured mnemonic experience in these films exists within, and is determined by, a broader historic context.

History adrift: mediating the past in *Russian Ark* and *Ararat*

Both *Ararat* and *Russian Ark* examine the instability of historical time, its mnemonic roots and its susceptibility to revision. In this respect, both are related to the project of temporal anchoring that inflects *Memento* and *Eternal Sunshine of the Spotless Mind*. Rather than opposing memory-films and history-films, then, I suggest looking at the common questions they raise regarding narrative, temporal experience and the archive. *Russian Ark* and *Ararat* articulate, through their games with time, a relationship between narrative and database structures that is framed in relation to historical loss and forgetting. The problems presented by forgetting and temporal disjuncture are also, fundamentally, problems of mediation. In *Russian Ark*, the enactments of historical moments appear as a series of narrative fragments, in which historical figures appear and disappear with little in the way of context. Any psychological or narrative grounding seems just beyond our reach. This parade of ephemeral moments is inflected by our knowledge that the Russian Revolution of 1917 was to sweep away all of this pomp and splendour. This sense of loss can be connected to the discourse of temporal crisis surrounding cultural postmodernism: the loss of historicity lamented by Jameson (1991), as well as the 'twilight memories' of Andreas Huyssen (1995). Central to this sense of historical loss is the question of mediation: Jameson's 'culture of the image' weakens historicity (1991, 6), while for Huyssen modern media bring the past into the present in such dramatic ways that collective amnesia is the result (1995, 5). *Russian Ark* shows an awareness of this relationship between history and mediation, by drawing our attention to multiple layers of representation. The film opens with the narrator (who travels with the camera's perspective throughout) remarking, over a blank screen, that he cannot see anything. As the images appear in front of us, and we move inside the museum, the narrator's mediating role continues to be reinforced through his voiceover. Yet the narrator in turn has his visit to the museum mediated by the curatorial figure of the Marquis de Custine, who contextualizes events and images for us, and provides his own acerbic commentary on them. In this way, the historic events on display are filtered through two subjective witnesses.

Also monitoring events is the ceaseless gaze of the video camera. Promotional materials for the film highlight the fact that it was the first feature film to be shot entirely in one take (although Mike Figgis's *Time Code* [2000] arguably achieves this feat, even though it displays four takes on screen simultaneously). In any case, we are invited to marvel at the film's well-choreographed technical accomplishment, made possible by a custom-built hard-drive recording set-up and a Steadicam rig. Even as the video camera links together temporally distant events via its real-time capture, it makes us aware of the vast gap between the slice of continuous time it captures, and the real events presented in this time. As a counterpoint to the digital gaze of the video camera, the film gestures towards earlier historical or mythical moments via the medium of painting. As Custine leads us through the great halls of the Hermitage, he stops to ponder upon the painted depictions of biblical scenes and the like. Yet as the camera follows his reverent journey, the surfaces of the paintings themselves are often obscured by reflected light. At these moments, the camera's photorealistic claims over the painting are weakened, and we are once again made aware of the camera's mediating role. Art, like history, recedes from the camera's representational grasp.

Ararat begins by foregrounding representational media: the camera pans across an artist's studio, revealing photographs and drawings. These, we

Figure 5.1   Ararat. Alliance Atlantis/TMN/ARP Selection/The Kobal Collection/
J. Eisen

later find out, belong to the Armenian painter Arshile Gorky, exiled from his home in Eastern Turkey following the 1915 massacre, and living in New York during the 1930s. Gorky's work, in particular his *Portrait of the Artist and his Mother*, serves as a focal point for the film's interrogation of historical memory. This painting is based upon a photograph of the young Gorky and his mother, taken before his departure from Turkey. As a memorial artefact, the painting already bears witness to the layering of mediation, having been copied from a photograph (which we see in Gorky's studio). Later, the painting appears in another format, projected onto a screen as part of a lecture on Gorky given by Ani, an expert on his life and work. Ani is of Armenian extraction, but lives in Canada. Ani's presentation of the Gorky painting illustrates the interweaving of archival, mediated history with cultural memory and personal significance. For Ani, the painting is not only a research object but also a key reminder of her own identity and ethnic roots. *Ararat* introduces a further layer of mediation by including a plotline regarding the production of a film about the massacre, which is also titled *Ararat*. Ani has been hired as a consultant on the film, and finds it difficult to come to terms with the screenwriter's fictionalizing of events. Scenes from this other *Ararat* are intercut with the present-day events;

these scenes are the sole means by which we have direct access to the events leading up to and following the 1915 massacre of the Armenians.

Mediated memory is also manifested in the video recordings made by Raffi, Ani's son. Spurred on by his confrontational stepsister Celia, Raffi travels to Turkey to visit and document the area where the Turkish Armenians lived. Like Ani's analysis of the Gorky painting, Raffi's videography is an important way for him to come to terms with his ethnic history. Raffi is stopped by a customs official, David, who wants to examine film cans in his luggage. Falsely claiming that he has been shooting additional footage for *Ararat*, Raffi suggests that the film was somehow lacking. His real footage of the Turkish landscape will remedy that. Despite the fact that the cans contain heroin rather than film, Raffi's claims are not baseless when applied to his videotapes. These tapes, which document the actual landscape of his ancestral home, do indeed supplement the fictional recreations of the dramatic film, which was shot in Toronto. By juxtaposing these different types of footage, the film evokes the uneven terrain of mediated history, its contradictions and instability.

Russian Ark and *Ararat* also acknowledge the mediating function of structure. As with other modular narratives, the interplay between continuity and disjuncture becomes a thematic as well as a stylistic element. Unlike most other modular narratives, however, *Russian Ark* is not divided into discrete segments. Rather, the temporal leaps in this film occur in the spatial movement from room to room within the Hermitage. The film's single long take affirms continuity, even as the spatio-temporal transitions within the film suggest the opposite. Indeed, the film itself effectively plots an archival journey. In this case, the rooms of the Hermitage store not only paintings, sculptures and other relics, but also ghostly scraps of the past. This linkage between archival storage and discontinuity brings to mind Michel Foucault's call for an 'archaeology' that would deprive history of its linear, teleological thrust, breaking it up instead into groups of ideas known as 'discourses'. These discourses are defined not by causality or categorization but by 'systems of dispersion' (Foucault 1972, 37–8). Discursive practices and statements together make up an 'archive', which does not unite them, but preserves difference instead (128). Foucault acknowledges his archaeology's devastating effect on the notion of historical time: 'Discourse is snatched from the law of development and established in a discontinuous atemporality' (166). He defends it by suggesting that it 'tries to show the intersection between necessarily successive relations and others that are not so' (168–9). Nonetheless, Foucault's approach favours rupture and discontinuity, and challenges narrative's claim on history. In *Russian Ark* the temporal succession of history is disrupted by the discontinuous articulation of archival time.

Russian Ark, however, dramatizes the retemporalization of the archive through its long-take aesthetics but also through what Paul Ricoeur describes as a 'fusion of horizons'. Ricoeur challenges Foucault's opposition between the archive and the notion of traditionality, and suggests that his emphasis on transformative ruptures runs the risk of turning time into a static element (Ricoeur 1984–8, 3:219). Instead, Ricoeur describes our relation to the past in terms of a 'traversed distance', which is 'opposed both to the notion of the past taken as simply passed and gone, abolished, and the notion of complete contemporaneity' (220). Traditionality overcomes the opposition between 'Uncrossable distance or annulled distance' (220). In this way, 'The past is revealed to us through the projection of a historical horizon that is both detached from the horizon of the present and taken up into and fused with it' (220). Traditionality lends meaning to the distance between the past and the present; it is 'an operation that can only make sense dialectically through the exchange between the interpreted past and the interpreting present' (221).

Russian Ark deploys traditionality in such a way, effecting a (qualified) fusion of horizons on several levels. Deploying images of the past as a way to reclaim lost fragments of Russian history, the film attempts to bridge the gap between the present and the days of pre-revolutionary Russia. Indeed, as Dragan Kujundzic notes, the film effectively erases the intervening Soviet period, firstly by choosing not to represent it for the most part, and secondly by eschewing its favoured cinematic aesthetics: Eisenstein's montage of attractions and Vertov's fast-cut documentation of everyday life via the *kino-eye* (2004, 227). By juxtaposing pre-revolutionary scenes with scenes showing present-day visitors to the Hermitage, Sokurov articulates an exchange between past and present, fusing them together in the same location.

At the same time, *Russian Ark*'s video aesthetic enables a fusion of two temporal modes: the historical time represented, and the 'real' time of its representation. The 'uncrossable distance' of the historical past and the 'annulled distance' of the film's contiguous scenes are partially overcome by the narrative action that links them. In this case, the narrative action in question is determined by Custine's and the narrator's journey through the museum. Yet on this level *Russian Ark* is a narrative only in the most minimal terms. It preserves the causal, spatial and temporal continuity of a narrative, and yet holds very little in the way of narrative content. The camera follows Custine from room to room as he offers commentary to the narrator, who responds occasionally. There are encounters with some of the other characters: Custine discusses sculptures with a blind woman, is ushered out of a room by some guards, and talks to the present-day curator of the Hermitage. These encounters, however, do not produce any significant narrative effects beyond themselves.

In addition, the causal connections between the various re-enacted historical scenes are weak at best. Peter the Great and Nicholas II are connected by succession, but the film leaves undeveloped the deeper historical connections between these ghostly figures. The fusion of past and present is undermined, in a sense, by these weak connections. They suggest something in between Foucault's archaeology and Ricoeur's narrative. Ultimately, the narrative itself runs up against an archival barrier. As the camera leaves behind the pageantry of the ball at the end of the film (shortly before the Revolution would overturn this privileged world), Custine refuses to accompany the narrator, remaining instead in the pre-revolutionary past. Finally, the camera looks out from the Hermitage (the 'Ark' of the title) across a watery expanse. Here, the misted horizon suggests that the act of historical retrieval has hit its limit, a horizon that cannot be reached. Tradition itself may not be enough to traverse this 'uncrossable distance' between present and past, after all. Despite its affirmation of continuity, the film acknowledges the defining role of historical disjuncture.

Russian Ark's dialectic between continuity and disjuncture is mapped onto historical coordinates. The former is associated with the past, a link manifested in the submerged linearity underlying the film's modular structure. For although the film leaps between the present and past in surprising ways, the scenes of pre-revolutionary Russia are arranged chronologically. The film begins with Peter the Great, and ends with the days preceding the Russian Revolution. The scenes that do not follow this chronology are those depicting the Soviet and post-Soviet days. Tellingly, these are the scenes that make most explicit reference to the immediate exterior of the Hermitage. In one, a man is building coffins during the Siege of Leningrad. In another, recent curators of the Hermitage comment upon the fact that the KGB placed bugging devices in the museum. In this way, temporal disjuncture is associated with more recent history, while the more distant past holds out the promise of chronological order. Beyond the specific historical disjuncture represented by the revolution itself, we may draw a connection with contemporary culture. *Russian Ark* acknowledges the growing museal fascination identified by Andreas Huyssen (1995, 2003), and the enhanced ability to bring the past into the present as a result of media technologies (in this case, the video recording apparatus that makes possible this rendezvous among historical moments). It also, like other modular narratives, uses database structure to query narrative's hold upon time. The database's role is ambiguous – on the one hand, it seems to continue the disjunctive tendencies of the revolution (which were directed at wiping away the imperial past), yet on the other it allows for past and present to be linked together in meaningful ways.

The narrative shape of *Ararat* also reflects this attempt to come to terms with the various strata of historical memory embodied in archival materials. From the very beginning of the film, a complex temporal relationship is established among a multitude of times and locations, including Raffi's conversation with David at Canadian customs and immigration, Gorky's time in New York and his memories of Turkey, Raffi's time in Turkey, the production of *Ararat* (the film-within-a-film) in Toronto, the premiere of the film and the historical scenes that it represents. The relative temporal position of these scenes is not always clear, but is eventually established in retrospect. Certain elements are given greater continuity: Raffi and David's encounter unfolds chronologically, although intercut with a variety of scenes that are not ordered in this way.

Although the system of the archive is a structuring element in *Ararat*, this film, like *Russian Ark*, has a strong investment in continuity. Like *Russian Ark*, *Ararat* attempts to retrieve lost elements from the past and reintegrate them with the present. Yet to a greater extent than Sokurov's film, *Ararat*'s affirmation of continuity is also an affirmation, though a cautious one, of narrative. In this respect, *Ararat* marks a greater departure from the archaeological approach to the past outlined by Michel Foucault (1972). On the one hand, *Ararat* parallels Foucault's concern with identifying ruptures and historical discontinuities, by challenging official historical accounts that have overlooked the Armenian genocide.[4] The film's aesthetics of disjuncture mimic this breaking open of official history, exposing its gaps and deficiencies. However, Foucault's approach is concerned not with individuals but with anonymous collectivities. It identifies the discourses that operate in a given social context, but is deeply mistrustful of historical continuity. *Ararat*, however, focusses upon history's impact on individuals. In this case, historical memory knits together archival materials, and inflects them with subjective meaning. Narrative plays a key role in this binding process. Thus, rather than critiquing narrative *per se*, *Ararat* exposes the mechanisms by which narrative creates continuity out of disjuncture.

Memory across borders

Modular narrative structures in *Russian Ark* and *Ararat* suggest a mnemonic approach to representing history. The temporal leaps in these films parallel the associative logic of human memory, and suggest alternative ways of conceptualizing historical narratives. In this respect, and in their foregrounding of mediation, they intersect with debates within postmodernist theory regarding the representation of history. Fredric Jameson, for example, criticizes E.L. Doctorow's historical novel *Ragtime* for representing the historical past indirectly, via popular ideas and stereotypes (1991, 25). Yet as Linda Hutcheon argues, *Ragtime* and other examples of 'historiographic metafiction' (1988, 5) do not do away with 'truth and reference', but 'make the reader aware of the distinction between the *events* of the past real and the *facts* by which we give meaning to that past, by which we assume to know it' (223). In this model, history is not abandoned, but the terms of reference relevant to the representation and understanding of history are placed in question and made part of literature's formal explorations.

This interplay between history and fiction is further developed in more recent theoretical debates regarding the relationship between history and memory. Underlying these debates, according to Andreas Huyssen, 'is a fundamental disturbance not just of the relationship between history as objective and scientific, and memory as subjective and personal, but of history itself and its promises' (2003, 2). Thus, the historicism described by Fredric Jameson may be regarded not simply as empty pastiche. Rather, by exploring history's fictive dimension and its relation to memory, contemporary art, literature and cinema can potentially challenge the authority of conventional, monolithic history and its relationship to received ideas regarding progress.[5] I would suggest that modular narratives form part of this tendency, and that they function as what Katharine Hodgkin and Susannah Radstone refer to as 'memory texts' (2003, 13). Hodgkin and Radstone note that recent decades have seen 'a broadening out of the category of the memory text into collective rather than subjective contexts, and non-narrative as well as narrative forms' (13).[6] Although both films under discussion here are narratives, both also make reference to archival forms of memory that are not in themselves narrative. Technologies of reproduction (in particular, video and film) take on an ambiguous role in this process, as agents of both remembering and forgetting. Huyssen remarks that modern media of reproduction, along with contemporary memory discourses, have weakened temporal boundaries: 'The past has become part of the present in ways simply unimaginable in earlier centuries' (2003, 1). Through their formal articulations, modular narratives examine these new relationships between past and present, re-imagining national history as collective memory.

Although *Russian Ark* gestures towards an archival aesthetic defined by disjuncture, its invocation of national memory is far removed from Michel Foucault's call for the dispassionate excavation of discourses and systems of dispersion (1972, 37–8). Firstly, the film imbues these past moments with an air of nostalgia. The Romanov daughters dance along a palace hallway in gauzy dresses, an image of beauty that can only seem all the more ephemeral when considered in relation to the family's imminent demise. At the same time, Custine and the narrator are far from detached observers. The narrator, who is Russian, has a stake in Russian national identity, and reacts with displeasure when Custine mocks Russian art and music, and the imitations of Italian art that he finds in the museum. The camera itself mirrors this dialectic between detachment and involvement. At times, it observes from a distance, but at others it almost becomes a participant, wheeling around among the dancers in the ballroom, or racing along a hallway with the Romanov sisters. The detachment of history is replaced by the experiential engagement of memory.

In *Ararat*, the narrative articulation of memory is a way of connecting individuals to history. For Ani, narrativizing Gorky's painting (by telling the story of its creation) connects her to Armenian history and culture. For Edward, the Armenian director of the film-within-the-film, the fictionalization of history brings it closer. For Raffi, the recounting of his personal and cultural narrative (in this case, to David) is a necessary step in the establishment of his identity. As David examines the materials that Raffi is bringing into Canada, Raffi narrativizes them verbally. In addition, he reads from the diary of Clarence Ussher, an American missionary who witnessed the atrocities of 1915. In this way, Raffi connects his personal narrative to the ethnic narrative of the Armenians, hence establishing the importance of the past to the immediate present.

The film's modular aesthetic further links memory and history. Many of the segments are juxtaposed in ways that mimic the associative operations of memory, without grounding these operations specifically or exclusively in the psychology of a particular character. For example, a scene of Gorky in his studio is followed by a 'flashback' of Gorky with his mother as their photograph is taken. Following this, we see Ani giving her lecture on Gorky's painting. We return again to Gorky in his studio, and back to the taking of the photograph. Although the latter scene can undoubtedly be seen as a conventional flashback in relation to Gorky in his studio, Ani's use of the photograph complicates this mnemonic device. It suggests that the photograph itself, and the painting that copies it, are the vehicles of memory in this case. The resulting externalization of memory creates complex temporal relationships between the present and the various layers of the past. History is revealed to us through collective and individual memory, which is inextricably bound up with the archival. The film's disjunctive narrative mimics both the traumatic eruption of repressed historical memory and the archival array or database. The search for historical truth is rooted in the material traces of the past that exist in the present, and in the associated efforts at mnemonic retrieval.

One crucial repository for such material traces is of course the museum, which has taken an increasingly central role in the contemporary era as a focal point for national memory. The tendency for nations, peoples and cultures to equate recognition in museums with broader cultural recognition is, notes Svetlana Alpers, a historically recent phenomenon (1991, 30). This contemporary development raises questions about the various possible articulations of national identity made possible by museum spaces. For example, Alpers argues that a chronological presentation of artworks or historical materials may not always be the most illuminating (27), and goes so far as to suggest that cinema and literature may be better equipped to articulate national identity (30). The modular structures of both *Ararat* and *Russian Ark* raise similar issues, indicating that a linear presentation of history is not the only option. *Russian Ark* literalizes this question of museal order and sequence by leading the viewer on a cinematic itinerary through a real museum space. In a sense, it is both film *and* museum. At the same time, both films undermine the 'programmed narrative' that Carol Duncan associates with many museal expressions of the nation (1991, 92). They achieve this by presenting the past as fictional, and by invoking personal memory as a crucial element of the archival process. As Susan Crane argues, museum exhibits that de-emphasize overarching official interpretations of the past (at the expense of historical certainty) can produce new perspectives on the *process* of writing history (1997). This perspective (which can be aligned with Linda Hutcheon's notion of 'historiographic metafiction' [1988, 5] in the literary sphere) suggests that memory itself is a dynamic force within the archival space of the museum (Crane 1997, 49). The 'problem' of historical 'distortion' is thus acknowledged and reframed as a vital aspect of both memory and museum culture (50). The overt re-enactments in *Russian Ark* and *Ararat* are, therefore, not simply false representations of history: rather, they are real instances of historical memory. National and ethnic identities in both films are thus mediated by an archival aesthetic, which is imbricated with mnemonic processes of storage and retrieval.

Furthermore, the modular structure of these narratives can be linked to contemporary changes in the structure of nationalism itself. As Benedict Anderson argues, the concept of the nation is a relatively recent invention, emerging late in the eighteenth century. The nation, for Anderson, can be defined as 'an imagined political community – and imagined as both inherently limited and sovereign' (1991, 6). Nations thus depend upon collective identification and a sense of distinct boundaries. They are defined not by the rule of a monarch, nor by the intimate social connections of a local community. Rather, they call upon a collective investment in narratives of identity. These narratives take place in a historical continuum that is, for Anderson, identifiable as the 'homogeneous, empty time' described and challenged by Walter Benjamin in his critique of modern, linear history (204). Thus, while the concept of nationality took on, upon its emergence, a 'modular' dynamic that allowed it to be 'transplanted ... to a great variety of social terrains' (4), this modularity did not extend to nationality's internal logic, which was emphatically linear. The past century, however, has witnessed a shift towards a more modular type of national identification. Andreas Huyssen points out that the spatio-temporal compression of modernity has 'expanded our horizons of time and space beyond the local, the national, and even the international' (2003, 4). Local and national borders have, over the past century, increasingly been traversed by global movements, whether of various national and ethnic groups, or of media transmissions and communications networks. In this way, cultural and ethnic memories have themselves become mobile. As a result, 'The form in which we think of the past is increasingly memory without borders rather than national history within borders' (4). Insofar as these national boundaries continue to restrict and shape global cultural flows, however, I suggest that we reframe Huyssen's definition to read 'memory *across* borders'.

This definition is particularly well-suited to the aesthetic and thematic projects of *Russian Ark* and *Ararat*. Both films undertake a *reinscription* of national identity, in which the local is infiltrated by the global, while spatial and temporal boundaries circumscribe the attempts to recall the historical past. Indeed, spatial and temporal boundaries are aligned in both films. In *Ararat*, Raffi's attempt to commemorate his homeland's violent past on videotape is held up at Canadian customs, so that

Canada's spatial boundary becomes a temporal boundary as well. In *Russian Ark*, the difficulty of representing the past is represented spatially, when the camera is 'stranded' inside the Hermitage at the end of the film. In both cases, collective memory is connected to the notion of nationhood in such a way that national identity itself appears as contingent and framed in relation to global concerns. In applying modular dynamics to their national and ethnic narratives, *Russian Ark* and *Ararat* produce a sense of national identity that is not simply monolithic and linear. Rather, Russian and Armenian identity, respectively, are complicated by their relationships with regional and global spaces and cultures. In this way, the modular structure of these films is directly connected to the network of disjunctures and traversals implied in the notion of 'memory across borders'.

As William Johnson comments, the art and décor in *Russian Ark* is dominated by European culture, suggesting 'less a Russian than a non-Russian Ark' (2004, 48). Similarly, Kriss Ravetto-Biagioli sees the film as a reminder 'that St. Petersburg itself was built as a Russian dream of Europe' (2005, 21). Furthermore, both Russia and Europe are revealed as imagined communities by the dialogue between the European Custine and his Russian companion behind the camera (22).[7] Russian history in the film is re-articulated as memory across borders. The Hermitage provides the location for this re-articulation, hinting at the transnational movements of cultures and peoples that contribute to the construction of identities. The memory-work of the film has its roots in the classical practice of mnemotechnics described by Frances Yates, involving a mental progression through an imagined space, in which images and thoughts might be stored (1966). *Russian Ark* represents just such a progression, in an even more literal fashion than the memory problem films described in Chapter 4. Custine leads us to various rooms and images, appearing in the process to summon up re-enactments of past events. At certain points, this mnemotechnic itinerary runs up against internal borders, as Custine is ushered out of certain rooms. At one point, a strange young man leans out of a doorway and blows air in Custine's direction, as if repelling him. These moments in the film suggest barriers to historical memory, a sense that is intensified by the ephemeral and distant nature of so many of the film's scenes. They also suggest the interconnectedness of time and space in relation to memory. As Hodgkin and Radstone point out, mnemonic disjuncture and complexity is often 'associated with changes in a place, registering the uncanniness of being at once the same and different, at once time and space' (2003, 11). Custine's spatial movement through the halls and rooms of the Hermitage is also a movement through time, a time defined both by continuity (the film's single take) and modularity (the segments of the past re-enacted in different rooms).

Ararat offers a similar sense of memory's basis in spatio-temporal relations. However, while *Russian Ark*'s spatio-temporal explorations take place entirely within the official space of the museum, with its authoritative status as a national site of memory, in *Ararat* the struggle for identity takes place across a range of institutional and extra-institutional sites. These sites are largely foreign. Raffi's ordeal at customs is one example of the film's meditation upon the question of memory in relation to spatial boundaries. His re-entry to Canada represents an attempt to carry memory (in the form of the videotapes, and his narrative account) *across* national borders. Similarly, Edward, the film's director, is told at customs that he may not bring a pomegranate into Canada. He promptly decides to eat the fruit, literally consuming this reminder of his homeland. These examples of memory traversing national boundaries suggest the contingent nature of national identity. This point is given heightened emphasis in *Ararat:* the Armenian victims of the 1915 massacre did not have a nation state to which they could lay claim. Raffi's journey to Turkey and his covert videotaping underline the fugitive quality that still attends these memories. Canada provides a refuge for Raffi's preserved memories, as well as the location for Edward's film. Despite the spatial and temporal distance from the events of 1915, the material reality of these events is affirmed. When Ani walks on set to withdraw her involvement, she is rebuked for the interruption by Martin Harcourt, the actor playing Clarence Ussher (the American missionary). Harcourt frames his rebuke not in relation to the present-day pragmatics of producing the film, but to the atrocities being enacted in the scene, as if they are occurring in the present tense. Ani is thus confronted by the reality of the massacre, spatially and ontologically displaced to a Canadian film set.

The art gallery in Toronto is another space that plays host to these fugitive memories by displaying Gorky's paintings. The paintings are, in a spatial sense, at two removes, as Gorky completed them in New York, not Turkey. This transnational movement of materials places responsibility upon outsiders as bearers of memory. Clarence Ussher, the American missionary who witnessed the massacre, is one such figure: his written account is a key piece of evidence establishing the truth of events. David, the customs officer, performs a similar role, as he bears witness to Raffi's story, and allows him to enter Canada with the videotapes (in a sense, these tapes carry time across spatial boundaries). Finally, Canada itself, by hosting the shooting of the film, becomes a caretaker of the Armenian story. This inside/outside dynamic is also evident in *Russian Ark*, in which Custine, a European, curates a journey through Russian history. However, the type of spatio-temporal displacement found in *Ararat* is quite different from the temporal displacement of *Russian Ark*, in which events are apparently enacted in the same places where they originally occurred, but at a later time. In *Ararat*, most of the scenes take place in Canada, meaning that the operation of mnemotechnics, which attaches memories to given places, is restricted. Furthermore, the constant mnemotechnic movement of *Russian Ark* contrasts with *Ararat's* relatively static dynamic. In fact, the most intense acts of memory in the film seem to occur at moments of physical stasis: Raffi's story to David is told while he is being held at customs and immigration, unable to enter Canada; Ani's evocation of Gorky's life is conducted in front of a lectern; while Gorky's recreation of his past occurs while standing at his easel. Both films associate memory with freedom of movement, but in *Ararat* this freedom is curtailed, and forgetting presents a greater threat. After all, while the historical figures depicted in *Russian Ark* are well-documented, the Armenian genocide is in real danger of being neglected altogether by history.

While both *Ararat* and *Russian Ark* enact the operations of historical memory via the content and form of their narratives, these operations are underwritten (as in the memory-problem films discussed in the previous chapter) by forgetting. As Andreas Huyssen points out, memory itself depends in part upon forgetting, in the sense that to remember something may involve erasing or neglecting to remember something else (2003, 4). Furthermore, the relationship between memory and forgetting has been intensified by the mnemonic plenitude of the current era, which has been made possible by modern technologies and museum culture. In this context, the overwhelming archival presence of the past becomes linked, paradoxically, with 'the threat of socially produced amnesia' (6). In *Russian Ark*, this is manifested in the forgetting of the Soviet era, which is 'presented as an ellipsis in Russian history that is left unnamed and unrepresented in the film' (Ravetto-Biagioli 2005, 19). Like other modern movements, the Soviet movement had a strong bias towards the future as opposed to the past, and was therefore grounded in forgetting. *Russian Ark's* memory-work, then, serves as a forgetting of modernist/Soviet forgetting.

From one perspective, this leaves the film open to historical critique, particularly of the Jamesonian kind. The film's strong investment in nostalgia would thus appear to be part of a regressive movement, in which true historicity is displaced by the resurrection of dead styles (Jameson 1991, 296). With the rise of such ahistorical fantasies comes the withering away of the utopian imagination, and of projects directed towards the future. Yet Andreas Huyssen suggests that this opposition between utopia and nostalgia is too one-sided: 'Nostalgia itself ... is not the opposite of utopia, but, as a form of memory, always implicated, even productive in it' (1995, 88). We may be witnessing, he suggests, 'a shift within the temporal organization of the utopian imagination from its futuristic pole toward the pole of remembrance' (88). Similarly, Pam Cook defends nostalgia by suggesting that 'where history suppresses the element of disavowal or fantasy in its re-presentation of the past, nostalgia foregrounds those elements, and in effect lays bare the processes at the heart of remembrance' (2004, 4). Nostalgia may thus work as a mnemonic strategy for resisting the ideology of progress and modernization, and 'the attack of the present on the rest of time' (Huyssen 2003, 88). In relation to this debate, *Russian Ark*'s deployment of nostalgia is ambiguous: on the one hand, it resists the forgetting of modernism; on the other, its wistful resurrection of the imperial past leaves out the historical pain and injustice that accompanied that past.[8] In any case, the film illustrates the processes of remembering and forgetting that are intertwined with the production of history and national identity.[9]

In *Ararat*, Raffi's insistence upon remembrance is also imbricated with active forgetting. For example, he tells David that his film cans contain exposed negative from Edward's film *Ararat*. When David discovers that Ani and the filmmakers are in fact en route to the film's premiere, Raffi concedes that bringing the film cans to Canada was the price for being allowed to record the video footage in Turkey. The man who gave him the cans assured him that they contained film. Yet Raffi contends that he had to tell his original story, because it 'meant something' to him. At this point, David takes on a role beyond his job as customs officer: it is up to him to judge whether Raffi's historical and personal narrative, laced with omissions and half-truths, is worthy of admission. Ultimately, despite discovering heroin and not film in the cans, David lets Raffi leave. Later, David confides to his son that he let Raffi go because he 'couldn't punish him for being honest'. The broader implication is that David has accepted Raffi's narrative about the massacre and his attempts to commemorate it. David's overlooking of the contents of the film can is effectively a forgetting that makes memory possible. This point is reinforced by the intercutting between the opening of the can and the premiere of the film, specifically with scenes showing the slaughter of the Armenians. Later on, showing his video footage to his half-sister Celia, Raffi tells her that he felt the ghost of his father as David opened the film can. In this way, the act of memory itself (which is inseparable from forgetting) has a conjuring effect, making the past appear within the present, and allowing for Raffi to establish a narrative of identity.

Celia's quest for identity is also inflected with memory and forgetting. She blames Ani for her father's death, and refuses to accept Ani's description of events implying either an accident or suicide. 'I can't remember it the way you want me to', Ani confesses to Celia. Ani's account contrasts with that of Raffi, who asserts to David that his father was killed while trying to assassinate a Turkish diplomat. Upon checking Raffi's background, David labels Raffi 'the son of a terrorist'. Thus, Ani's story about her husband's death is revealed as another lie – but one that is designed to protect Celia. Celia, for her part, resists this benevolent forgetting. Gorky's painting forms a focal image for this resistance. Remarking on the fact that Gorky's mother's hands appear unfinished in the painting, Celia confronts Ani with the suggestion that the artist erased the hands after having painted them. Later, we see a short scene of Gorky in his studio that confirms this hypothesis – taking his own hands, Gorky smears paint across the hands in the painting. It is an image that links creation and forgetting together, suggesting the present's incomplete grip on the past. Following the confrontation with Ani, Celia takes forgetting into her own hands by running into the art gallery and attacking Gorky's painting with a knife. This attempted act of erasure has as its goal the recognition of past events, providing another example of the complex relationship between remembering and forgetting. As Michael Roth says of Alain Resnais's *Hiroshima mon amour*, *Ararat* is 'a film that remembers forgetting' (1995, 101).

Anchoring the archive

The ambiguity regarding nostalgia, memory and forgetting in *Russian Ark* and *Ararat* is parallelled by the unstable relationship between floating time and temporal anchoring. With regard to floating time, Maureen Turim concludes her book on the history of cinematic flashbacks with a rumination on the future of the flashback form. Turim sees value and potential in 'avant-garde modes of expression that reconstruct narrative time and space so as to dissolve the definitive sense of a past the present can clearly access' (1989, 246). Turim favours such films as Marguerite Duras's *India Song* (1975) which destabilize the represented past; in these films, 'past history is always a story, always itself in question' (246). These avant-garde disarticulations of flashback structures produce 'floating temporalities', which 'do not maintain the points of reference necessary to the flashback as a device' (246). *Russian Ark* at the very least gestures towards this avant-garde disarticulation of time. The flashes of past events we see in the film cannot properly be described as flashbacks; rather, they seem to emerge unbidden, as ghostly re-enactments of the past, without being placed in firm temporal context. The camera itself appears to float through the museum's archive of unmoored temporalities. The archival structure of the film is thus linked to the temporal disarticulation described by Turim, which draws both representation and history into question. As with other modular narratives such as *Eternal Sunshine of the Spotless Mind*, the database structure in *Russian Ark* and *Ararat* is linked to temporal instability. In shuttling between different layers of time, these films create a cloud of uncertainty around the past, which appears subject to the errors and erasures of human memory.

The floating temporalities of *Russian Ark* can, however, be placed into productive tension with Andreas Huyssen's notion of 'temporal anchoring', which attempts to slow down the fragmentary and chaotic movement of mediated time, re-establishing a relationship between the past and the present (1995, 7). *Russian Ark* is, effectively, a cinematic extension of the museal impulse that Huyssen detects in contemporary culture. In *Russian Ark*, the curatorial figure of Custine represents one way in which the film attempts to anchor its drifting temporalities. Custine offers asides to the camera indicating the events and personages being depicted. His mnemotechnic itinerary through the Hermitage is itself a kind of temporal anchoring. The submerged chronology of these historical scenes indicates that the film's historical order is anchored to the spatio-temporal order of Custine's guided tour. With a few exceptions, Custine leads us on a kind of historical journey that is largely linear.

The memory-work of the film does not, however, lead us to some definitive account of the past. Indeed, the metaphor of temporal anchoring retains a sense of movement and drift, even as it attempts to find a grounded anchoring point beneath the surface. Floating temporalities and temporal anchoring are thus not completely opposed terms. Rather, temporal anchoring acknowledges the floating connections between memories and historical events. Yet it refuses to see temporal disarticulation as an end point. To extend the dialectic between floating and anchored time, one may turn to the ark imagery that underwrites the film. As Dragan Kujundzic points out, Noah's ark in itself might be seen as an archive of sorts: 'the first attempt at taxonomization of the animal world, and a museum of 'natural' selection' (225). The Russian ark, as a museal record of Russian history, is itself adrift. At the end of the film, the ark appears to be surrounded by water, as if the Hermitage had been set adrift. This image indicates the instability of the ark/ archive's relation to the present – the anchoring of Custine's mnemotechnic itinerary is circumscribed by forgetting and historical loss. History itself floats away, unmoored from the present.[10] This final image indicates the fragile and contingent nature of temporal anchoring, offering forgetting and temporal drift the final word.

Ararat also deals directly with the dialectic between floating time and temporal anchoring, but resolves this dialectic in favour of the latter term. The film sets history adrift with its narrative structure, bringing past events into immediate proximity with the present, but also suggesting the disjunctures of historical forgetting. At the same time, it insists upon the importance of historical grounding. An intertitle at the end of the film proclaims: 'The historical events in this film have been substantiated by holocaust scholars, national archives, and eyewitness accounts, including that of Clarence Ussher'. This statement encapsulates the film's affirmation of memory, narrative and identity, and the connections among them. Its acknowledgement of forgetting and discontinuity complicates but does not diminish this affirmation. Raffi and Ani in particular serve as agents of temporal anchoring, as they contextualize places and events by telling and retelling the history of the Armenians. While the database aesthetic of the film appears to present us with floating temporalities, these temporalities are grounded and given historical context through storytelling.

As in *Russian Ark*, the archive is imagined as an ark. Mount Ararat, the mountain upon which Noah's ark is said to have come aground, is a central image in the film. The massacred Armenians, it can be argued, have been swept away by the flood of history, and their story is now threatened with exclusion from the historical ark/archive. The film's task is to rescue the scraps of this forgotten story, and give them their place in the archive. Whereas Sokurov's video camera surveys the inside of his Russian Ark, ending upon the misty waters of the Neva, Raffi's camera records the landscape *outside* the ark, after it has been inundated by the flood of history. This flood is by implication also a flood of forgetting, wiping away the memory of a people and leaving them outside the ark of history. Temporal anchoring in the film is given literal expression in Raffi's desire to ground his identity in a direct encounter with the Turkish landscape. Raffi's trip to Turkey, and his sense that the original film (which was shot in Canada) is lacking something, are thus motivated by his conviction that temporal anchoring depends upon spatial anchoring.

Accordingly, the Turkish landscape itself appears to lose its sense of stability when remade in a foreign context. Ani points out to Reuben that the film set's painted backdrop erroneously places Mount Ararat in proximity with Clarence Ussher's house. With their painted backdrop, the filmmakers effectively unmoor Mount Ararat itself from its true location. As in *Russian Ark*, history is set adrift in the process of its representation. Yet *Ararat* balances out this sense of drift with Raffi's trip to the real location of the genocide in Turkey. At the same time, Raffi's realization that he has been used as a drug courier has tempered his naïve belief in unmediated history. There is no film in the cans, and David's selective forgetting is therefore the only way that Raffi can bring his video-memories into Canada. While the shifting of Mount Ararat emphasizes difference and spatio-temporal distance, the film within the film serves to bring the past closer through re-enactment.

This dialectic between distance and proximity returns us to Paul Ricoeur's notion of a 'fusion of horizons'. For Ricoeur, historical narratives maintain a tension between notions of the past as either absent or contemporaneous (1984–8, 3:220). *Ararat* confronts this issue via its modular structure by juxtaposing the past with the present, so that the former threatens, on the one hand, to overwhelm the latter, and on the other, to disappear from it altogether. For Ricoeur, historical narratives ameliorate these twin threats by mediating between the past and the present, projecting a 'historical horizon that is both detached from the horizon of the present and taken up into and fused with it' (220). *Ararat* achieves this fusion of horizons by anchoring its modular segments in ethnic and personal narratives of identity. Raffi, Ani and Edward are all involved in constructing historical narratives that affirm the contemporary relevance of the past, and its difference from the present.

Egoyan's film also manifests this fusion of horizons spatially, in the image of the fake Mount Ararat on the backdrop of the Canadian film set. Here, two spatial horizons (Armenian and Canadian) become aligned with the temporal horizons of the past and the present. Thus, a relationship is established between the fictional horizon depicted in the film-within-a-film, and the real horizon captured in Raffi's footage, as well as between the experience of the present-day characters and that of their ancestors. The reconstruction of the past through historical detail brings the past into the present, but the distance from the past is upheld in the constant references to the production of the film-within-the-film. Without erasing the sense of a real past, the film acknowledges mediation's role in reconstructing the past in the present, establishing a dialectic 'between the interpreted past and the interpreting present' (Ricoeur 1984–8, 3:221). In this way, *Ararat* attempts a reconciliation between archival knowledge and historical narrative.

Russian Ark also fuses spatio-temporal horizons, but in the absence of a clear narrative the past fluctuates between the states of disappearance and omnipresence. The film's final image of the waters of the Neva highlights this fluctuation. For it represents both the end of the single shot that has traversed the entire film, and the end of Russia's tsarist era. This image of the horizon therefore unites past and present in the same location. Yet it is an indistinct and misty horizon at best, and the water seems to emblematize the 'uncrossable distance' that signifies the absence of the past (Ricoeur 1984–8, 3:220). This sense of uncrossable distance is heightened by the fact that Custine (from the past) and the narrator (from the present) have just parted company. By omitting the narrative relations that might mediate between past and present, *Russian Ark* creates an unstable relationship between detached and fused horizons, in which temporal anchoring ultimately falls prey to temporal drift.

Ararat and *Russian Ark* thus present two related, but distinct, ways of using modular narrative to interrogate the mediation of history. Although the direct treatment of history seems relatively rare in contemporary modular narratives, these two films demonstrate that modular structure can contribute towards a rethinking of the relationship between present and past. In both *Russian Ark* and *Ararat*, modular temporal structure performs a complex function, articulating memory and forgetting, temporal instability and temporal anchoring. This archival aesthetic imbues history with the qualities of memory, inflecting it with the personal and nostalgic.

While the database structures of these films are not explicitly linked to digital technology (as in *Eternal Sunshine of the Spotless Mind*, for example), they share a focus upon memory and audiovisual mediation that is very much of the current moment. As Andreas Huyssen points out, the turn to memory in contemporary society reflects a 'loss' of the past in relation to an excess of representation (1995, 6–7). Whereas modernist artists and thinkers such as Freidrich Nietzsche felt compelled to resist 'official' history through forgetting (1983, 62), their postmodern counterparts occupy a situation in which forgetting and fragmentation are central features of cultural life, and in which historical unity cannot be taken for granted (Huyssen 1995, 7). Accordingly, *Russian Ark* and *Ararat* seem at times to display contradictory impulses, towards unity and fragmentation, memory and forgetting. For example, forgetting in these films is associated with particular instances of historical crisis (the Russian Revolution of 1917 and the Armenian genocide of 1915) but also with the attempt to overcome these crises. In each case, the modular narrative structure mediates between these contradictory impulses.

While both films invoke discontinuity, in relation to upwellings of violence as well as in relation to archival systems generally, both also affirm continuity. In *Russian Ark*, this is achieved through an insistence upon the 'real time' of filming, while *Ararat* emphasizes narrative's mediating role. This struggle for continuity is also a struggle for identity, a struggle that is by no means a straightforward affirmation of national qualities, circumscribed by clearly defined boundaries. Rather, identity is inflected with otherness in both films (the European perspective of Custine in *Russian Ark*, and Canadian perspectives in *Ararat*). Physical and temporal distance is a kind of precondition for these attempts to establish identity. Taking us outside of conventional history as well as the interiority of memory, the modular structures of these films stage the relationship with the past from a perspective that is both inside and outside, now and then. In the dialectic between continuity and disjuncture, they enact the crisis and qualified redemption of history. The key difference between the films is in *Ararat*'s insistence upon temporal anchoring. The oddly timeless figure of Custine guiding us through the ark contrasts with Ani, Raffi and David, whose connections to the past are all firmly grounded in the present.

6
Deciphering the Present: Simultaneity, Succession and Mediation

Modular narratives put the narrative future in jeopardy by suggesting that events may be predetermined, and put the past in jeopardy via the destabilization of memory and history. The direct representation of the present, however, is less obviously fraught, since films generally appear to unfold in the present tense by default. Yet a number of modular narratives do test the boundaries of cinema's ability to represent simultaneous events. The scope of this challenge varies among the different types of modular narrative. This chapter will focus particularly upon *Time Code* (Mike Figgis, 2000) and *Code Unknown* (Michael Haneke, 2000), which represent examples of the split-screen and episodic modular narrative, respectively. These two films directly address the relationship between simultaneity and succession. Modern-day Los Angeles and Paris, respectively, are the focus of their examination of urban synchronicity. Their formal workings (characterized in one case by visual excess and in the other by narrative austerity) explore the limits of contemporary cinema's attempts to represent simultaneity in the context of the contemporary city.

Other types of modular narrative also address simultaneity, although few contemporary films do so with such directness. Anachronic narratives may invoke synchrony by revisiting events a number of times or from a number of perspectives. In *Elephant* (Gus Van Sant, 2003), the events leading up to a massacre at an American high school are examined in non-linear fashion. Encounters among the students in and around the school are replayed from different perspectives. In the context of the upcoming massacre, the narrative shuttles back and forth over the low-key moments of the day, as if searching for causal connections.[1] The two boys who undertake the killings are also observed, but there is no single element in their lives that can properly explain their actions. The temporal modularity of this film does not directly throw into crisis any notion of the present tense. Rather, it suggests the lack of a clear causal explanation for the massacre (visiting and revisiting the preceding events yields no clear motivation), and articulates a type of nostalgic longing for the 'innocent' moments preceding the massacre. In this way, the film invokes the past (memory) as much as the present (especially given the way that it plays upon the public memory of the Columbine shootings).

While anachronic modular narratives generally present a temporally fractured but ontologically unified world, films that present alternative narrative possibilities may challenge the notion of a unified present (or, for that matter, time itself). Kay Young remarks upon this tendency, noting the way that forking-path films can lead us to consider not only alternative futures, but also 'different modes of being in the *present*' (2002, 117). In this way, contemporary forking-path narratives provide us with ways of thinking about narrative's claim on the simultaneous present. For example, the romantic comedy *Sliding Doors* (Peter Howitt, 1997) bifurcates into two possible worlds. Helen, a PR consultant who has just been made redundant, enters a London Underground station on her way home. After missing her train, she arrives home late. However, the film goes on to show a parallel reality in which she catches the train and arrives home in time to discover her boyfriend Gerry's infidelity. Leaving Gerry, she finds career success, and falls in love with a charming young man named James. In the meantime, the 'initial' Helen is forced to take a job in a café and is, until the end of the film, ignorant of Gerry's unfaithfulness. Despite the temporal divergence between these two worlds, they are consistently coded as simultaneous, mainly through classical cross-cutting. Cross-cutting is already, at the beginning of the film, used to shift between Helen's voyage to work and Gerry's affair. This technique is continued after the bifurcation at the train station. The two Helens experience day or night at the same time, and even appear in the same location simultaneously, so that spatial contiguity reinforces narrative simultaneity.[2]

Eventually, both Helens are admitted to hospital after suffering accidents. The 'successful' Helen dies, and by implication we realize that her experiences have been a fantasy experienced by the 'real' Helen. Upon her release from hospital, however, Helen meets James, the love interest from her parallel life. At the resolution, the multiple threads are effectively domesticated, as *Sliding Doors* re-affirms linear time. By maintaining the synchronicity of the two worlds, the film ensures that the idea of the present is preserved. Just as the two Helens miss the train at the same time, for example, they also witness James's rowing race simultaneously. The urban space of London is the vehicle for personal choice and contingency, the engine driving these parallel temporalities. This urban space always runs on time, its perfectly synchronized events allowing us to chart the differences between the two worlds. The potential threat to the notion of a unified present is defused, firstly through cinematic conventions, and secondly through the discovery that one of the two possible presents was more 'real' than the other.

While these anachronic and forking-path modular narratives draw narrative order into question, threatening to make the past or future either inaccessible or excessively manifest in the present, episodic and split-screen modular narratives are less obviously tales about time. These narratives, which create a narrative chain out of lesser narratives or spatially distinct screens, would appear rather to be tales about space, in which the geographical linkages between characters and situations drive the narrative. Certainly, both *Time Code* and *Code Unknown* explore the limits of narrative's ability to unite urban, national or global spaces. As well as displaying the spatial complexity produced through these phenomena, however, both films create a context in which time itself is put into question. For this reason, the fact that both films feature the word 'code' as part of the title is no coincidence; in each case, time threatens to become unreadable, and audiences must decipher the codes determining temporal relations. Thus, both films suggest that time is never natural, but always comes to us via mediation. Through the exploration of different forms of mediation – technology, narrative and music – these films dramatize the attempt to redeem time, to reinvest it with its proper dimensionality.

Simultaneity, narrative and cinema

The rise of industrial modernity and literary modernism ushered in a heightened questioning of 'whether the present is a sequence of single local events or a simultaneity of multiple distant events' (Kern 1983, 68). This questioning accompanied the rise of new technologies that linked distinct spaces and made possible simultaneous reception: the radio, the telephone, the high-speed rotary press and the cinema (68). Meanwhile, modernist authors made simultaneity a central organizing principle (Heise 1997, 50). In *Ulysses*, James Joyce utilized multiple perspectives and the repetition of narrative events, as well as charting spatial itineraries that linked characters and places. (Kern 1983, 77). He experimented with cinematic montage techniques to represent the life of Dublin in the present moment, 'spatially extended and embodying its entire past in a vast expanded present' (77). Joyce thus made the present the locus of real experience, compressing the past and the future into the present in the form of memories and expectations, especially via interior monologue (86).

These literary examples highlight simultaneity's differing connotations. Benedict Anderson has noted the way that the rise of nationalism after the late eighteenth century was connected to the emergence of simultaneity. As opposed to the medieval conception of time, which did not distinguish sharply between the past and the present, the modern era treated simultaneity as 'transverse, cross-time, marked not by prefiguring and fulfilment, but by temporal coincidence, and measured by clock and calendar' (1991, 24).[3] It was made possible by the eighteenth-century emergence of the novel and the newspaper, which could be consumed by large numbers of spatially dispersed individuals, thereby providing 'the technical means for "re-presenting" the *kind* of imagined community that is the nation' (25). Simultaneity was also central to modern power relations. As Helga Nowotny notes, its rise was prepared for by 'the spatial extension of state control, then with the economic one of the market, and finally with that of technologies' (1994, 23). The notion of simultaneity, then, was imbricated with the rise of modern cities and nations, which were crisscrossed by these flows of technology, capital and political power.

By contrast, modernist literature tended to resist this homogeneous brand of simultaneity. Through the use of multiple perspectives and interior monologues, and his representation through language of different temporal rhythms and speeds, James Joyce offered a sense of time as heterogeneous (Kern 1983, 17). Although these personal, private temporalities can be seen as an alternative to the homogeneity of public clock-time, it does not follow that modernist novels are concerned solely with individual experience. As Ursula Heise argues, the aggregation of perspectives in such novels as *Mrs Dalloway* and *Ulysses* 'adds up to an alternative social time, a time beyond the individual that is less alienating and impersonal than the globally standardized one of the Greenwich mean' (1997, 51). The modernists told stories that allowed for the emergence of 'temporal succession, and more generally a coherent external reality … far from excluding or invalidating each other, the differing and sometimes unreliable accounts in the novels mentioned do in the end allow the reader to infer a fairly consistent story …' (50).

This sense of unity and succession was abandoned by many of the later modernists, who would eventually eschew psychological realism and juxtapose logically irreconcilable narrative sequences (53).[4] There is simultaneity in these works, but it is a simultaneity produced through techniques of repetition and recursion, 'in which past and future are indistinguishable, and in which the present manifests itself only as the difference between two versions of the (almost) same' (115). This 'schismatic' notion of simultaneity is formally consistent with certain developments in science, including Einstein's Special Theory of Relativity, which suggested that different objects and observers have their own distinct temporality (Nowotny 1994, 36). In this view, simultaneity as it is generally understood is in fact an illusion, as it is based upon the false perception of a common temporal continuum.

Yet the notion of simultaneity has retained its currency within social, political and cultural spheres. Indeed, Helga Nowotny remarks upon 'a recurring discovery of simultaneity' in the late twentieth century (28). The spread of telephone networks and growth of broadcast media such as television have extended the experience of simultaneity to an ever-widening segment of the world's population, to the point where it is no longer the domain of an elite group. In industrialized countries, it has become the norm for most people (29): 'What was euphorically celebrated at the turn of the century has become prosaic reality today, but with non-trivial consequences ...' (30–1). These consequences have not been universally welcomed. While enabling subjects to participate in global simultaneity, communication technologies have also challenged the boundaries that distinguish private from public, hence undermining the notion of private time that was so important to the early modernists (31).

The 'discovery' of simultaneity has been given new impetus in recent years with the growth of mobile telephony and Internet use, which has facilitated communications among diverse and globally dispersed individuals. New technologies, however, can also be associated with a countervailing tendency towards asynchrony. William J. Mitchell notes that the 'controlled asynchrony' of voicemail, email and online forums allows for more efficient and convenient communication (1995, 16). The synchronic spatiality of the modern city is thus overtaken by the asynchrony of electronic media. In this context, the 'temporal rhythm' of the tangible city (dictated by seasonal, weekly and daily cycles) 'turns to white noise' (17). The television news, for example, often presents us with scenarios in which 'the distinction between live events and arbitrarily time-shifted replays becomes difficult or impossible to draw' (17). Temporality becomes unmarked and resists decoding.

Simultaneity is thus the subject of increasingly complex and ambiguous relationships in the digital era. For modernist writers and thinkers, the dominant mode of urban and global simultaneity was associated with the implacable march of linear, rational time. Insofar as they embraced simultaneity, then, they used it to link together the heterogeneous temporal experiences of a diverse range of characters. In the current context, simultaneity is no longer the unquestioned dominant. Rather, it coexists with the multiple asynchronous temporalities of electronic media. The communal temporality of cities and nations is therefore no longer a given. As Mitchell points out, the electronic era has hastened and intensified the division between '*urbs* (the territory of the civic formation, such as the seven hills of Rome)' and '*civitas* (families or tribes joined together because they shared the same religious beliefs, social organization, and modes of production)' (1999, 96). The time-space of the physical city is no longer directly identified with that of the community.

A number of contemporary films base their narratives around this disjuncture between urban and civic spatio-temporal relations. This is most evident in a group of films that can be called 'multiple protagonist narratives' (Bordwell 2005). These films, which display to some extent the influence of episodic television, knit together a multitude of characters and storylines, often highlighting points of convergence among them. In this manner, distinct stories gradually interconnect, and 'threads become webs' (Bordwell 2005). Prominent examples of the multiple protagonist film include *Nashville* (Robert Altman, 1975), *Short Cuts* (Robert Altman, 1993), *Magnolia* (Paul Thomas Anderson, 1999), *Amores Perros* (Alejandro González Iñárritu, 2000) and *Love Actually* (Richard Curtis, 2003), as well as such looser narrative constructions as *Chungking Express* (Wong Kar-wai, 1994), *Night on Earth* (Jim Jarmusch, 1991) and *Toute une nuit* (Chantal Akerman, 1982). Similarly, Fredric Jameson notes the resurfacing, within international cinema, of a narrative paradigm based upon the representation of simultaneity, which he dubs the 'narrative of simultaneous monadic simultaneity' (or SMS) (1992, 116).[5]

Jameson sees a melancholy note in SMS narratives. Remarking on the literary uses of plot coincidences in novels such as Henry Fielding's *Tom Jones*, Jameson notes that such coincidences 'generally involved the mysteries of birth and genealogy' (114). Modernist novels such as André Gide's *The Counterfeiters* (1926), on the other hand, find no such solace in their coincidences, which serve rather to reinforce the isolation of individuals and the incommensurability of their perspectives (115).

In the modernist context, individuals cross paths without knowing it, and the narrative coincidences merely emphasize the ephemerality of human connections. In sum, 'the Providence-effect is little more than an aesthetic one: the bravura gesture of a Romantic or a modern, which corresponds to nothing in lived experience' (115). To this assertion one can respond that the ephemeral encounters in the modernist text may serve as a source not only of alienation but also of pleasure. Furthermore, Jameson downplays the extent to which the diverse perspectives of the modernist novel create an aggregate shared temporality. The 'Providence-effect' is not simply an aesthetic gesture – it is also a way of revealing the common temporal medium that unites these disparate characters.

This argument also applies to such recent cinematic examples of the SMS as Robert Altman's *Short Cuts*. This film allows its narratives to play out as short stories, without weaving them together into an overarching narrative structure. The only thing connecting these various stories together is coincidence. However, these coincidences do serve a unifying purpose: they affirm that these stories are taking place in a geographically connected space, in a common temporality. There is no indication in the film that we are moving through time in anything other than a linear fashion. This sense of temporal unity is confirmed towards the end of the film, when an earthquake rocks Los Angeles and the film cuts between the various characters experiencing and reacting to it at the same time. In this moment, the sprawling, disconnected story worlds and urban spaces of the film are drawn together. *Short Cuts* may emphasize the spatial dislocations of contemporary urban life, but the temporal unity of the narrative remains virtually unquestioned.

Simultaneity and technological time: *Time Code* and *Code Unknown*

Although they offer divergent views on the possibility of representing simultaneity, *Time Code* and *Code Unknown* both have an investment in preserving temporal unity and succession. In this respect, they are closer to modernist literature than to the radically fractured temporal worlds of late modernism. However, they also use modular aesthetics to draw temporal unity into question. These modular SMS narratives, unlike *Short Cuts* and *Magnolia*, suggest that narrative form itself may not be enough to contain the diversity of spatio-temporal threads. By intensifying and foregrounding the modular structures implicit in multi-protagonist narratives, they insist that we not take the unifying power of narrative time for granted. In this respect, they are preceded by films such as *Toute une nuit* and *Night on Earth*, which present diverse narrative strands without connecting them directly. Yet in *Time Code* and *Code Unknown*, simultaneity is treated in a particularly direct and literal fashion, both formally and thematically. In *Code Unknown*, temporal segmentation displaces the 'natural' flow of linear narrative, while in *Time Code* parallel narrative threads are presented onscreen simultaneously. These two films thus demarcate the formal limits of the SMS or 'multiple protagonist' narrative, one via an aesthetic of absence, the other via an aesthetic of excess. In so doing, they question whether narrative can reconcile simultaneity and succession, and test its ability to traverse the spatially and temporally heterogeneous terrain of the contemporary city.

Time Code's promotional tagline boldly places the film's production techniques as central to its appeal: 'Four cameras. One take. No edits. Real time'. Indeed, the film is overtly concerned with the notion of real time, and of technology's role in mediating narrative time. The film follows a number of narrative strands that eventually coalesce in a followable plot. Throughout the film's 97 minutes, the screen is split into four quadrants, with each offering a different perspective on the narrative. Shot simultaneously with four cameras and without internal editing, these images sometimes depict different characters and spaces, and sometimes converge to offer different perspectives on the same situation. The story itself revolves around the personnel of a Los Angeles film company named Red Mullet. Head producer Alex Green is late for a production meeting. He appears to be suffering emotional problems; his wife Emma, who has been undergoing therapy, announces that she is leaving him. As auditions for a new film go on at Red Mullet, hopeful actress Rose arrives in a limousine with her lover Lauren, who suspects Rose of infidelity. Planting a microphone in Rose's handbag, Lauren later has her suspicions confirmed. Waiting outside in the limousine, Lauren listens in as Alex and Rose engage in a covert sexual encounter inside the building. Despite Alex's unwillingness to further Rose's acting ambitions, she later has a promising audition with Lester, an intense but undistinguished film director. After tossing around various film ideas, many of them absurd, the Red Mullet team listens to a pitch from Anna, an aspiring director. In a self-conscious mirroring of *Time Code*'s own structure, Anna imagines a film that will 'go beyond' montage, offering four simultaneous video images as a vehicle for its story. Meanwhile, a furious Lauren confronts Rose outside, then enters the Red Mullet offices bearing a gun and searching for Alex. As the room empties of people and Alex lies bleeding on the floor, Anna stays behind to film him with her video camera.

Time Code represents a marked departure from the norms of narrative cinema. It is, however, far from unprecedented. Experimental filmmakers and video artists long ago discovered the possibility of multiple screens, of course, but there are also examples of narrative filmmakers exploring this territory. Abel Gance's *Napoléon* (1927) used multiple projectors to create a triptych effect. Split-screen effects are also prominent in a number of Brian De Palma films, such as *Sisters* (1973) and *Carrie* (1976), in *Chelsea Girls* (Andy Warhol, 1966), *Numéro deux* (Jean-Luc Godard, 1975) and *The Boston Strangler* (Richard Fleischer, 1968). Peter Greenaway's films *Prospero's Books* (1991) and *The Pillow Book* (1996) make extensive use of frames-within-the-frame. More recently, *The Hulk* (Ang Lee, 2003), *Run Lola Run* (Tom Tykwer, 1998) and the television series *24* (Fox Network, 2001–) have utilized split-screen sequences to represent moments of fraught action. Yet few of these films use the effect in such a sustained manner, or as a means of interrogating the status of cinematic time.[6] For this reason, *Time Code*, which displays neither the disjunctive temporality of anachronic or forking-path narratives, nor the segmented structure of an episodic narrative, can productively be discussed in the context of modular narrative. Unlike the other films I have discussed, *Time Code* represents its modular structure spatially, as a relationship between synchronic channels of time rather than segments of time organized diachronically. Yet it raises similar questions regarding the dimensionality of time, and narrative's role in representing time.

Michael Haneke's *Code Unknown* (2000) displays many parallels with *Time Code* beyond the mutual resonance of the films' titles. However, its temporal aesthetic is far removed from the synchronic excess of *Time Code*. Like *Time Code*, *Code Unknown* concerns itself with a number of narrative threads, but in this case the threads are much less tightly woven. The narrative consists of a series of loosely connected fragments, separated by brief periods of blackness. In one thread, Anne, an actress, is filming scenes for a thriller in which she plays the victim of a serial killer. Anne's partner, Georges, is a war photographer. While Georges is on assignment in Kosovo, his brother, Jean, approaches Anne to ask if he can stay at her Paris apartment. Jean no longer wants to work with his father on the family farm. Anne agrees to let Jean stay for a while, but soon after their conversation, Jean gets himself into trouble. In a scene that links the various story strands together, Jean drops a piece of rubbish in the lap of Maria, a Romanian immigrant who is begging on the street. Jean is challenged for his thoughtlessness by Amadou, a teacher of deaf children. Following a confrontation between Jean and Amadou, Amadou and Maria are arrested, and Maria is deported. After this scene, the stories of Anne, Jean, Amadou and Maria largely diverge. Anne later spots Amadou dining in the same restaurant as her, and she and Georges console Georges's father after Jean runs off a second time. Yet for the most part *Code Unknown* appears to emphasize the way these stories *fail* to coincide. Amadou teaches his students to drum. Maria makes her way back to Paris illegally, and ends up begging on the streets once more. Jean vanishes from the film altogether. Meanwhile, returning from another assignment abroad, Georges discovers that Anne has had the entry code to her apartment changed. Here, the spectator is explicitly denied the formal consolations of the modernist SMS, in which the random connections between the characters add up to a shared social time. Although *Code Unknown* eschews non-linear temporal leaps or repetition, it can be described as a modular narrative, because its episodic structure undermines temporal and causal connections. In order to make sense of the narrative, we are forced to assume that the segments are ordered chronologically, although in many cases there is no evidence to confirm this. As with anachronic and forking-path modular narratives, we must adopt an analytical perspective in order to decipher the organization of time.

Just as the modern emergence of simultaneity accompanied the rise of such new technologies as the radio, the telephone and the cinema, technological mediation in these films plays an important role in conceptualizing urban simultaneity. Yet *Time Code*'s opening images, which directly establish a digitally driven information aesthetic, initially suggest technologically mediated *asynchrony*. As saxophone-driven jazz music plays on the soundtrack, the four quadrants of the screen come alive with various images of digital readouts, waveforms and video effects. The film's title appears, in digital letters. We hear electronic noises, and indecipherable scraps of dialogue. To use Lev Manovich's term, *Time Code* 'transcodes' the modular, database logic of digital media into the world of the film, acknowledging the informational underpinnings of its representation of time (2001b, 45). Here, the film gestures towards asynchrony by revealing the status of time as digital data. Ultimately, however, simultaneity definitively asserts itself, as a numeric countdown leads to the image of a video play button, before the upper right quadrant stabilizes, showing Alex's wife Emma in her therapy session. This opening sequence, lasting two and a half minutes, hints that *Time Code* will be concerned as much with its own form and production as with its narrative content. The images to follow, we are made aware, will consist of coded digital information. In addition, this opening sequence sets up the central negotiation between synchrony and diachrony, encouraging the audience to parse the images for similarities and differences. This decoding operation continues throughout the film.

In displacing diachronic montage into synchronic collage, *Time Code* creates a tension between duration and simultaneity. However, the four quadrants are connected by spatial overlaps, universally experienced events and by technology, so that this tension is reconciled. First of all, although the effect of monitoring four distinct areas of the screen depicting four distinct spaces may initially disorient audiences, the film soon ameliorates this effect. Very early on in the film, some of the quadrants converge, so that we are given two perspectives on the same space at the same time. For example, when an itinerant masseur named Quentin arrives at the Red Mullet reception desk, we watch him from two perspectives (one is a wide shot taken from the lobby, and the other is a closer perspective taken from within the reception area). These spatial overlaps, which recur throughout the film, stabilize the film's narrative world in two ways. Firstly, they indicate that the quadrants represent a consistent, contiguous space. Secondly, they affirm that these events are occurring simultaneously. This type of verification-effect is enabled by the restricted spatial reach of the diegesis. In comparison with other SMS narratives, *Time Code* represents a relatively contained world. All of the characters are connected to Red Mullet in one way or another, and no one travels a significant distance from the company office. Here, the characters are connected spatially and socially, and the story is therefore less dependent on the device of the unlikely coincidence. Secondly, as in *Short Cuts*, earthquakes are used to indicate narrative synchrony. In this case, three earthquakes punctuate the narrative. At these moments, characters in all four quadrants simultaneously experience the shaking and react in fright. Their spatial proximity (they are all within the earthquake's radius) serves to guarantee that they inhabit the same moment in time.

Thirdly, *Time Code* invokes technological mediation as a way of unifying its temporal threads, and reconciling simultaneity and succession. Indeed, one of the four quadrants begins by showing a surveillance monitor, itself split into quadrants By invoking surveillance technologies, *Time Code* assures us that each of the quadrants is unfolding in the same temporality. The threat of excess presented by *Time Code*'s hypermediated aesthetic is therefore neutralized by its affirmation of liveness.

In fact, as Thomas Levin has pointed out, *Time Code*'s claims on cinematic realism are based on 'the unprecedented temporal coherence of its conditions of production' (2002, 593).[7] Surveillance is a critical element of the diegesis, as Lauren's quest for revenge is triggered by her ability to listen in on Rose via a remote audio device. Yet *Time Code* does not invoke surveillance in order to examine its use as an instrument of power and control. As Lev Manovich remarks, *Time Code* marries its surveillance aesthetics to a relatively conventional story, thereby utilizing a 'telecommunication-type interface to a traditional narrative' (2001a, 15). To use Bolter and Grusin's term, *Time Code* constitutes a 'remediation' of surveillance aesthetics (1999, 5). Remediation is characterized by the interdependence of hypermediacy (which foregrounds mediation) and immediacy (which disavows it) (34). In this case, the hypermediacy of the four quadrants acknowledges mediation, while making possible the temporal immediacy of the four simultaneous long takes. The sinister connotations of surveillance are thus eclipsed by its ability to unite simultaneity and succession. In this sense, the film sidesteps the urban crisis described by Mike Davis, in which, developers and municipal authorities have conspired to create a compartmentalized Los Angeles, where the wealthy are insulated from the poor by architectural and legal barriers (1990, 226). This 'privatization of the architectural public realm' is paralleled and enhanced by surveillance technologies and 'restructurings of electronic space' which restrict access to 'the invisible agora' (226). *Time Code*, which takes place entirely within the bounds of well-to-do Hollywood, confronts the spatio-temporal boundaries of its surveillance aesthetic, without having to confront the socio-economic barriers that circumscribe its narrative world. In contrast, as I will argue, *Code Unknown* aligns its spatio-temporal and social disjunctures in representing urban Paris.

In *Time Code*, then, surveillance and communications technologies, rather than presenting a menace to freedom and privacy, become a means of linking the screens together. Lauren's reactions to what she can hear (and what we can see in another quadrant) guarantee that the events we are witnessing are simultaneous. A similar function is performed by the various mobile phone calls that punctuate the film, uniting disparate images in a mutual dialogue. Although it threatens to alienate us from time, digital technology in *Time Code* knits together (public and private) urban space, thus affirming temporal unity. This runs counter to the relationship between urban and electronic space described by William J. Mitchell, in which the 'asynchronous city' constituted by electronic media challenges the relevance and spatio-temporal integrity of physical

Figure 6.1   Time Code. Red Mullet Prod./The Kobal Collection/Elliott Marks

cities (1995, 16). Similarly, Scott Bukatman argues that science fiction films such as *Blade Runner* (Ridley Scott, 1982) articulate a movement beyond the lived space of the city and into the 'terminal space' of the computer screen (1993, 137). *Time Code*'s hypermediated split-screen aesthetic certainly gestures towards this terminal space, grounding its narrative relations in a digitally mediated, two-dimensional plane, and the film begins by acknowledging the technological–informational base underlying its representation of time.

Time Code, however, reassures us that this techno-temporality can be decoded. Just as the art of memory attempts the recovery of the past through spatial navigation (as demonstrated in *Memento* and *Eternal Sunshine of the Spotless Mind*), the spatial explorations of *Time Code*'s distinct quadrants allow for the recovery of the present. However, whereas *Memento* and *Eternal Sunshine* depict circumstances in which the practice of mnemotechnics is disabled by spatio-temporal disloca-tion, *Time Code* appears to overcome the spatio-temporal dislocation of its split screens. Here, the disjunctures associated with electronic media are overcome not by denying mediation but by embracing an *excess* of it. Thus, *Time Code* illustrates the way that modular aesthetics can invoke not only spatio-temporal breaks but also spatio-temporal connections.

In *Code Unknown*, this type of spatio-temporal mapping is deliberately made inaccessible to the audience. The film begins by implying that it will, like other SMS films, undertake an exploration of interconnected stories within an urban environment. The first major dramatic scene charts the meeting between Anne and Jean, Jean's subsequent mistreatment of Maria and his confrontation with Amadou. These urban coincidences play out on a Parisian street, shot in a single long take. Yet as it unfolds, the film frustrates any attempts to draw closer connections among these characters, and effects a type of spatial dispersal. While the film is principally centred on metropolitan Paris, it also visits rural France and Romania, as well as an unidentified location in Africa. Even within the Parisian sections, it is more often than not impossible to intuit the spatial relations between various locations. We know that certain scenes (the confrontation between Jean and Amadou, and Georges's return from overseas) take place in the street outside Anne's apartment. Yet most of the scenes unfold within discrete spatial capsules: a cemetery, a supermarket, a restaurant, a theatre, an airport boarding tunnel. Many of the characters move further away from this urban context, and the prospect of connecting them spatially becomes less and less likely. Technological mediation offers little help in this regard. Like *Time Code*, *Code Unknown* features a number of phone calls (featuring Amadou's father, Georges and Anne), but these do not serve to affirm simultaneity. In this case, we are only ever allowed to hear one interlocutor, and the content of the discussion is often difficult to decipher.

Technological mediation is also featured, in both films, in the recording of actors' performances. In this way, the theme of mediation is given concrete form. In *Time Code*, Rose's audition is recorded on video. We are able to see her reading her lines, as a TV monitor shows the same action unfolding in real time (formally, this image mimics the frame-within-a-frame aesthetic of the film itself). Here, the film's yoking of real time and mediated time is played out in miniature. *Code Unknown* sets out to achieve the opposite effect. In one scene, Anne acts out a scene from her movie, addressing her lines directly to the camera (a video camera). In the scene, Anne is locked in a soundproof room by a serial killer. However, it becomes difficult to tell whether the male voice giving instructions from behind the camera belongs to the film's director or to one of the characters. 'The camera is the door', he says, as if giving screen directions. Yet subsequent lines such as 'I want to watch you die', and 'Be spontaneous', combine in confusing ways, suggesting that we may be watching a film-within-a-film in which the killer videos his victim. In this case, the diegetic time of Anne's film and 'real time' become indiscernible. This also occurs in later scenes. In one, Anne is shown around an apartment by a realtor. The action is interrupted by the director's call of 'cut', and we realize that we are watching another scene from the thriller. Following this, we watch Anne playing out another scene in the same location. At the end of the take, the dialogue repeats what we heard at the beginning of the first take. In other words, we have been watching the two shots in reverse chronological order. By allowing these realizations of temporal discontinuity to emerge only towards the end of each take, the film destabilizes our sense of temporal indexicality. The cuts that divide up these recorded segments thus articulate a chain of definitive breaks, creating a series of discrete and disconnected pieces of space-time. Although implicitly inviting us to connect these pieces, the film refuses to underwrite their veracity. Real time is a fundamentally unreliable notion in *Code Unknown*.

These differing thematic and aesthetic approaches to real time are also played out in relation to the notion of 'clock time' that underwrites it. The concept of clock time was integral to the modern era, and supported the modern systematization of factories, train timetables and global trade. As Stephen Kern notes, modernist writers searched for ways to resist the linear thrust of this measured, public clock time by representing the heterogeneity of private time (1983, 17). In the electronic era, by contrast, the integrity of public time is itself arguably under threat, as a result of asynchronous communication technologies and practices (Mitchell 1995, 16). Accordingly, and in sharp contrast to its modernist forebears, *Time Code* attempts nothing less than the reconciliation of private time and public, clock time. At one point early in the film, one quadrant shows a shot of a clock on the wall, as the film's private dramas unfold in the other quadrants. This analogue clock affirms the reliability of digital time that underwrites the whole narrative. Director Mike Figgis notes that the shooting of the film required that the cameras as well as the actor's watches be synchronized. Shooting commenced at 11:00 am precisely, after a countdown. The audience's ability to synthesize the strands of the narrative depends upon the clock-based synchronicity of its production. On the other hand, *Code Unknown*, with its multiple incommensurable temporalities, rejects clock time as an answer to contemporary asynchrony. One scene in particular highlights this fact. As Amadou and his female friend sit down in a restaurant, she asks him if he likes her watch. He responds neutrally, and she places the watch in an ashtray. This inconsequential moment subtly underlines the uselessness of clock time in the context of the film's disjunctive temporal structure. However, *Code Unknown* offers no affirmation of private time as per the modernist tradition. Rather, both public and private time are subject to disjuncture.

Mediation and mobility

In both films technological mediation is connected to a dialectic between movement and stasis, which plays itself out across the contemporary cityscapes of Los Angeles and Paris. One of the four quadrants in *Time Code* begins by showing a surveillance monitor, split into four images. At once, the camera moves away from this screen to show us the security guard who is monitoring it. In this camera movement, *Time Code* implies that its visual mobility marks it out as superior to 'ordinary' surveillance. This mobility allows us to traverse both public and private spaces, looking in, for example, on Emma's psychotherapy session and Alex and Rose's covert tryst. This mobility is grounded, paradoxically, in stasis. Just as the security guard appears tethered to his monitor (he strolls outside at one point, but always stays close to his desk), Lauren remains parked outside in the limousine while listening in on Rose. Her continued presence in the limousine provides an anchoring point for this surveillance. To this extent, the visual mobility of the other screens is grounded in Lauren's relative stasis. The limousine, apparently a self-sufficient capsule in which to traverse the city, is stopped outside the building, immobilized by its function as a base for surveillance. In this regard, *Time Code* is less emphatic in its embrace of technology's unifying effects. For Lauren, the synchronicity of surveillance leads to isolation and violence (she eventually shoots Alex as revenge for Rose's affair with him).

In *Code Unknown*, the character of Georges (Anne's partner, a war photographer) engages in a limited type of surveillance, strapping a still camera around his neck so that he can photograph unsuspecting commuters on the Paris Métro. It is an awkward operation that requires extreme stillness on Georges's part. In contrast with *Time Code's* real-time aesthetic, there is no 'liveness' in this form of mediation. We are not allowed to view the images from Georges's camera until a later scene, in which the photos are displayed in slide-show fashion, while Georges's letter from Afghanistan is read by Anne in voiceover. Here, the dialectic between movement and stasis is also a dialectic between moving and still images. Just as the movement of the train allows for the stasis of its occupants, Georges's acts of surveillance produce a series of frozen instants. Both travel and surveillance are thus divested of any association with simultaneity. Georges's subsequent voiceover, rather than narrativizing or remobilizing the still images, refers to another time and context altogether (his trip to Afghanistan). The disjunctures here are multiple: between Georges and the anonymous subjects of his photographs, between movement and stasis, between the disconnected temporalities of Paris and Kabul, and between the time of photographing/writing and the time of viewing/reading. Here, in sharp contrast to *Time Code*, urban surveillance, travel and communication are radically asynchronous.

Paul Virilio has addressed this paradoxical sense of stasis and asynchrony amidst an environment of speed and simultaneity. In a world dominated by movement and speed, the notion of the instant and the 'illusion of inertia' both depend upon 'our remaining unconscious of our own speeds' (1991a, 108). In order to explain this idea, Virilio refers to Einstein's example of two trains which 'seem immobile to travellers while they are really launched at top speed one beside the other' (108). In this context simultaneity is an illusion, in which 'the inertia of the moment' is produced through rapid motion (108). In spite of this revelation of simultaneity's illusory nature, 'our historical discourse has remained tied to a culture based on a common conception of space and time' (110). This common conception is nonetheless distinct from the old notion of duration, attached to the 'unique historical time' of individual subjects. Rather, the contemporary subject finds him/herself 'in motion and in transit in railroad car compartments, that are also, for their user, compartments of space and time' (110). Both *Time Code* and *Code Unknown* articulate the desire for a common space and time. Only the latter film, however, exposes the illusory underpinnings of this common temporality by portraying a city-space traversed by heterogeneous rates of movement.

Time in *Code Unknown* is mediated by travel. Central to the film's representation of flows and disjunctures is the motif of the journey (The film is subtitled 'Tales of Several Incomplete Journeys'). Each narrative segment concludes with a blunt cut, in several cases cutting off conversations or actions in mid-flow. These scenes function in themselves as a series of journeys without a destination. Journeys in the film traverse urban, rural and global spaces, but rather than uniting these spaces they serve mainly to demonstrate disjuncture. First of all, most of the journeys are presented as solitary. These include Maria's deportation from

France via aeroplane, Georges's assignment in Kosovo (we never meet any of his travelling companions) and Amadou's father's arrival in Africa (he remains alone in his car as he drives out of the container). When people in the film do share a journey, their status as fellow-travellers is usually unsustainable. Thus, after receiving a call regarding his son's arrest, Amadou's father drives his taxi fast enough to panic his passenger, who is then insulted when Amadou's father insists he get out. When Anne travels by metro, she is harassed by an Arab youth who sarcastically wonders why she is not travelling in a chauffeured car. The association between modes of transport and the failure of interpersonal connections also extends to the relationship between Jean and his father. In an apparent attempt to encourage Jean to stay on the farm, Jean's father unloads a motorbike from the back of his van. However, as soon as he is summoned to view it, Jean climbs on and rides out of shot. Rather than linking him more closely to the farm, the bike offers him the means to leave it. Vehicular journeys in *Code Unknown* thus isolate characters within separate worlds, or place them within worlds that they refuse to share. In this film, the temporal continuity of the journey is not a shared continuity.

The separate spatialities and temporalities experienced by these characters thus parallel the formal disarticulation of the narrative, as their incomplete journeys are manifested in the film's truncated narrative segments. Furthermore, travel in *Code Unknown* is shorn of its traditional connotations of freedom. Indeed, the most well-off characters are those that have the freedom *not* to move. Maria's return to Paris ultimately finds her walking aimlessly along the street, before finally deciding to return to begging. However, upon selecting a space to sit down, she is immediately moved on by some shopkeepers. This sense of undesired mobility contrasts with the security of Anne's nearby apartment, which is protected by an electronic lock. In this sense, the film aligns itself with critiques of urban-global simultaneity. As Helga Nowotny points out, simultaneity may unite diverse subjects and spaces, but it 'does not automatically become translatable into equality' (1994, 33). In fact, it may exacerbate socio-economic disparity by obliging individuals and groups (such as developing nations) to participate in technological and economic systems in which the terms favour the most powerful participants (33). In *Code Unknown*, all of the characters have access to global mobility, but not all of them benefit from it. Thus, just as the film's aesthetics of disjuncture undermine the representation of simultaneity, its thematics of alienation and inequality attack simultaneity's utopian underpinnings. The dominant associations of simultaneity are with ideas of national identity and progress: on the one hand, it supports the shared national time of the 'imagined community' (Anderson 1991, 24); on the other, it supports the irreversible 'progress of humanity conceived in evolutionary terms' (Nowotny 1994, 33). Yet simultaneity in *Code Unknown* fails to underwrite either shared national time or irreversible progress. Similarly, urban and global travel in the film drives its representation of simultaneity, but is a vehicle neither for national identity nor for utopian visions of the future.

The radical discontinuity of the narrative, furthermore, is linked to the film's attempt to follow characters and situations across an extremely heterogeneous spatial field. In this sense, the film's structure is animated by what can be described as an 'aesthetics of globalization'; the formal features of globalization are experienced by the characters as well as embodied in the shape of the narrative. According to Arjun Appadurai's influential description, globalization is characterized by a relationship between flows and disjunctures (1996). In the era of globalization, the world is traversed by global flows, shaped by the movements across national boundaries of people, culture, technology, capital and ideology (described by Appadurai as ethnoscapes, mediascapes, technoscapes, financescapes and ideoscapes) (33). Yet the relationships among these dimensions of global flows are increasingly disjunctive (37).[8] For example, in third-world nations international flows of culture may occur where flows of technology do not, producing a disjuncture between lived and represented experiences of technology. *Code Unknown* displays a similar understanding of the 'complex, overlapping, disjunctive order' of globalization, and seeks to represent it both thematically and formally (32). It depicts a transnational ethnoscape defined by flows of immigration (legal and illegal) that are not always commensurate with flows of capital and culture, a fact illustrated by the differing fates of immigrants in the film. For example, whereas Amadou draws upon African culture in teaching drumming to his students, Maria's return to Paris highlights her cultural *dislocation* (she leaves behind her family and musical culture despite having failed before to find work in the French capital). When Amadou's father arrives in Africa, the car he drives out of the container represents a movement of technology and capital that appears to insulate him from his immediate sociocultural environment (the camera is located inside the car for the duration of the scene, and he does not interact with any of the people milling around outside). This sense of interrelated flows and disjunctures in the world of the story is duplicated formally in the narrative structure. Rather than heightening the sense of simultaneity, this thematic and formal articulation of global dynamics emphasizes the production of incommensurable temporal flows and spatial disjunctures.

Accordingly, the representation of journeys in *Code Unknown* is characterized by temporal elisions and interruptions. This disjunctive effect applies no less to the scenes in which actual travel is being depicted. Georges's journeys to Kosovo and Afghanistan are presented as a series of still photographs, while Georges narrates the contents of his letter to Anne in voiceover. The continuity of Georges's letter is set in counterpoint to the series of still images, in which images of war and death compound the sense of disjuncture. Furthermore, a number of the journeys are wholly elided. We see Maria being escorted aboard the plane in Paris, but nothing of her trip to Romania. When she returns, we see her climbing into her hiding place (inside a truck or a container). The next time we see her, she is already back in Paris. Similarly, Amadou's father arrives in Africa with no prior context (save for an oblique reference to Africa in an earlier conversation), and his journey is not depicted. Nor is Jean's arrival in Paris and his subsequent return to, and departure from, the farm shown directly. Furthermore, the contrasts among the narrative depictions of journeys in *Code Unknown* contribute to the overall sense of temporal incommensurability. Thus, while Maria's and Georges's journeys seem to be all but left out of the film, in another scene we watch as Jean's father ploughs a field in his tractor. The extended length of this take, in which the tractor makes its way up and down the field, measures an elongated temporality that is at odds with the compressed and elided presentation of Georges and Maria's international trips. This disjuncture between instantaneity and duration is effectively a structuring principle for the entire film. Causal connections among these different times and spaces are de-emphasized, exaggerating the sense of disjuncture. Here, it is difficult to envision the type of spatial mapping exemplified by *Time Code*'s intersecting monadic journeys. The connections among characters and scenes tend towards the schismatic. As a result, we are offered scant assurance that the characters in *Code Unknown* occupy a common temporal continuum.

Duration, instantaneity and the long take

Time Code and *Code Unknown* are both distinguished by their use of long-take aesthetics. As Mary Ann Doane comments, the continuity of the long take is intimately connected with the concept of 'real time' (2004, 265–6). The pre-history of this concept is to be found in the modernists' exploration of the relationship between temporal continuity and discontinuity, inspired in part by new technologies such as photography and cinema (268). In the current context, a fascination with real time can be found in the instantaneity of live television and the internet (264). Doane's concern is to critique this concept, firstly because it is associated with the human will to control time (280), and secondly because it is based upon unacknowledged disjunctures. On the one hand, film archives an experience of time that is discontinuous with the present (272); on the other, 'real time' only makes sense in relation to 'the possibility of an "unreal time", the time, for instance, of an edited temporal flow' (265). Real time, like simultaneity itself, is therefore an illusory concept. For this reason, Doane favours avant-garde, non-narrative works that expose the ruptures underlying real time (275). *Time Code* and *Code Unknown*, however, engage with this relationship between duration and real time, succession and simultaneity, in a more ambivalent way. Formally and thematically, they embrace ruptures as well as continuity. Here, I will argue that both *Code Unknown* and *Time Code* have an investment in the relationship between succession and simultaneity, and therefore in the notion of real time. However, while *Code Unknown* directly challenges this relationship, *Time Code* is generally less circumspect.

Despite its insistent emphasis on spatio-temporal disjuncture, *Code Unknown*, like *Time Code*, issues an affirmation of the cinematic long take. This affirmation is grounded in an attachment to cinematic realism, which is reminiscent of the theories of André Bazin. For Bazin, classical cinema of the 1920s and 30s was characterized by its use of montage, which, notes Bazin, generated sense and meaning from the relationship between adjacent images rather than their intrinsic properties (1967, 25). In post-1940 cinema, however, Bazin detects a renewal of cinematic realism that constitutes 'a decisive step forward in the development of the language of the film' (38). Without doing away with montage altogether, this new cinema placed emphasis on long takes and deep focus. Bazin singles out Orson Welles for praise, commenting that he 'restored to cinematographic illusion a fundamental quality of reality – its continuity' (1971, 28). This type of realism meant that cinema was 'capable once more of bringing together real time, in which things exist, along with the duration of the action, for which classical editing had insidiously substituted mental and abstract time' (Bazin 1967, 39). Thus, Bazin's aesthetic theories privilege the long take for its ability to unite cinematic time and real time, which montage had previously rendered separate. Although Bazin's theories are generally associated with 1950s and 60s movements such as Italian neorealism and the documentary genres of direct cinema and *cinema verité*, they continue to be a reference point for contemporary approaches to cinematic realism.[9]

In *Code Unknown*, one scene in particular appears to illustrate Bazin's argument. In this scene, we see Anne enjoying a romantic encounter with a male companion. Suddenly, Anne reacts in shock. A boy clings to the wall surrounding the pool, which is atop a tall apartment building. He appears in danger of falling. Anne and her male partner rush to rescue the boy, named Pierrot. This dramatic sequence is markedly different from the sequence shots that make up most of the scenes in the film, because it makes use of conventional continuity editing. Anne's look of shock motivates a reverse-shot of the boy, while a series of quick edits heightens the action as the couple rush to save him. At the conclusion of these events, the narrational status of the scene is immediately undermined. We discover that it is merely a scene from one of Anne's films, as Anne and her fellow actor view the scene from a recording studio, recording lines of replacement dialogue over the looping images. Here, the sleight of hand of classical continuity editing is exposed, and this scene is made to seem an inferior simulacrum in relation to *Code Unknown*'s dominant mode of exacting long takes. *Code Unknown* reveals the artificial unity made possible through editing, echoing André Bazin's concern that continuity editing constitutes a demonstrably untrustworthy representation of the world.

Time Code, too, takes seriously the connection between realism and spatio-temporal continuity, and the assumption that editing is a disunifying practice. Describing Robert Flaherty's *Nanook of the North* (1922), Bazin comments upon a scene in which Nanook hunts a seal. While 'montage could suggest the time involved' in waiting for the seal to appear, Bazin praises the director's single-setup approach: Flaherty 'confines himself to showing the actual waiting period; the length of the hunt is the very substance of the image, its true object' (1967, 27). Similarly, the notion of waiting time is an integral part of *Time Code*'s durational aesthetic. The four cameras dutifully record the uneventful moments in between actions, decisions and confrontations. Thus, the upper-left quadrant devotes a large amount of time to Lauren as she sits in the limousine, waiting for Rose to return or listening in on her activities. Emma's conversation with her therapist occupies the upper-right quadrant for over 20 minutes, despite the fact that we hear very little of what she has to say. This dedication to recording the 'reality' of waiting time is also, like Bazin's perspective on cinematic realism, grounded in humanism. For Bazin, the Italian neorealist cinema's 'documentary quality' enabled its anchoring in social reality (1971, 20). The concomitant humanism of these films was, according to Bazin, their 'chief merit' (21). Although *Time Code* is far removed from the working-class settings of Italian neo-realism, and is billed by its director as a 'black comedy' (Figgis, DVD featurette), its focus on human relationships and connections betrays a humanist perspective. The film's lack of editing, combined with its modular, split-screen aesthetic, enables it to explore these human connections, and implicitly affirms their value.

This perspective is not shared by *Code Unknown*, in which the long take is rigorously divorced from humanism. The scene in which Jean and Amadou have their confrontation illustrates the limits of the long take's unifying powers. Following this scene, Anne, Jean, Amadou and Maria will have very little to do with one another. Yet this dynamic of dispersal is evident within the scene itself. Shuttling backwards and forwards among the characters, the camera fails to plot a unified relationship among them. The camera's persistent movement mimics the sense of placelessness felt by characters such as the runaway Jean and homeless Maria. Neither camera movement nor duration are able to fulfil their promises of freedom and unity, respectively. Furthermore, just as the swimming pool scene undermines the veracity of continuity editing, other scenes reveal that the sequence shot is almost as suspect. When Anne acts out scenes from her film, we are misled or confused regarding the truth-value of what we are seeing. In one scene, Anne's direct-to-camera address leaves us unsure whether she is addressing the director or the character of the serial killer. In another, we are led to believe that Anne herself is looking for a new apartment, when it is in fact her character. Both of these scenes unfold as long takes, although the second is interrupted by a slate. Although *Code Unknown* displays a commitment to the long take, it disrupts the long take's claims on both unity and veracity. The long take is marked as epistemologically superior to continuity editing, but is also revealed as potentially misleading.

Ultimately, *Code Unknown* departs from Bazin's perspective on realism and duration by suggesting that time itself is subject to codes that must be deciphered. Although Bazin is far from being a naïve realist, his approach is characterized by a commitment to the spatio-temporal indexicality of cinematic images. In *Code Unknown*, indexicality is invoked by the use of the long take, but is undermined by the emphasis on mediation and codes. The 'code' of the title is a motif that runs throughout the film. The opening scene establishes the centrality of this idea: a deaf child mimes for her classmates, who are unable to decipher her gestures. Similarly, Georges is left locked out of Anne's apartment because he does not know the code. By extension, Maria is locked out of French society, as if unable to translate its socio-economic codes. Our experience of watching the film is also one of decoding: scenes are presented to us devoid of context, and we are forced to parse locations, character behaviour and dialogue for narrative clues. In certain scenes, minimal or misleading information effectively locks out the audience (as with the bewildering scene in which Anne addresses the director/killer behind the video camera). Just as space, causality and meaning are subject to this system of codes, so is time.

Again and again, time in *Code Unknown* appears to be unreadable. First of all, the film fosters uncertainty as to the temporal relations between scenes. The scenes tend to work as self-contained segments, not referring beyond themselves spatially or temporally. In the absence of any other indication, one assumes that the scenes are ordered chronologically, even though it is possible, in many instances, that they are not. Secondly, clues as to temporal duration are omitted. We are unsure as to the length of time covered by the film, and in certain cases (namely, the photographic slide-shows) by individual scenes. Finally, by deliberately confusing scenes from Anne's thriller with those from the diegetic 'real' world, the film forces us to decode these temporalities, distinguishing filmic from real time. In deciphering the narrative, the audience must decode the various relations between duration and instantaneity. In *Code Unknown*, time is constituted not simply by the sequence of images, but in a series of interlocking codes relating to order, duration and ontological status. Time is a language that can be mistranslated and misunderstood.

Time codes: narrative, technology, language and music

In both *Time Code* and *Code Unknown*, the acknowledgement of coded temporality draws narrative into question, suggesting that narrative itself may be little more than one code among many. Both films imply that the diachronic mode of cinema may not be equipped to capture the synchronic, multiple nature of modern urban life, yet both ultimately allow for the recuperation of narrative time. Whereas one film allows us to navigate its aesthetic of excess, the other allows us to compensate for its aesthetic of absence. *Time Code*, despite its overt synchrony, establishes a diachronic narrative path. Firstly, the soundtrack assists by, for the most part, accompanying one quadrant at a time. In this way, our attention is directed to significant narrative events as they occur. Secondly, narrative excess is controlled by making certain quadrants into temporal placemarkers, in which the narrative content is minimal. For example, Emma's therapy session goes on without requiring much direct attention. Similarly, other characters such as Lauren and the security guard function as observers, who watch or listen as more significant events unfold in the other quadrants. Thirdly, the film resolves itself into a fairly conventional narrative, in which Alex's affair with Rose triggers Lauren's revenge. Although there are a number of other threads, they eventually arrange themselves around this straightforward plot. *Code Unknown* also allows us to decode its narrative, although its lack of classical structure and resolution makes it more resistant to decoding. Nonetheless, the film does not prevent us from assuming a chronological structure, and in effect demands that we knit together a narrative, however minimal, out of its disconnected segments.

The two films' narrative workings can be contrasted in terms of their treatment of endings and mortality. Georges's photographs of the war dead, for example, make literal Roland Barthes's association between still photography and death. According to Barthes, the photograph, by turning its human subjects into objects, allows one to 'experience a micro-version of death (of parenthesis): I am truly becoming a specter' (1981, 14). In *Code Unknown*, this deathly stillness, this parenthetical fissure produced by the photograph is implicitly linked to a disjunctive narrative aesthetic. Georges's images of the dead appear and disappear abruptly, breaking the flow of the moving images with their unassimilable sense of contingency. These fatal disjunctures are paralleled by the sudden cuts to black that prematurely terminate each segment of the film. Here, the equation of mortality and narrative endings places *Code Unknown* within the modernist tradition described by Frank Kermode (1967). For Kermode, the ending of a traditional Western narrative text, typified by the archetype of the biblical apocalypse, constituted the mortal moment that conferred meaning and order on all that preceded it. Modernist writers such as James Joyce and Virginia Woolf, however, detached mortality from the ends of narratives and distributed it through their texts as a generalized sense of crisis. Thus, although the notion of the End/Apocalypse has 'lost its naïve *imminence*, its shadow still lies on the crises of our fictions; we may speak of it as *immanent*' (Kermode 1967, 6). In a similar way, *Code Unknown*'s endings are multiple, distributed and immanent. In the absence of a cohesive ending for the narrative, the film is punctuated by multiple endings that are represented as a loss of consciousness, a falling into oblivion. The structural codes and successive temporality of classical narrative cannot be taken for granted in *Code Unknown*.

In *Time Code*, by contrast, death retains its traditional place at the end of the narrative. Lauren shoots Alex, and although his death is not confirmed, his quadrant cuts to black before the others, implying that the end has arrived for him. Indeed, the film producer's death at the end is, by comic extension, the death of traditional single-channel filmmaking. Fittingly, Alex's plight is videotaped by Anna, the young filmmaker who has just unsuccessfully pitched a multichannel film project to the Red Mullet team. Anna, like Georges, becomes a chronicler of mortality. Yet the placing of the shooting as the climactic moment affirms the film's essentially diachronic tendency, a tendency that is supported by the selective sound mixing and the use of 'dead time' to restrict narrative excess.

Time Code and *Code Unknown* both challenge and then recuperate narrative's ability to cope with synchronic events. Yet this affirmation of time also goes beyond narrative, and into the realms of sound and music. James Tobias suggests that cinematic narratives can be described in terms of their inherent musicality. That is, musicality inflects not only the soundtrack but the visual and narrative rhythms of the diegesis. This concept is related to Eisenstein's 'theories of rhythmic montage' (Tobias 2004, 27). *Time Code* is, for Tobias, a strong example of this, because the soundtrack of the film, which oscillates between the different visual channels, 'pinpoints the film's emotional highs and lows in a *musique concrete*' (26). The final scene of the film addresses the 'musicality of sound-image relations' by showing Anna's film proposal accompanied by her musician friend playing the keyboard (26). For Tobias, films like *Time Code* and *Run Lola Run* show that 'narrativity and musicality are not opposed in the first place' (31). Although Tobias's approach illustrates the interdependence of these different time codes, analyses that view music as inherently narrational fail to address what *distinguishes* narrative from music, namely its basis in a distinctly *causal* succession. For this reason, I treat music and narrative separately here.

Code Unknown eschews non-diegetic music. There is background music in the restaurant scene, and singing and dancing during a Romanian wedding attended by Maria. This music, however, is used neither to connect together scenes nor to foster emotional identification in the audience. On the first point, Mary Ann Doane notes that Hollywood cinema generally creates an 'illusion of uncodified flow' by using sound, including music, to divert attention from visual cuts (1985, 57). *Code Unknown*'s abrupt caesurae, by contrast, synchronize sound and image cuts, undermining cinema's uncodified flow. On the second point, Anahid Kassabian writes of the way that music in Hollywood films invites 'perceivers' into 'identifications' with characters, situations and nations (2001, 2–3). By largely rejecting music, *Code Unknown* refuses to make any such identificatory invitation. Kassabian notes that American films from *Birth of a Nation* (D.W. Griffith, 1915) to *Mission to Mars* (Brian de Palma, 2000) have conducted their address to American nationalism through their musical scores. *Code Unknown*, however, generally refuses to ameliorate the fragmentation of French society via musical means.

However, the drumming performed by Amadou's deaf students takes on a unifying function at the end of the film. We see and hear this drumming in two scenes, and it continues over the concluding scenes of the movie, in which Maria searches for a begging spot, Anne returns to her apartment, Georges finds himself locked out. Finally, the music stops, and a deaf child mimes something to his classmates. The drumming is the only element in the film that overlays the disjunctive scene-breaks. After the failure of narrative connections and language to connect the characters, this gesture towards temporal unity is striking. Yet this is a heavily qualified gesture. First of all, the drumming does not actively link the characters, except aesthetically. The final scenes emphasize the fact that no-one is any closer together at the close of the narrative. Secondly, it is significant that drumming is used. There is no transcendent harmony that might suggest a higher level of commonality among the characters. This music is, to use Michel Chion's term, 'anempathetic music' (1994, 8). Whereas empathetic music adopts 'the scene's rhythm, tone, and phrasing' in order to evoke associated emotions directly, anempathetic music proceeds 'in a steady, undaunted, and ineluctable manner' creating a 'backdrop of "indifference"' (8). Although anempathetic music can intensify emotion, it does not directly invite emotional *identification*. The drumming in *Code Unknown* thus gestures towards unity while maintaining a sense of difference and disjuncture. Thirdly, the drummers are in fact Amadou's deaf students. The sound of the drumming may reverberate across the final scenes, but it is at best a muffled sound for the students.

Here, however, lies the element of faith at the heart of *Code Unknown*. The students are engaged in a communicative act that, because of their deafness, is also an act of faith. Similarly, in the final shot of the film, one of the deaf children mimes for his classmates, as at the start. As before, the concept being mimed is virtually impossible to decipher. However, the act of miming has an aesthetic, performative quality to it.

Like the music, these gestures communicate without communicating anything in particular. Importantly, this is a communicative gesture not assisted by modern technology. It is a moment shared in open, public space. Accordingly, the collective rhythm of the drumming contrasts with Georges's inability to negotiate the high-tech electronic lock of Anne's apartment. The private space of the apartment contrasts with the public space where the drummers perform. This public space is transformed into public *time* via the temporal flow of the performance. The temporality of the film at this point is not simply disjunctive; it is constituted in the tenuous relationship between unity and disjuncture. Whereas the narrative and visual movements of the film have failed to bring a sense of unity, the staccato movement of the drumming overlaps spatio-temporal disjunctures. This in turn fosters a sense of community, however abstract or tenuous. As James Tobias suggests, 'In music, perhaps, the subject of discourse is first-person plural' (2004, 34). The narrative of *Code Unknown* ultimately stakes its claim to temporal unity upon a musical metaphor.

Time Code also uses sonic metaphors, but in a less qualified manner. In this case, language is not a barrier to unity, as in *Code Unknown*. In fact, language is able to traverse the four quadrants easily, via the medium of mobile telephony. Yet the film depends for narrative clarity upon selective audio mixing, which allows one quadrant to be supplied with a soundtrack as the others are muted. In other words, the hypervisibility of the four channels is countered by a kind of selective listening. Whereas the miming of the deaf children in *Code Unknown* asserts the communicative value of acts that are narratively unfathomable, virtual deafness becomes the pre-condition for narrative clarity in *Time Code*. The synchronization of narrative time and real time is made possible through this virtual deafness. Yet these times are further connected via the medium of music. For one, non-diegetic music appears periodically throughout the film, artificially linking the quadrants. Furthermore, director Mike Figgis notes that he did not write a conventional script for the film. Rather, he created a kind of 'score', in which each bar corresponded to a minute of screen time, the quadrants were represented by staves, and the various characters by blocks of colour. Although much of the dialogue was improvised, the score indicated in advance the timing and location of each characters' actions. This 'musical' score, therefore, allowed for the creation of a fully synchronized narrative. As James Tobias points out, cinematic images are themselves 'scored' by the 'simultaneous reception of the audible' (35). An awareness of this fact can reveal the way that musical structures intertwine themselves with cinematic narrative forms.[10] Figgis's emphasis on music extends further: he notes that he mixed the score live at the premiere, like a DJ, and draws attention to his trumpet playing on the soundtrack (he holds a trumpet during the interview, and is proud to note that one audience member mistook his playing for that of Miles Davis). Via this emphasis on musical improvisation, Figgis offers a way of negotiating between narrative time and clock time, in which the former is not simply subordinated to the latter.

The emergence of musical metaphors in both films suggests a common project of thinking beyond narrative's exclusive claim on time. Music offers its own mediation of the temporal that is distinct from narrative's. However, the films are divergent in their deployment of these time codes. In *Time Code* the various codes (narrative, clock time, musical time) turn out to be translatable and mutually affirmative. In this way, the film recalls once more Lev Manovich's notion of 'transcoding', which refers to the way that the logic of digital technology (characterized by lists, arrays and modular structures) emerges within other contexts and media forms (2001b, 45). *Time Code* appears to assimilate this digital logic via the digital camera and surveillance technologies through which it tells its relatively conventional story. In doing so, the film suggests that the technological codes underpinning digital technology are compatible with the formal and communicative codes underpinning its narrative.

By contrast, *Code Unknown* presents these codes as a list of alternatives. Technology fractures time, whereas narrative presents a false claim on unity. However, narrative time is partially redeemed by way of musical time, which does not underwrite its unifying project but instead supplements its deficiencies. The failure of narrative connections at the end of the film is balanced by the suggestion of temporal commonality. Music is an alternative time code that can reconcile unity and disjuncture without resolving them into a synthesis. While maintaining narrative sense and chronology, both films offer ways of questioning narrative's mediation of time, and regarding it in relation to other time codes.

While *Time Code* affirms a homogeneous, technologized temporality as a way of uniting its various temporal strands, *Code Unknown* suggests that such an affirmation is based in an illusory notion of simultaneity. In *Code Unknown*, time is heterogeneous and any attempts to 'decode' it are fraught at best. *Time Code* sets up a challenge to diachronic narrative, but limits the scope of this challenge by restricting the screen to four quadrants and by using spatial and sonic clues to facilitate narrative understanding. Yet the discussion of these two films should not conclude with a simple validation of *Code Unknown*'s critical rigour against *Time Code*'s naïve faith in technology. What is significant about both films is the way that they revisit one of the most significant narrative modes of the twentieth century, the narrative of 'synchronous monadic simultaneity' (Jameson 1992, 116), and test its limits in relation to the contemporary city's complex weave of synchronous and asynchronous networks. They question the assumption of temporal continuity underlying most SMS films, even as they attempt to reaffirm temporal succession. In foregrounding the codes that hold time and space together, *Time Code* and *Code Unknown* articulate a desire to maintain a relationship between simultaneity and succession, and to preserve the notion of the present tense within an increasingly asynchronous urban-global milieu.

7
Coda: Playing Games with Cinema

Collectively, cinematic modular narratives represent encounters between linearity and non-linearity, narrative and database, memory and forgetting, temporal anchoring and temporal drift, simultaneity and succession and chaos and order. The terms in this list are not simple opposites, and the negotiations between them take different forms. All of these films attempt to reconcile different ways of structuring time. In this sense they serve as a collective referendum on the status and value of narrative in the digital era. Each film suggests a limit to narrative's ability to mediate our experience of the world, although each also recuperates narrative in one way or another.[1] Meanwhile, the popular embrace of modular narrative structures suggests, on the one hand, that audiences are now comfortable with complex articulations of time; indeed, they take pleasure in them. On the other, the fraught temporality of these narratives suggests a residual anxiety regarding the effects of temporal mediation, which is traceable across a variety of genres and national cinemas.

How, then, do the thematics of modular time extend beyond these works and into the surrounding mediascape? After all, the syntagmatic modularity of these films is arguably exceeded by a much more literal intertextual modularity that extends across media platforms and genres. Even if we confine ourselves to cinema's immediate network of ancillary texts, the varieties of formal modularity are overwhelming. Firstly, DVD releases allow viewers to browse deleted scenes and alternative endings, so that secondary narrative possibilities open up alongside the 'official' story. As Carol O'Sullivan notes, alternative endings can 'alter the film on a molecular level, activating the "failed stories" lying behind the apparently monolithic film artefact' (2006).[2] Secondly, media producers are increasingly making use of what Henry Jenkins calls 'transmedia storytelling' (2006). Thus, fans of *The Matrix* (1999–2003) can not only watch the three movies, but also play the video game or watch *The Animatrix* (2003), a DVD containing several short films by different directors based in the same narrative world. They can also engage with the world of *The Matrix* through a host of merchandise including toys, music and books. Thirdly, fan culture itself produces a network of related texts including fan videos and fiction, much of which generates supplementary or contradictory narrative paths based upon the original franchise.

Fourthly, interactive media allow for enhanced modular encounters with narrative content. This includes video games that are based upon existing stories (*Scarface*, 2006) and those that draw upon cinematic iconography and generic plotlines (the *Grand Theft Auto* series, 1998–). It can also include experimental interactive works like *Tracing the Decay of Fiction* (2002), in which elements of filmic narrative surface intermittently as users explore virtual spaces. Furthermore, promotional websites for films will sometimes provide puzzles or 'experiences' that supplement or explore the film narrative, or provide alternatives to it. This can even become the basis for entirely web-based 'remix' projects such as *Stray Cinema* (2006), which offers users a collection of video assets with which to create their own films; these are then displayed on the *Stray Cinema* site. Peter Greenaway's *Tulse Luper Journey* (2005) is a web-based work in which users play games in order to unlock brief video sequences, gradually piecing together the story of the main character's life. This project is another example of transmedia storytelling because it is accompanied by a series of feature films and by Greenaway's own 'VJ' performances in which he remixes images and sounds from the films for a live audience.[3]

Fifthly, gallery installations can foster a modular approach to cinema, either by offering different entry-points to the films, or by linking them with ancillary materials. For example, a 2007 exhibition of Rainer Werner Fassbinder's 15-hour opus *Berlin Alexanderplatz* (1980) in New York allowed visitors to view the film in its entirety, or to 'browse' the film via a video installation showing segments from each of the film's episodes on 14 separate screens. In Pierre Huyghe's *The Third Memory* (2000), a large split-screen projection shows extracts from the bank heist drama *Dog Day Afternoon* (Sidney Lumet, 1975), juxtaposed with a present-day staged re-enactment featuring the real bank robber, John Wojtowicz (who was played in the film by Al Pacino). An adjacent room maps out the real events through newspaper clippings and TV shows from the time.

The boundaries of cinematic time

How, then, should we describe the temporality of these works, and what is their relationship to cinematic narrative? First of all, the modular relations within and among these texts produce an almost infinite variety of temporal models. These modular intertexts and hypertexts can establish tightly woven temporal relations, or they can leave such relations open to speculation. They can lend themselves to sense and order, or can foster ambiguity and confusion. By dwelling on a few of them I hope to explore the way that they relate to the form and thematics of modular narratives. One feature of much of the writing about interactive digital media has been a tendency to focus on spatial analysis at the expense of addressing time. Certainly, the temporality of these works is harder to map than that of literary or cinematic narrative. Nonetheless, I suggest that both new media works and the critical discourse around them are deeply concerned with time. The temporal discourse around these works, I argue, is marked by a particular combination of retrospection and prospection.

The first place where this is evident is in the often heated debates about narratives and games. In one corner are those who feel that new media will and should produce new variations on classical narrative (Laurel 1993 and Murray 1998). In the other are those who see many or most new media texts as games rather than narratives (Aarseth 1997, Frasca 1999 and 2003, Eskelinen 2004, Juul 2004,). In this debate, the narrative camp draws upon literary and dramatic forms from the past and projects them into the future, while the 'ludologists' attempt to define a new form, at least partly, by cutting ties with a past one. At stake in these differing accounts of media are important questions regarding the relationship between time and narrative.

One difficulty in addressing 'new media' is that the term does not define a single media form or genre. Within new media there is a diversity of distinct forms, from games to literary hypertext, from online news to net art. Espen Aarseth, however, has suggested a useful way of addressing games and related new media forms collectively as 'ergodic' works. In these works, 'nontrivial effort is required to allow the reader to traverse the text' (Aarseth 1997, 1). An ergodic work 'includes the rules for its own use' and 'automatically distinguishes between successful and unsuccessful users' (179). Significantly, Aarseth defines such work as distinct from narrative. He frames this distinction in terms of the structuring opposition of 'aporia' and 'epiphany'. In narrative, aporias (blockages or points of confusion) and epiphanies (moments of realization) are

framed in relation to the total work. In the 'game of narration' represented by hypertext fiction, this is not the case, because the reader lacks
access to the whole work. To encounter a hypertext aporia is to be lost
in a maze, while the hypertext epiphany 'is a salvaging detail/ link out'
(91). This is a useful opposition, but Aarseth overstates its significance,
failing to recognize the overlap between games and narratives. He
argues, for example, that the hypertext aporia is, in contrast with James
Joyce's use of the device, immanent and pre-planned rather than contingent (92). These arguments do not acknowledge that narratives are
just as pre-planned as games, or that narrative comprehension can also
proceed without access to a total, finished structure.

A more balanced perspective is offered by Henry Jenkins, who argues
that video games (which are included under Aarseth's definition of
ergodic works) can be considered as a type of 'narrative architecture'
(2004, 119). Games offer the space in which different types of narrative
can occur. Their spatial emphasis, argues Jenkins, links them to existing
narratives, from *The Odyssey* to *Lord of the Rings*, that are structured
around journeys (122). According to Jenkins, game environments create
the space for four different modes of narrative:

> spatial stories can evoke pre-existing narrative associations; they can
> provide a staging ground where narrative events are enacted; they
> may embed narrative information within their mise-en-scene; or
> they provide resources for emergent narratives.
>
> (123)

Thus, Jenkins offers a way of understanding games that allows for their
difference from narratives while capturing the way that the two forms
overlap. The current media environment is one in which this overlap
has become increasingly pronounced.[4] Just as computer games have
taken on codes and structural elements from cinema, modular narratives arguably constitute a set of films that operate like games, challenging viewers with temporal and narrative puzzles.

What, then, is the temporality of games or 'ergodic' works, and how
does it intersect with cinematic narrative time? Markku Eskelinen draws
upon Christian Metz's discussion of narrative to distinguish between
narrative time and game time. Eskelinen argues that whereas narratives
present one time scheme through another (the syuzhuet-fabula or plot-
story distinction), games have only one necessary time scheme (2004,
39). Similarly, for Jesper Juul games take place in the present: 'there is a
basic sense of *now* when you play a game' (2004, 135). Nonetheless, Juul

identifies a distinction, in those games that present a fictional world, between 'play time' and 'event time' (131). The relation between these two times is one of 'mapping', and it can vary greatly. It can also be interrupted by other temporal modes (the cinematic temporality of 'cut scenes', for example) or by the caesurae that separate different levels in arcade games. On the whole, action and arcade games tend to display a 1:1 relation between play and event time, while strategy and simulation games offer a variety of temporal ratios. Indeed, in many cases these games offer players the chance to speed up or slow down event time (131). Here, we find another example of the analytic perspective on time that inflects modular narratives.

This control over time is, however, accompanied by certain restrictions. For example, such cinematic devices as flashback and flashforward are uncommon, because they would be in conflict with the player's attempts to direct events within the game (136). Thus, game-worlds demand a degree of contingency, however pre-programmed the overall structure may be. In this sense, then, the temporality of games is prospective or future-directed, and not simply rooted in the present: it invokes a structure of anticipation and fulfilment. Moreover, games may also display a retrospective dimension. As Juul points out, certain games require that the players uncover clues or artefacts revealing information about 'past' events in the game-world. The adventure game *Myst* (1997) is one example of this. Finally, games may be 'fixated' historically (that is, set in a particular time period) (135). In this way, the location of game-time in the present is complicated by criss-crossing operations of anticipation and recollection. As James Newman points out, such operations are shared by games and narratives (2004, 97). They are, however, further complicated in the instance of 'save games', those 'manipulations of game time' that allow players to replay a task or level until it is successfully completed (Juul 2004, 137). Here, parallel temporalities (corresponding to the forking paths of Borges and of *Run Lola Run*) are encountered as a series of draft versions. In this instance, recollection and anticipation are projected into 'play time', as the player draws upon the memory of past attempts in anticipation of future success.

The temporality of games is at once more and less complex than that of cinematic narratives. On the one hand, games allow for variations in the mapping of play time to event time, in the store of textual 'memories' that a player draws upon in playing the game, and in the future possibilities offered by the game (although all of these are of course circumscribed by the game 'architecture'). On the other hand, games are generally less complex than narratives in their syntagmatic articulation of time. This is less the case, however, with other ergodic genres such as literary hypertext, which are more concerned with the representation of time and memory. In many of these works, past events are encountered out of chronological sequence as the reader makes their way through a network of hyperlinks, often organized according to an associative logic. Time is conditional in this context, or 'subjunctive' as Graeme Weinbren argues (1995). Thus, it must be acknowledged that there is not one temporal model for ergodic works. The model varies depending on a number of factors, including the work's main organizational principle (game or narrative) and on its degree of narrative coherence. However, these works do not simply project an 'eternal present'. Rather, they consistently invoke the retrospective and prospective cognition of their players, readers or viewers.

Indeed, prospection and retrospection are structuring operations in the debates regarding games and 'post-cinematic' works. As Peter Lunenfeld points out, much of the discourse around 'interactive cinema' has been so future-directed that the ongoing absence of the idealized aesthetic object has barely slowed down the production of theories around it (2002, 145). At times, such discussions have taken on the rhetoric of the avant-garde without always acknowledging the historical roots of that rhetoric in the early twentieth century. The futurist tendency is particularly evident in volumes such as *Future Cinema* (2003). In the introduction to this work, Jeffrey Shaw argues that 'the hegemony of Hollywood's movie-making modalities is increasingly being challenged by the radical new potentialities of the digital media technologies', which make possible 'a new poetics of narrative' (2003, 19). Although Shaw's vision of an open and innovative narrative culture is undeniably attractive, it depends too heavily on technology as the driving factor in a vector of aesthetic 'progress'. Indeed, as R.L. Rutsky notes, the rhetoric of high technology has repurposed the discourse of avant-gardism, revealing a 'postmodern techne', in which technology is an aesthetic end in itself (101). Some of the more sophisticated analyses of cinema and digital media, by contrast, have combined their perspective on future developments with a more thorough acknowledgement of the contribution and relevance of modernist practice to the present moment. Lev Manovich, for example, sees aesthetic parallels between new media and Dziga Vertov's influential experimental film of 1929, *Man with a Movie Camera* (Manovich 2001b, 239–43). Meanwhile, Marsha Kinder sees a productive connection between contemporary 'database narratives' and the narrative innovations of late modernist filmmakers including Resnais, Marker, Bunuel, Varda and Rivette (2002b). Despite taking quite divergent positions regarding the database-narrative relationship, both Manovich and Kinder are attentive to the relationships among past, present and future media aesthetics.

Games about time

A number of new media works and ancillary texts deal explicitly with temporality, displaying a thematics of time that is very similar to that found in cinematic modular narratives. Here, I will look briefly at three such works: a website, a CD-ROM and a DVD-ROM. The first of these examples is the website (Hi-Res, 2001) for the film *Donnie Darko* (Richard Kelly, 2001). Although there has been a surge in web-based 'experiences' linked to feature film properties in subsequent years, the *Darko* website remains particularly interesting because of the way it reflects upon the narrative and thematics of the film, extending its exploration of conditional temporality. The main character in the film, Donnie, is a suburban teenager plagued by visions of a sinister rabbit-man named Frank, who spouts predictions about the end of the world. After surviving an incident in which a jet engine falls on his house, Donnie proceeds towards Frank's apocalyptic deadline, while his teachers and parents fret about his mental condition. Eventually Donnie's troubled state precipitates an incident in which he burns down the house of a motivational speaker who, it is revealed, is also a paedophile. Finally, Donnie's ongoing fascination with time-travel is parallelled by a 'wormhole' that sends the story back through time. The end of the film reveals that Donnie was actually at home when the engine landed on his house, and was killed as a result.

Although the film's narrative does not display the pronounced modularity of the other films discussed in this book, it does have a submerged forking-path structure, in which the end of the film returns us to an alternative temporality which invalidates everything else that has gone before. By ending in this way, *Donnie Darko* offers a sense of foreclosed possibilities. The main question in the film until that point has been whether Donnie's visions are the sign of mental illness or the window on to another world. With its final gesture, the ending suggests that Donnie is doomed either way: he has been crushed either by the fantastical world of Frank and his apocalyptic pronouncements, or by the mundane world in which nobody believes in these things. The time travel plot and the film's unstable ontology together articulate a conditional temporality.

The film's website extends this conditional temporality into an inter-active context. The site consists of three 'levels'; completing one level grants the user a password to the next one. Like the Hi-Res site for *Requiem for a Dream* (Darren Aronofsky, 2000), this site repurposes nar-rative elements in order to fashion an experience that shifts between poem and puzzle. Both of these sites, notes James C. Beck, demand a puzzle-solving attitude from users, who must try to figure out the rules and objectives of the game (2004, 71). At the same time, however, they 'revel in purposeful misdirection' (72). Hyperlinks are often concealed; when clicked upon, they launch unpredictable combinations of text, images and video that are not organized according to an internal narra-tive logic. What, then, is the relationship between these fragmentary elements and the film's narrative? Beck suggests that the *Donnie Darko* website generates a 'narrative effect' because of its relationship with the existing story (77). For those familiar with the film, the site offers infor-mation that supplements the narrative. It includes excerpts from a book on time travel written by one of the characters, Roberta Sparrow, and news reports detailing the fates of others. There is also a 'spoiler' at the end of level three, which furthers the film's parallel universe conceit by informing us that the fatal engine belongs to a plane that has had no reported technical problems. Despite the puzzle-based dynamic, how-ever, the site arguably adds little to our understanding of the story. For the most part, it presents users with a collection of disarticulated refer-ences and images from the film. Indeed, I would suggest that the site is primarily poetic and evocative rather than directed towards any solu-tion, narrative or otherwise.

The site is also designed, like most other promotional sites, to give minimal information about the film in order to stimulate the interest of potential viewers. From this perspective, the site's narrative fragments cannot be viewed as part of a necessary structure. The modular relation between the film and the website takes quite a different form depending on which experience occurs first. Thus, the retrospection-prospection pair operates in *Donnie Darko* on at least two levels. Firstly, the time-travel narrative of the film, supplemented by material from the website, sets up a conditional temporality in which the apocalyptic moment (the jet engine falling on the house) exists both in the past (Donnie is already dead) and the future (he is heading for oblivion). Secondly, the website is deliberately designed to frame the narrative both prospec-tively and retrospectively, depending on which text is encountered first.[5] These variable textual relations produce different narrative and temporal results: users can encounter the website as a game that mitigates the confused temporal relations in the film, or as a poetic, associative work that projects a schismatic temporality. Like many cinematic modular narratives, this ancillary text fluctuates between order and chaos, between control and the loss of control, between subjectivity and the end of the subject, between floating time and anchored time.

A more oblique relation with cinematic time is evident in Chris Marker's CD-ROM, *Immemory* (1997). This work combines text and images (plus a handful of video and audio clips) in a hyperlinked structure. Much of the material is drawn from Marker's previous films and installations. The work is organized into seven 'zones', under the titles Cinema, Travel, Museum, Memory, Poetry, War and Photography. It also includes an 'X-Plugs' section which recombines images and text in a series of layered collages. Part memoir, part travelogue and part essay, *Immemory* mixes media and discursive modes. Rather than constructing a coherent narrative, Marker explores 'the geography of his own memory' (Lupton 2005, 205). This spatial metaphor points not to the irrelevance of time. Rather, it gestures towards time as both prospection and retrospection: as an open and contingent temporality in which images and ideas recombine, and as a mnemonic temporality in which past events and memories float to the surface of consciousness. In *Immemory*, comments Catherine Lupton, 'photos taken apparently by chance, postcards chosen on the whim of the moment, begin once they mount up to sketch an itinerary, to map the imaginary country which spreads out inside of us' (206). Time and space, contingency and memory are thus complementary forces in *Immemory*.

What, then, is the relationship between new media and cinematic narrative time in this work? First of all, *Immemory* orients itself in relation to existing representational traditions. It contains video clips, photographs, poems, prose and essayistic passages. It also refers directly to literary and cinematic antecedents: the first screen in the 'Memory' zone confronts us with images of Marcel Proust and Alfred Hitchcock. Following the link attached to either images leads to the motif of the madeleine. Here, Marker is interested in a coincidental connection between Proust's novel *In Search of Lost Time* (1913–27) and Hitchcock's film *Vertigo* (1956). In the former, the narrator's drift through memories of the past is triggered by the taste of a madeleine (a small cake) dipped in tea. In the latter, Madeleine is the name of the mysterious woman followed by the protagonist, Scotty. After Madeleine dies, Scotty finds another woman who resembles her and tries to remake her as Madeleine, unaware that it is in fact the same woman and that he has been caught up in an elaborate hoax. Marker's whimsical linking of the two texts suggests a sort of ghostly hypertextual memory, in which *Vertigo* 'remembers' Proust's novel. *Immemory*, in turn, remembers both.

Memory is addressed immediately in the *Vertigo* section: if you don't know the film by heart, warns the first screen, there's no use in proceeding further. As with many other sections in *Immemory*, this one is quite linear on a local level (while the overall shape of the work is determined by numerous bifurcations and loops). Our encounter with *Vertigo* is through a series of still images and textual overlays, which are explicitly concerned with temporality: for Marker, the vertigo referred to in the film's title is a 'vertigo of time'. The second half of the film, in which Scotty attempts to recreate Madeleine, is a 'step through the mirror', which embodies 'the insane, maniacal and terrifying attempt to deny time'. *Immemory* replays this temporal desire by revisiting and describing a number of the film's locations, some of which have been demolished. We also see a shot of the Golden Gate Bridge in 1982, which is replaced by a still of the same location as seen in the film. These reflections and juxtapositions offer a keen sense of time's passing, and of the possible futures that have been snuffed out in the process. For example, Marker's text notes that Hitchcock had planned a final scene for *The Birds* (1963), in which the Golden Gate Bridge was to be covered with beating wings. The description of this unrealized vision forms another layer over the images of the bridge from 1956 and 1982. There is a distinctly literary (and even Proustian) perspective on memory in Marker's assemblage of images and text. Memory is an attempt to preserve what has been lost or unrealized, but it can also manifest as a sickness, as the desire to halt time.

Vertigo may look backwards towards Proust, but it also, claims the text on the final screen in this section, looks forward to video games. These embody the desire to cheat death and start over, the desire for a 'free replay'. After reaching this final screen, the user of *Immemory* is given no choice but to return to the menu and start again. This starting over, however, does not reset time. Rather, it allows us to reflect on the mortal moments contained in any history, the points at which certain possibilities were extinguished in favour of others. Furthermore, *Immemory*'s modular structure sets up a dual temporality. On the one hand, it untethers temporal relations by juxtaposing apparently disconnected images and accounts. On the other, it anchors time by supplying contextual details and dates, and by pursuing an associative logic that is explicitly aligned with Marker's personal actions of recollection.

Cinema's place in this structure of recollection is a privileged one, not least because Marker's life has been devoted to filmmaking. Yet the structural metaphors that animate *Immemory* are varied: it is at once a museum, a novel, a photograph album and a film. We are thus made aware that cinema is only one element among an array of media forms. It is also the subject of some ambivalence. Cinema, reflects Marker, is quite possibly dying. This is not simply an occasion for mourning, however, and may in fact constitute an 'honorable destiny': 'perhaps cinema has given all it can give, perhaps it must leave room for something else'. If death is considered as a return to what one has loved and lost, then the end of cinema will reconstitute it as 'an immense memory'. Rather than trying to halt time (like Scotty in *Vertigo*), we can affirm the persistence of time in the cinema by allowing it to be distributed across the mediasphere.

For Marker, memory and contingency are mutually affirming concepts. Memory is not static but must be constantly reconfigured through encounters between different spaces, moments and events. *Memories of the Future*, the title of Catherine Lupton's book on Marker's works, is thus particularly appropriate to *Immemory*. It captures the way that the work animates previous possible futures while reflecting on the perseverance of our own present into the future, and its status as a memory-to-come. Moreover, *Immemory* was produced in 1997, and its own status as a viable memory is challenged by subsequent technological shifts. The CD-ROM requires Apple Computer's OS 9, an operating system that will not run on newer machines. Thus, viewing the work now involves an archival operation in which 'old' technology is put in the service of 'new' media. *Immemory*, like cinema, faces its mortal moment.

Death and cinema are also intertwined in the interactive DVD-ROM *Tracing the Decay of Fiction: Encounters with a Film by Pat O'Neill* (Pat O'Neill, Rosemary Cornella, Kristy H.A. Kang and the Labyrinth Project, 2002).[6] In this work, the user navigates through the Ambassador Hotel in Los Angeles, represented by stills and film clips from Pat O'Neill's film *The Decay of Fiction*. Using 'hot spots', the user can trigger audio-visual clips that refer both to the history of the hotel and to scraps of cinematic narratives that appear to haunt it. Cinema is invoked in a multitude of ways. Firstly, the Ambassador itself is intimately connected to Hollywood history. For example, it was the location for many industry award ceremonies and gatherings. One part of the work displays a series of images of the hotel's 'Cocoanut Grove', and highlights a number of well-known Hollywood figures in the crowd. Secondly, in *Tracing the Decay of Fiction*, the Ambassador is crisscrossed by a multitude of (often fleeting) scenes that serve as cinematic micronarratives. In many cases, the audio consists of clips 'recycled' from Hollywood classic films, with a particular emphasis on *film noir*. These fragmentary scenes are restaged with different actors, who appear as black-and-white semitransparent ghosts superimposed on O'Neill's present-day footage of the deserted hotel. These ghostlike figures, combined with the use of slightly wide-angle lenses to emphasize spatial depth, recall in turn another cinematic haunted hotel, the Overlook, from Stanley Kubrick's *The Shining* (1980).

Cinema is also invoked by one of the key visual tropes of the work, which destabilizes the relationship between still and moving images. In certain areas of the hotel, an icon appears at the edge of the frame. Mousing over this icon initiates a tracking shot in that direction. Moving the mouse away will freeze the shot, turning the frame back to a still image. The user then has the option to resume the tracking shot as before, or reverse it by mousing over the opposite frame-edge. These tracking shots are thus movements in time as well as space. By allowing us to reverse directions, *Tracing the Decay* suggests a reversible space-time. This mirrors in turn the fluid movement between different moments in history, both the history of the hotel (where Kruschev stayed in 1959 and Robert F. Kennedy was assassinated in 1968) and the history of cinema itself (represented by the recycled audio clips from old films). The tracking shot is also itself a distinctly cinematic movement. By allowing us to freeze and reverse this cinematic movement, however, *Tracing the Decay* turns cinema itself into a ghostly presence.

This malleability of cinematic time is evident in Pat O'Neill's time-lapse sequences showing the outside of the hotel. It is also extended to some of the fragmentary scenes inside the hotel, in which the black-and-white figures flit by in fast-forward. In one area users encounter a 'hot spot' which, when clicked upon, triggers a sped-up silent playthrough of the Joan Crawford film *Sudden Fear* (David Miller, 1952). The film elapses in a matter of seconds, and Crawford's panicked face, briefly glimpsed, almost appears as a reaction to this sudden onslaught of time. As in *Immemory*, the idea that cinema is dead or dying is central to the operation of the text. Here, this idea is given literal weight by the crumbling walls of the hotel's rooms, and the fact that the Ambassador's demolition is imminent (a fate which finally arrived in 2006). The scenes that play out in these rooms, drawn extensively from old *films noirs*, have a palpable air of fatalism. In one scene, a middle-aged man, flanked by two young beauties, insists that his chest pain is 'just heartburn'. In another, a man and woman stroll in the gardens, planning an 'accident' for some unfortunate third party.

The ghostliness of cinematic and narrative time is paralleled by the presence of historical ghosts in the hotel. Most notably, the work dwells upon the assassination of Robert F. Kennedy. We are shown clips of Kennedy speaking at the hotel, the corridor where he was shot, and present-day images of the room in which he spoke, overlaid with voiceover accounts of the assassination from different witnesses. Other historical moments are invoked by the work too. One segment, for example, gives a window on racial politics, through an account of debates surrounding the requirement that black performers enter the hotel by the service door. By exploring these different strands of the hotel's history, *Tracing the Decay of Fiction* reflects on the contingent processes that continually produce the present. It does so not by creating a single coherent narrative but by uncovering the traces of multiple fictional and historical narratives.[7] In its non-linear structure, this work blends fiction and history, treating both as forms of memory. It functions as a museal space, in which the mnemotechnic journey from room to room gives rise to artefacts of the past (images, sounds and sequences).

Like *Immemory*, this work succeeds in communicating what might be described as the otherness of time. It achieves this through techniques of repetition and juxtaposition. The scenes from old films are replayed by ghostly actors, who do not belong to the voices they inhabit. By replaying these scenes differently, *Tracing the Decay of Fiction* introduces an alternative temporality. Similarly, clicking on 'hot spots' at different times can trigger different combinations of sound and image. For example, the account of Kennedy's assassination is delivered by two separate people. Clicking on the appropriate link will bring up the same series of shots of the empty ballroom each time, but will overlay it with one of the two possible voiceover accounts. This structure encourages users to repeat portions of the work in order to explore the different combinatorial possibilities. In this way, *Tracing the Decay* combines its retrospective dimension with a prospective dimension that seeks to produce, as much as possible, new juxtapositions and imaginative projections. Its mnemotechnic strategies are aimed at recovering not just the past but also the presents that failed to materialize.

In this respect, these new media works are very similar to cinematic modular narratives. Indeed, Kinder notes that 'database narratives' in general (a group which would include the modular narratives discussed in this book) produce structures that 'reveal the arbitrariness of the particular choices made and the possibility of making other combinations, which would create alternative stories' (2002b, 127). Although these new media works tend to operate at or beyond the boundaries of narrative, they produce thematic effects that are markedly similar to those found in the modular narrative. By externalizing memory and combining it with history, they suggest the ways that database structure can both anchor the past and set it adrift.[8] By foregrounding alternative possibilities, they invoke questions of contingency and determinism. Finally, by juxtaposing different media forms and different modes of linking, they foreground the mediation of time and the codes that make temporal experience communicable.

The futures of cinematic time

In this chapter, I have argued that despite the distinct structural articulations of films and new media, certain new media works explore the same temporal themes as cinematic modular narratives. I have also suggested that cinematic temporality is itself reworked and re-examined within the modular temporal structures of these works. Returning to the films that have formed the principal subject of this book, it is now worth asking how these works fit in relation to the history and future of temporal mediation. On the one hand, they hark back to much earlier innovations of modernist literature and cinema. On the other, they point forward to future textual forms, of the type hinted at by *Immemory* and *Tracing the Decay of Fiction*. In this sense, cinematic modular narratives occupy a middle ground between traditional narrative and experimentation. Yet rather than privileging one over the other, I suggest that the value of these films lies in their agnosticism, in their implicit questioning of both linear narrative and the non-linear forms that would seek to displace it.

Do these films herald the beginning of an ongoing period of experimentation in mainstream cinema, or simply a passing phase? The answer is not clear at the time of writing. It is quite possible that modular narratives are part of a cyclical movement in cinema, and that the current cycle is reaching its end. After all, when critics write about the experimentation in European cinema in the 1960s and early 1970s, it is easy to forget that they are generally talking about a relatively small group of films. The vast bulk of narrative cinema, then as now, adheres largely to classical norms. At the same time, an undeniable shift is taking place in the broader context of consumption practices and media platforms. For example, video games and films have become more closely aligned than ever before. Meanwhile, digital software and online distribution channels have offered users enhanced opportunities for mixing and matching media. Films are among the texts that are subject to these operations of search, selection and recombination.

The significance of modular narratives in relation to these shifts, I would argue, is that they take an active role in thinking through the relations between time and narrative. They are, to return to Paul Ricoeur's distinction, not simply 'tales in time' but also 'tales about time' (1984–8, 2:101). While new media provide a new set of resources for representing and conceptualizing time, they are not by necessity better equipped than their cinematic counterparts to deal with the thematics of time. Indeed, the interplay between non-linear and linear narrative dynamics is one of the most interesting aspects of cinematic modular narratives. Furthermore, emergent multiplatform and interactive forms do not simply supersede cinematic narrative time, but enter into complex relations with it. It may be that, as the new media works discussed in this chapter imply, the digital mediascape will both precipitate and accommodate a ghostly afterlife for cinematic narrative time.

The tension between schism and modularity in cinematic modular narratives parallels the technological and social changes underpinning the contemporary experience of time and its representability. For example, the phenomenon of accelerated globalization suggests both networks and disjunctures. Global time can produce the sense of a new connectedness, or it can highlight the inequalities, delays and time-shifts that shape temporal experience (Nowotny 1994, 41). Similarly, digital technology allows for an unprecedented level of control over representations of time. This can mean, on the one hand, the production of ever more disjunctive temporal experiences, because time (or rather its representation) can be shuffled, reversed and rearranged at will. On the other hand, digital media can facilitate new articulations of time that are compatible with narrative ends, structuring memory, history and contingency in meaningful ways. Modular narratives, directly or indirectly, intersect with these contemporary articulations of time.

At the least, these films bear witness to a persistent need to be able to give meaning to time, and to articulate relationships among present, past and future. The structure of these films mediates between schism and modularity, representing time at a moment in which social and technological changes have prompted a further examination of the dimensions of temporal experience. As to the duration of this historical moment and the precise shape of future narratives, only time will tell.

Notes

1 Modular Narratives in Contemporary Cinema

1. Evan Smith also notes the success during the late 1990s of films featuring complex narrative structures, in terms of 'impressive reviews, Oscar wins, and dollar-for-dollar returns' (1999, 94).

2. Lev Manovich argues that narrative and database are two distinct and competing cultural forms: 'the database represents the world as a list of items, and it refuses to order this list. In contrast, a narrative creates a cause-and-effect trajectory of seemingly unordered items (events)' (2001b, 225). As I discuss in Chapter 2, Manovich's argument must be qualified by an understanding of narrative's ability to make use of the database for its own ends.

3. Manuel Castells, for example, argues that the dominant temporality of today's 'network society', produced through technologization, globalization and instantaneous communication, is *'timeless time'* (2000, 494): 'Time is erased in the new communication system when past, present, and future can be programmed to interact with each other in the same message' (406).

4. Ricoeur's analysis centres upon Mann's *The Magic Mountain* (1924), Woolf's *Mrs. Dalloway* (1925) and Proust's *In Search of Lost Time* (1913–27).

5. Syuzhet patterning, argues Bordwell, is medium-independent; the same pattern could be reproduced, for example, across literature, theatre and cinema (1985, 49).

6. In his treatment of order, duration and frequency, Bordwell is drawing upon the work of narratologist Gérard Genette. Like Bordwell, Genette distinguishes between the narrative content ('story') and the way this content is organized and expressed ('discourse') (1980, 27). A similar distinction is made by Seymour Chatman (1990, 9) and by Christian Metz, who describes narrative as 'A doubly temporal sequence' that conveys 'the time of the thing told and the time of the telling' (1974, 18). A key function of narrative is thus 'to invent one time scheme in terms of another time scheme' (18).

7. Bordwell, Staiger and Thompson contrast these narrative rules with the ambiguity, unreliable narration and open-endedness of non-classical films of the 1950s and 1960s such as those of Jean-Luc Godard and Alain Resnais. Godard's attitude towards narrative structure is encapsulated in this attributed quotation: 'A story should have a beginning, a middle and an end, but not necessarily in that order'. In these modernist films, 'spatial and temporal systems come forward and share with narrative the role of structuring the film' (Bordwell, Staiger and Thompson 1985, 381). This multitude of organizational systems draws unity into question, and 'a dynamic of unity and fragmentation is set up within the text' (381). Whereas these films progress towards endings that can prove to be inconclusive or even false, classical Hollywood cinema privileges clarity and resolution: 'in the classical narrative, the corridor may be winding, but it is never crooked' (41).

8. Amongst other films that gesture towards modularity, one could include the Chinese film *Hero* (Zhang Yimou, 2003), Thailand's *Tropical Malady* (Apichatpong Weerasethakul, 2004) and Iran's *10* (Abbas Kiarostami, 2002).

9. David Bordwell addresses the broad sweep of complex narrative forms in *The Way Hollywood Tells it* (2006), but does not provide a focussed typology of films that play with temporal structure. Charles Ramirez-Berg (2006) has assayed a more comprehensive taxonomy, but it is more a loose catalogue of tropes than a tool for illuminating formal dynamics.

10. The distinction between modernism and postmodernism is notoriously contentious; I will address this distinction at length in Chapter 2. At this point, it will suffice to point out that many theorists see modernism as more concerned with time, while postmodernism is assumed to have a spatial focus (see, for example, Jameson 1991, Cubitt 2004 and Manovich 2001b).

2   The Shape of Narrative Time: Subjective, Schismatic and Modular

1. Mittel draws the notion of the 'operational aesthetic' from Neil Harris's description of P.T. Barnum's mechanical tricks and stunts (Harris, 1981).

2. The philosopher Henri Bergson went so far as to suggest that public time was not a true temporality; rather, it gave rise to a distorted perspective on the experience of duration and represented it 'spatially, as on a clock' (Kern 1983, 26). Bergson was opposed to Einstein's relativized space-time, insisting that time consisted of a unified duration (see in particular Bergson's *Creative Evolution* [1912]).

3. In Woolf's novel *Mrs. Dalloway* (1925), argues Paul Ricoeur, the experience of time belongs not to individual characters, but is constituted by the network that exists among them. This collective, unified time 'confronts, in a complex and unstable relationship, monumental time, itself resulting from all the complicities between clock time and the figures of authority' (1984–8, 2: 112).

4. It is notable that certain parts of *Ulysses* were influenced directly by cinema: in the 'Wandering Rocks' segment, Joyce deliberately used montage techniques to show a variety of perspectives on the same events (Kern 1983, 77).

5. As Brian Henderson notes, this structure is to be found in such prominent examples as *Citizen Kane, Double Indemnity* (Billy Wilder, 1944), *Sunset Boulevard* (Billy Wilder, 1950) and *All About Eve* (Joseph L. Mankiewicz, 1950) (Henderson 1983, 6).

6. As Anne Friedberg points out, different art forms have been associated with the term 'postmodernism' at different times: it has been used 'in literature since the early 1960s, since the middle 1970s in architecture, since the late 1970s in dance and performance, and applied to film and television only in the 1980s' (1993, 157). In the face of this theoretical impasse, I propose to call the literary and cinematic experiments of the 1960s 'late modernist'. There are two significant features that distinguish these works from the broader tendencies within the postmodern: they retain an intense focus upon innovation, striving to create new modes of representation, and they are at odds with the populist orientation of mainstream postmodernism.

7. The notion of a breakdown in narrative order is also central to Jean-Francois Lyotard's definition of the postmodern in terms of its 'incredulity towards metanarratives' (Lyotard 1984, xxiv).

8. Heise designates these novelists as 'postmodernist'. However, for reasons noted above, I propose to call the literary and cinematic experiments of the 1960s 'late modernist'.

9. According to Alain Robbe-Grillet, time 'played the lead' in the nineteenth century realist novel, typified by the work of Balzac, while 'in the modern narrative, one might say that time was cut off from its temporality. It doesn't flow any more. It isn't the agent for anything any more' (1965b, 151).

10. Another key film in terms of thinking about modular narrative structures is Luis Bunuel's *The Phantom of Liberty* (1974), which consists of a series of tangentially linked, surreal scenes.

11. For an overview of complex television narratives, see Mittel 2006; for a detailed account of the 'neo-baroque' narrative formations of television series and serials, see Ndalianis 2005.

12. For more on science fiction's relation to postmodern 'schizophrenia', see Sobchack 1997, 282; Telotte 1995, 133; and Telotte 2001, 56–58.

13. Brooks Landon connects science fiction and non-linear narrative structure directly, by pointing to the possibilities for non-linear narrative forms afforded by digital hypermedia (1999, 43).

14. Anxiety around the representation of time effectively spans the modern and postmodern, stretching from Bergson (1912) to Jameson (1991) and to the more recent work of Sean Cubitt (2004) and Andreas Huyssen (1995, 2003).

15. Digital culture in its present form can be traced to a number of key factors, including the rise of global capitalism, the development of military technologies during World War II and the Cold War years, the emergence of certain techno-scientific discourses and post-war avant-garde artistic movements (Gere 2002, 75).

16. Nye argues that the 'computerization of society' has been contemporaneous with cultural postmodernism in the same way that electrification accompanied the emergence of aesthetic modernism (1997, 162).

17. The approach promoted by Landow and his colleagues is also well articulated in the collection *Hyper/Text/Theory* (Landow, 1994).

18. The notion of *lexias* is itself borrowed from Barthes's book *S/Z* (1974). Barthes suggests a mode of reading and analysis that interrupts 'the flowing discourse of narration' and 'the "naturalness" of ordinary language' by segmenting it arbitrarily 'into a series of brief, contiguous fragments, which we shall call *lexias*, since they are units of reading' (13).

19. Here, Manovich echoes Walter Benjamin's earlier warning that an information culture (characterized by the rapid dissemination of news) is displacing storytelling (Benjamin 1968a, 89).

20. Manovich argues that formal modularity is not only integral to computer-based media; it is also a feature of contemporary society, in which 'everything from objects to people's identities is assembled from ready-made parts' (126).

21. For a brief account of the aesthetic promise of database narrative, addressing the contributions of both Kinder and Manovich, see Anderson 2004.

3 Projecting the Future: Order, Chaos and Modularity

1. This contradiction perhaps explains the divergent responses to early cinema among modernist thinkers. Henri Bergson, for one, saw it as yet another example of the division and spatialization of time (Kern 1983, 101). James Joyce, however, was 'deeply impressed with cinematic montage' (76), and even deliberately introduced filmic montage techniques into *Ulysses* (6).
2. Literary theorist N. Katherine Hayles counters Prigogine and Stengers' brand of chaos theory, which shows how order *emerges* from complex systems, with another theory, more favoured within scientific circles, which 'emphasizes the hidden order that exists *within* chaotic systems' (1990, 9). According to Hayles, cultural postmodernism functions according to a similar dynamic. Echoing Fredric Jameson, Hayles states: 'Time still exists in cultural postmodernism, but it no longer functions as a continuum along which human action can meaningfully be plotted' (279). Although Hayles's account is comprehensive and persuasive, she overemphasizes the fragmentation of time, without acknowledging the way that space can be fragmented or deprived of meaning via travel, commodification and global communication networks.
3. For example, Alain Robbe-Grillet, writing in the late 1970s, invokes a persistent sense of ambivalence when he suggests that societies, cultures and readers of novels all oscillate between a desire for the freedom associated with chaos and the security associated with order (1977, 2–3).
4. In a manner reminiscent of Katherine Hayles, Cubitt's analysis of cinematic modular narratives suggests the notion of order masquerading as chaos.
5. Drawing upon Lev Manovich's work on new media aesthetics, Cubitt situates modular narratives in relation to the contemporary cultural influence of database structures, suggesting that the database form is not only an aspect of new media but is also 'intrinsic to Hollywood market research, scriptwriting, and editing' (237).
6. *Irreversible* is not the first film to equate anality and temporal disorder: *Pulp Fiction* features an anal rape as a central moment in its reshuffled narrative, as well as a scene in which the young Butch is told about the anal concealment of his father's watch during the Vietnam War (a twisted tale that makes even more literal the temporal analogy). Similarly, Alain Resnais's *Providence* (1977) features a novelist whose chaotic narrative imagination is accompanied by recurrent rectal pains. In each case, the temporal disorder of the narrative is also figured as a violation or affliction of the human body.
7. On a similar note, Doane comments that the modern era's increasingly secular orientation effectively undermined religion's traditional ability 'to confer a meaning upon death, to domesticate it by bringing it back within the realm of the knowable' (2002, 254, n. 10).
8. Heise refers to the novels in question as 'postmodernist'. For reasons outlined in Chapter 2, I prefer the term 'late modernist'.
9. Brian McHale, commenting on postmodernist fiction, and David Harvey, on postmodern culture in general, have both argued that such ontological concerns are a defining feature of postmodern narratives. For McHale, key postmodernist questions include 'Which world is this? What is to be done in it? Which of my selves is to do it?' (1987, 10; see also Harvey 1990, 48).

10. The spiral patterns in *Run Lola Run* are also reminiscent of the spiralling camera work in *Irreversible*. In both films, spirals function as emblems of a temporality that has ceased to run in linear fashion.
11. To extend Branigan's argument, it can be argued that narrative displays a more complicated and subtle temporality than is often assumed, because of the way it addresses memory. Frank Kermode identifies three kinds of memory: mere physiological persistence; recollections that can be accessed via introspection; and anticipatory memory or expectation. This third kind of memory is manipulated by any fiction, as our expectations are fulfilled or subverted, in the form of the *peripeteia*. (Kermode 1967, 54). In this way, demonstrates Kermode, the reception of narrative has a non-linear dimension, in which readers or viewers connect or contrast disparate moments. It might be suggested that this aspect of narrative also challenges determinism by allowing audiences to imagine events having followed a different course.

4 Navigating Memory: Temporal Anchoring and the Modular Subject

1. See, for example, *Abre los ojos* (*Open Your Eyes*, Alejandro Amenábar, 1997), later remade as *Vanilla Sky* (Cameron Crowe, 2001), *The Butterfly Effect* (Eric Bress and J. Mackye Gruber, 2004) and *The Jacket* (John Maybury, 2005).
2. For Sigmund Freud, a variation on the wax tablet, the 'Mystic Writing Pad', served as an appropriate metaphor for memory. (Freud 1961, 228). The wax slab, which held traces even after they have been erased from the sheet above, mimicked the role of human memory and the unconscious (231). Jacques Derrida, however, suggests that even this metaphor is imbricated with forgetting, because the process of writing is not continuous – the pen must be lifted from the sheet, and therefore some things are not recorded at all: 'Writing is unthinkable without repression' (1978, 226).
3. Norman Klein points out that mnemonic aids have in many cases been suspected of undermining our ability to remember. According to Plato's account, Socrates had thought that writing itself would erode the human capacity for memory, because of our reliance on an external substitute for what should be performed within the mind (14).
4. The notion of memory loss as desirable or necessary also extends to the later modernism of Argentinian writer Jorge Luis Borges. In the short story 'Funes the Memorious', Borges shows us a young paralyzed man who remembers every detail of his life, from 'the forms of the southern clouds at dawn on 30 April 1882', to 'the many faces of a dead man throughout a long wake'. However, incapable of forgetting differences and making generalizations, Funes is therefore unable to think, and dies finally and perhaps appropriately of congestion of the lungs.
5. Here, Jameson uses Lacan's definition of schizophrenia as 'a breakdown in the signifying chain', in which signifiers are unmoored from their customary order, reducing the signified to 'a meaning-effect' or 'mirage of signification' (1991, 26). Lacking the temporal unification which is a function of language itself, the schizophrenic's experience of 'pure material signifiers' is therefore also the experience of 'a series of pure and unrelated presents in time' (27).

6. This sense of nostalgia is carried through to the production techniques of the film itself. On the DVD commentary, director Michel Gondry is at pains to point out the number of visual effects achieved via old-fashioned techniques such as forced perspective, lighting and in-camera effects (although the film displays a number of sequences that conspicuously make use of digital effects).

7. Interviews with Gondry and Kaufman indicate the indirect nature of Resnais's influence on the film. Asked by an interviewer from *Ecranlarge.com* about his influences, Gondry responded: 'Elles vont de Chaplin à Jean Vigo en passant par Alain Resnais ou David Lynch tout en essayant de garder mon identité et en évitant de recopier des images qui existent déjà' ('They extend from Chaplin to Jean Vigo by way of Alain Resnais or David Lynch while trying to preserve my identity and avoiding copying images that exist already'). Asked by an interviewer from *Reverseshot.com* whether Resnais or any other filmmaker was an influence on the writing of the screenplay, screenwriter Charlie Kaufman responded: 'No. I don't know about Michel's influences, but we talked about the visuals a lot'.

8. This collapse of work and leisure time is also a feature of *Groundhog Day*. Upon discovering that he is trapped in an endless repetition of the same day, Phil initially loses interest in his work and loafs around. However, Phil becomes increasingly concerned with spending his time productively. These efforts ultimately make him worthy of a relationship with Rita, who is not only the object of his desire but is also his work colleague.

9. In Marcel Proust's *In Search of Lost Time*, the narrator awakes adrift in time, unable to remember which bedroom he is in. It is an experience that is both disorienting and pleasurable. Similarly, in *Eternal Sunshine* rooms are combined, so that doorways change place and far apart spaces become contiguous.

10. In *Groundhog Day*, by contrast, Phil's mnemotechnic system works all too well. Phil attempts suicide as a way of overcoming repetition, hoping to liberate himself from reified memory. Death and forgetting are associated, not with play and disorder as in *Eternal Sunshine*, but with the attempt to assert narrative order.

11. This confusion between places and images is enhanced by the film's digital visual effects. For example, as Joel and Clementine race through a railway station, the other people are wiped out by sudden erasures that appear to transform them into two-dimensional images.

12. *Groundhog Day* also attaches its romantic plot to a sense of seasonal progression. Phil's inability to move beyond February 2 leaves him in a perpetual winter, which will only begin to pass once he has resolved his relationship with Rita.

13. The definition of *film noir* is contentious. Here, I am simply using the term to describe a cycle of films that emerged between 1941 and 1958, which were characterized by their focus on crime stories, usually in urban settings, and a 'dark' aesthetic featuring high-contrast visuals and relatively complex narrative structures. In relation to these films, *Memento* can be classified as 'neo-*noir*'.

14. Arguably, such 'philosophical noir' is related to other modernist and postmodernist reworkings of the detective tradition in which epistemological or ontological certainty is undermined. See, for example, the works of Alain Robbe-Grillet, Jorge Luis Borges, Umberto Eco and Paul Auster.

15. For further Jamesonian analyses of memory and identity in science fiction cinema, see Bukatman 1993 and Landon 1992b. See also Charles Tryon's analysis of *Dark City* (Alex Proyas, 1998), a film which 'both evokes and disavows ... anxieties regarding digital technologies' malleable and thus potentially misrepresentative capabilities' (2003, 58).
16. It might also be suggested that forgetting plays a different role in each film: in *Eternal Sunshine* it is associated with play, while in *Memento* the emphasis is upon work. Leonard goes about his quest like a detective doing his job, and forgetting helps him to complete that job.
17. In contrast, Christopher Williams (2003) argues that *Memento* confuses the epistemological and the ontological. However, I would argue that *Memento* displays the *relationship* between epistemology and ontology, and allows for a critical perspective on it.
18. In this respect, *Memento* is the opposite of *Groundhog Day*, in which Phil's decision to behave ethically leads to narrative resolution. In *Memento*, however, Leonard appears able to achieve his narrative goals only by abandoning ethics. While *Memento* opens up a breach between Leonard's forgetting and the audience's memory, *Groundhog Day* offers us a main character with whom the audience becomes progressively more identified. In this sense, *Groundhog Day* lets its audience off lightly, declining to question the contingencies of personal identity in the manner of *Eternal Sunshine* and *Memento*. Repetition and modularity in *Groundhog Day* in no way undermine the integrity of Phil's subjective consciousness.
19. A number of writers have attempted to describe contemporary cinema in relation to Deleuze's theory. See, for example, Clarke 2002, Bianco 2004, Pisters 2003, Martin-Jones 2006. Both Clarke and Bianco discuss *Memento* directly, but overemphasize the ontological dimension of the film at the expense of the epistemological.
20. Deleuze's discussion of *Je t'aime, je t'aime* acknowledges mediation to some degree. However, the film's experiment leads its protagonist into a memory-world that is beyond the grasp of mediation, evading any attempt at control by either Ridder or the scientists.

5 Articulating History: Archival Aesthetics and the National Narrative

1. The packaging from the Australian release of the *Russian Ark* DVD opines: 'A groundbreaking feat of filmmaking, Alexander Sokurov's amazing journey through 300 years of Russian art and history is the first ever feature to be shot in a single, unedited take' (Madman Entertainment, 2004).
2. Here, Burgoyne draws upon Hayden White's argument that 'modernist techniques of representation' foster a critical perspective on history, because they 'provide the possibility of de-fetishizing both events and the fantasy accounts of them which deny the threat they pose, in the very process of pretending to represent them realistically' (White 1996, 32). I would qualify this argument by pointing to *Russian Ark*, which demonstrates that 'modernist' narrative techniques may be compatible with the nostalgic fetishization of the past.

3. This weakening of historicity is, according to Jameson, produced by 'a new depthlessness, which finds its prolongation both in contemporary 'theory' and in a whole new culture of the image or the simulacrum ... ' (1991, 6). The 'eclipse of historicity' is accompanied by a voracious historicism, 'in the bad sense of an omnipresent and indiscriminate appetite for dead styles and fashions; indeed, for the styles and fashions of a dead past' (286).

4. This is still a major issue in Turkey, where prominent author Orhan Pamuk was prosecuted by the government in 2005 for publicly acknowledging the 1915 genocide, and thereby engaging in the 'public denigration' of Turkish identity. See 'Turk "genocide" author faces jail'. *BBC News Online*, September 1, 2005. http://news.bbc.co.uk/2/hi/europe/4205708.stm. The charges against Pamuk were later dropped, possibly as a result of Turkey's bid to avoid international censure as it attempted to join the European Union (Eakin, 2006).

5. For variations on this argument, see Robert Rosenstone's suggestion that 'a push beyond the confines of realistic representation ... serves to probe the limits of rationalistic discourse – the heart of the historical enterprise since the eighteenth century' (1995, 11) and Pam Cook's recuperation of the critical dimension of nostalgia (2004). Cook suggests that an aesthetic of nostalgia can articulate 'a desire to question linear progression, and the way we think of social progress and history' (2004, 16).

6. Hodgkin and Radstone also comment that cinema's 'flashbacks, fadeouts and affective immediacy may offer a more appropriate medium or model for memory work than more traditional media' (2003, 14). 'What makes a film a memory text ... may not be so much a matter of its explicit content as of its form: it may enact mnemonic processes as well as, or instead of, being about memories' (14).

7. Comments Ravetto-Biagioli, 'By allowing the European stranger to assume a superior position, the Russian speaker subtly undermines it, showing that Europe's identity is also an imaginary construction that is contingent on its others, and ironically, it is the Hermitage that houses and preserves the various dreams, memories, and histories of Europe' (2005, 22).

8. William Johnson comments that while 'some viewers may feel that Sokurov takes too uncritical or nostalgic [a] view of the tsarist era ... the tsars and their guests are hardly placed on pedestals' (2004, 48). While I agree with this statement, it does not do full justice to the sense of historical longing the film attaches to the cultural and material wealth of the tsars.

9. Kriss Ravetto-Biagioli describes the film's critical perspective thus: 'As *Russian Ark* participates in mass amnesia – treating the Bolshevik Revolution as both a rupture with and an interruption of Russian history – it draws attention to the problems caused by such erasures and desperate attempts to scour the national archives (or treasures) in order to salvage or reinvent some form of legitimacy' (2005, 21). Benedict Anderson has also commented upon the way that the writing of a nation's biography is 'marked by deaths' which are inscribed with meaning retrospectively (1991, 205). 'To serve the narrative purpose, these violent deaths must be remembered/forgotten as "our own"' (206).

10. Comments made by Sokurov prior to the production of the film describe the virtual collapse of the past: 'History in our films is only a more or less elaborated background, sometimes detailed, sometimes as one finds it in Leonardo's works: an abstract perspective, a line of mountains in the mist,

an opening sky, a shore, an ocean or river. There is no past or future in history, just as there is no past or future in art, only the present' (2001, 127).

6 Deciphering the Present: Simultaneity, Succession and Mediation

1. For the discussion of an earlier example, see Stephen Mamber's analysis of *The Killing* (Stanley Kubrick, 1955). Mamber offers a formalist account of the use of complex flashback structures in the film, which create repetition and temporal overlap in order to represent simultaneous events (1998).
2. Here, cross-cutting effectively translates the narrative's parallel worlds into a form compatible with the serial logic of traditional narrative. Noting that Borges's story 'The Garden of Forking Paths' 'writes of time as a fabric of simultaneous possibility', Kay Young remarks that most forking-path narratives nevertheless account for the limits of our cognitive abilities by focussing our attention upon one thread at a time (2002, 117–8). *Time Code*, notes Young, is a partial exception to this rule, although the film limits cognitive overload by restricting itself to four simultaneous threads (117).
3. This treatment of simultaneity is analogous, argues Anderson, to Walter Benjamin's pejorative notion of 'homogeneous, empty, time' (Anderson 1991, 24). For Benjamin, this uniform national time is associated with a linear model of history that privileges progress and universalizing narratives at the expense of genuine historical analysis (Benjamin 1968b, 263–5).
4. Here, Heise is referring to later Robbe-Grillet novels such as *La maison de rendez-vous* (*The House of Assignation*, 1965), *Projet pour une révolution à New York* (*Project for a Revolution in New York*, 1970) and *Souvenirs du triangle d'or* (*Recollections of the Golden Triangle*, 1978). For Heise, the abandonment of causality and psychology in these later works marks them out as 'postmodernist' (115). For reasons outlined in Chapter 2, I prefer to retain the term 'late modernist' to describe these novels.
5. The notion of the monad is associated with the eighteenth-century philosopher Leibniz. For Leibniz, 'The Monad ... is nothing but a *simple* substance, which enters into compounds' (1973, 217). Individual subjects are such monads. Collectively, they form a 'totality ... of all spirits', which 'must compose the City of God', a total state of existence that is perfect because it is universal (267). In a passage reminiscent of the themes of the modern novel, Leibniz uses an urban metaphor to explain this situation: 'And as the same town, looked at from various sides, appears quite different and becomes as it were numerous in aspects ... ; even so, as a result of the infinite number of simple substances, it is as if there were so many different universes, which, nevertheless are nothing but aspects ... of a single universe, according to the special point of view of each Monad' (248).
6. Although some narrative films, such as *The Thomas Crown Affair* (Norman Jewison, 1968) and *Napoléon*, have incorporated split- or multiple-screen flashbacks, most have tended to use these techniques in order to represent *simultaneously* occurring events. This may be because the most crucial implications of dividing the screen are, as Julie Talen suggests, temporal: 'cutting up the screen unmoors the images in time' (2005, 3). Experimental filmmakers,

notes Talen, have made much more extensive use of the temporal possibilities of the mosaic aesthetic: 'Nam June Paik, Bill Viola, Gary Hill and other video artists have long used multiple monitors to fracture time and images' (2005, 2).

7. In the digital age, Levin argues, a number of films draw upon the aesthetics of surveillance, replacing the 'spatial indexicality' of classical cinema with a 'temporal indexicality, an image whose truth is supposedly 'guaranteed' by the fact that it is happening in so-called 'real time and thus – by virtue of its technical conditions of production – is supposedly not susceptible to post-production manipulation' (2002, 592).

8. Similarly, political economist Saskia Sassen points out that globalized and technologized economic activities, occurring at differing rates, 'can engender differing temporalities' (2001, 267).

9. For example, Nicholas Rombes makes extensive reference to Bazin in discussing the return to long-take aesthetics and realist principles in contemporary digital video projects such as the 'Dogme 95' films, as well as *Time Code* and *Russian Ark* (2005, 5). Similarly, Lev Manovich, while sceptical about the value of 'DV realism', connects films such as *Time Code* to cinema verité's embrace of immediacy and realism (2001a, 8). For Jean-Pierre Geuens, *Time Code*'s merging of digital technology with the long take produces a type of reality-effect absent from much contemporary cinema, because it embraces contingency (Geuens 2002, 24).

10. James Tobias also notes that the *Time Code* DVD uses the motif of the graphical score in its menu design, creating a 'narrativized interface' for the film (2004, 35).

7   Coda: Playing Games with Cinema

1. Although most modular narratives ultimately affirm narrative, there is at least a certain agnosticism regarding its reach and value. Thus, these films echo Peter Brooks's comment regarding the contemporary ambivalence towards narrative: 'If we cannot do without plots, we nonetheless feel uneasy about them, and feel obliged to show up their arbitrariness, to parody their mechanisms while admitting our dependence on them' (1984, 7).

2. In 'The Choice Of An Ending: DVD And The Future(s) Of Post-Apocalyptic Narrative' (2006), O'Sullivan offers an excellent analysis of how the alternative ending has functioned as a narrative device in DVD releases of feature films (particularly post-apocalyptic science fiction). Writing about *28 Days Later* (Danny Boyle, 2002), she suggests that the multiple endings available on the DVD release 'invite users to share in the filmmakers' overlapping visions of potential, and sometimes contradictory, futures, thus expressing doubts central to the genre itself'.

3. For a discussion of these and other cross-platform works, see Dena 2007.

4. Jenkins's approach also has the benefit of describing present media realities rather than speculating on the future ascendance of an idealized victorious form (whether game or narrative). For Peter Lunenfeld, the contemporary mediascape reflects neither the end of narrative nor the consolidation of its classical form. Instead, the omnipresence of narrative across all media forms now means that it is enough to refer to it in passing in order to call up its codes

and meanings (2002, 151). Thus, cinematic and literary narratives increasingly inhabit a series of distributed afterlives across other media, including the video games that Jenkins describes.

5. The website for *Hard Candy* (David Slade, 2005) pursues a similar approach successfully. In this site, users are invited to explore spaces from the film, uncovering narrative clues that offer enough information to enlighten those who have seen the film, but are sufficiently cryptic to attract new viewers without giving away too much.

6. For a description of the Labyrinth Project's approach to database narrative, see Kinder 1999 and 2003.

7. Marsha Kinder, who was extensively involved with this project, would describe it as a narrative. Against Lev Manovich's rigid opposition between database and narrative, she proposes that they are 'two compatible structures that always function together' (2002b, 126). Although it is true that database and narrative are not always in competition, I do not agree with Kinder that the relationship is necessarily complementary. Part of the problem here is that Kinder's definition of narrative as 'a discursive mode of patterning and interpreting the meaning of perceptions' (121) is simply too broad.

8. For a discussion of the implications of presenting history through non-linear and interactive new media works, see Paul Arthur's 'Multimedia and the Narrative Frame: Navigating Digital Histories' (2006). Arthur notes that the combination of narrative with the informational architecture of new media can produce a situation in which the narrative 'voice' is drowned out by the sheer volume of available information. Works with narrative intentions may thus be misperceived, in some cases, as '"purely" informational'.

Bibliography

Aarseth, Espen. 1997. *Cybertext: Perspectives on Ergodic Literature*. Baltimore: Johns Hopkins University Press.

———. 1999. 'Aporia and Epiphany in *Doom* and *The Speaking Clock*: The Temporality of Ergodic Art'. In *Cyberspace Textuality: Computer Technology and Literary Theory*, ed. Marie-Laure Ryan, 31–41. Bloomington and Indianapolis: Indiana University Press.

Alpers, Svetlana. 1991. 'The Museum as a Way of Seeing'. In *Exhibiting Cultures: The Poetics and Politics of Museum Display*, ed. Ivan Karp and Steven D. Lavine, 25–32. Washington, DC: Smithsonian Institution Press.

Anderson, Benedict. 1991. *Imagined Communities: Reflections on the Origins and Spread of Nationalism*. 2nd ed. London: Verso.

Anderson, Steve. 2004. 'Select and Combine: The Rise of Database Narratives'. *Res Magazine* (January/February): 52–3.

Andrew, Dudley. 1984. *Concepts in Film Theory*. Oxford: Oxford University Press.

———. 2000. 'Tracing Ricoeur'. *diacritics*, 30 (2): 43–69.

Appadurai, Arjun. 1996. *Modernity at Large: Cultural Dimensions of Globalization*. Minneapolis: University of Minnesota Press.

Aristotle. 1982. *Poetics*. Trans. James Hutton. New York: W.W. Norton & Company.

Arthur, Paul. 2006. 'Multimedia and the Narrative Frame: Navigating Digital Histories'. *Refractory: A Journal of Entertainment Media* no. 9. http://www.refractory.unimelb.edu.au/.

Augé, Marc. 1995. *Non-places: Introduction to an Anthropology of Supermodernity*. Trans. John Howe. London: Verso.

Bakhtin, M.M. 1981. 'Forms of Time and of the Chronotope in the Novel'. In *The Dialogic Imagination: Four Essays*, 84–258. Trans. Caryl Emerson and Michael Holquist. Ed. Michael Holquist. Austin: University of Texas Press.

Barthes, Roland. 1974. *S/Z*. Trans. Richard Miller. New York: Hill and Wang.

———. 1977. 'Introduction to the Structural Analysis of Narratives'. In *Image Music Text*, 79–124. Trans. Stephen Heath. London: Fontana.

———. 1981. *Camera Lucida*. Trans. Richard Howard. New York: Hill and Wang.

Baudrillard, Jean. 1983. *Simulations*. Trans. Paul Foss, Paul Patton and Philip Beitchman. New York: Semiotext(e).

Bauman, Zygmunt. 2000. *Liquid Modernity*. Cambridge: Polity Press.

Bazin, André. 1967. *What Is Cinema?* Trans. Hugh Gray. Berkeley: University of California Press.

———. 1971. *What Is Cinema?* Vol. II. Trans. Hugh Gray. Berkeley: University of California Press.

Beck, James C. 2004. 'The Concept of Narrative: An Analysis of *Requiem for a Dream*(.com) and *Donnie Darko*(.com)'. *Convergence: The International Journal of Research into New Media Technologies*, 10 (3): 55–82.

Benjamin, Walter. 1968a. 'The Storyteller: Reflections on the Works of Nikolai Leskov'. In *Illuminations*, 83–109. Ed. Hannah Arendt. Trans. Harry Zohn. New York: Harcourt, Brace, and World.

——. 1968b. 'Theses on the Philosophy of History'. In *Illuminations*, 255–66. Ed. Hannah Arendt. Trans. Harry Zohn. New York: Harcourt, Brace and World.

——. 1968c. 'The Work of Art in the Age of Mechanical Reproduction'. In *Illuminations*, 217–51. Ed. Hannah Arendt. Trans. Harry Zohn. New York: Harcourt, Brace and World.

Bergson, Henri. 1912. *Creative Evokution*. Trans. Arthur Mitchell. London: Macmillan.

——. 1988. *Matter and Memory*. Trans. Nancy Margaret Paul and W. Scott Palmer. New York: Zone Books.

Bianco, Jamie Skye. 2004. 'Techno-Cinema'. *Comparative Literature Studies*, 41 (3): 377–403.

Bizzochi, Jim. 2005. '*Run Lola Run* – Film as Database Narrative'. Paper presented at the Fourth Media in Transition Conference, May 6–8, MIT, Cambridge, MA.

Bolter, Jay David. 1991. *Writing Space: the Computer, Hypertext, and the History of Writing*. Hillsdale, N.J.: L. Erlbaum Associates.

Bolter, Jay David, and Richard Grusin. 1999. *Remediation: Understanding New Media*. Cambridge, MA: MIT Press.

Bordwell, David. 1985. *Narration and the Fiction Film*. London: Routledge.

——. 2002. 'Film Futures'. *SubStance*, 31 (1): 88–104.

——. 2005. Paper on alternative narrative forms in Hollywood cinema, presented at LaTrobe University, Melbourne, Australia, March 11.

——. 2006. *The Way Hollywood Tells It: Story and Style in Modern Movies*. Berkeley: University of California Press.

Bordwell, David, Janet Staiger and Kristin Thompson. 1985. *Classical Hollywood Cinema: Film Style and Mode of Production to 1960*. London: Routledge.

Borges, Jorge Luis. 1970a. 'The Garden of Forking Paths'. Trans. Donald A. Yates. In *Labyrinths: Selected Stories and Other Writings*, 44–54. Ed. Donald A. Yates and James E. Irby. London: Penguin.

——. 1970b. 'Funes the Memorious'. Trans. James E. Irby. In *Labyrinths: Selected Stories and Other Writings*, 87–95. Ed. Donald A. Yates and James E. Irby. London: Penguin.

——. 1970c. 'A New Refutation of Time'. Trans. James E. Irby. In *Labyrinths: Selected Stories and Other Writings*, 252–70. Ed. Donald A. Yates and James E. Irby. London: Penguin.

Branigan, Edward. 2002. 'Nearly True: Forking Plots, Forking Interpretations'. *SubStance*, 31 (1): 105–14.

Brooks, Peter. 1984. *Reading for the Plot: Design and Intention in Narrative*. Oxford: Clarendon Press.

Brottman, Mikita and David Sterritt. 2004. Review of *Irréversible*, dir. Gaspar Noé. *Film Quarterly*, 57 (2): 37–42.

Bruno, Giuliana. 1987. 'Ramble City: Postmodernism and *Blade Runner*'. *October*, 41:61–74. Reprinted in *Alien Zone: Cultural Theory and Science Fiction Cinema*, ed. Annette Kuhn, 183–95. London: Verso, 1990.

Buckland, Warren. 1998. 'A Close Encounter with *Raiders of the Lost Ark*: Notes on Narrative Aspects of the New Hollywood Blockbuster'. In *Contemporary Hollywood Cinema*, eds Steve Neale and Murray Smith, 166–77. London: Routledge.

Bukatman, Scott. 1993. *Terminal Identity: The Virtual Subject in Postmodern Science Fiction*. Durham: Duke University Press.

Burgoyne, Robert. 1996. 'Modernism and the Narrative of Nation in *JFK*'. In *The Persistence of History: Cinema, Television, and the Modern Event*, ed. Vivian Sobchack, 113–25. New York: Routledge.

Calvino, Italo. 1979. *The Castle of Crossed Destinies*. Trans. William Weaver. New York: Harcourt Brace Jovanovich.

——. 1992. *If on a Winter's Night a Traveller*. Trans. William Weaver. London: Minerva.

——. 1997. *Invisible Cities*. Trans. William Weaver. London: Vintage.

Cameron, Allan. 2006. 'Contingency, Order and the Modular Narrative: *21 Grams* and *Irreversible*'. *The Velvet Light Trap*, no. 58: 65–78.

Carroll, Noël. 1982. 'The Future of Allusion: Hollywood in the Seventies (and Beyond)'. *October*, 20 (Spring): 51–81.

Castells, Manuel. 2000. *The Rise of the Network Society*. Malden, MA: Blackwell Publishers.

Chatman, Seymour. 1990. *Coming to Terms: The Rhetoric of Narrative in Fiction and Film*. Ithaca: Cornell University Press.

Chion, Michel. 1994. *Audio-Vision: Sound on Screen*. Ed. and trans. Claudia Gorbman. New York: Columbia University Press.

Clarke, Melissa. 2002. 'The Space-Time Image: The Case of Bergson, Deleuze, and *Memento*'. *The Journal of Speculative Philosophy*, 16 (3): 167–81.

Collins, Jim. 1995. *Architectures of Excess: Cultural Life in the Information Age*. New York: Routledge.

Cook, Pam. 2004. *Screening the Past: Memory and Nostalgia in Cinema*. London: Routledge.

Cortazar, Julio. 1966. *Hopscotch*. Trans. Gregory Rabassa. New York: Avon Books.

Crane, Susan A. 1997. 'Memory, Distortion, and History in the Museum'. *History and Theory*, 36 (4): 44–63.

Cubitt, Sean. 2002. 'Spreadsheets, Sitemaps and Search Engines: Why Narrative is Marginal to Multimedia and Networked Communication, and Why Marginality is More Vital than Universality'. In *New Screen Media: Cinema/Art/Narrative*, ed. Martin Rieser and Andrea Zapp, 3–13. London: British Film Institute.

——. 2004. *The Cinema Effect*. Cambridge, MA: MIT Press.

Currie, Mark. 1998. *Postmodern Narrative Theory*. London: Macmillan.

Darley, Andrew. 2000. *Visual Digital Culture: Surface Play and Spectacle in New Media Genres*. London: Routledge.

Davis, Mike. 1990. *City of Quartz: Excavating the Future in Los Angeles*. London: Verso.

Deleuze, Gilles. 1986. *Cinema 1: The Movement-Image*. Trans. Hugh Tomlinson and Barbara Habberjam. London: Athlone Press.

——. 1989. *Cinema 2: The Time-Image*. Trans. Hugh Tomlinson and Barbara Habberjam. London: Athlone Press.

——. 1990. *Bergsonism*. Trans. Hugh Tomlinson and Barbara Habberjam. Cambridge, MA: MIT Press.

Deleuze, Gilles, and Félix Guattari. 1987. *A Thousand Plateaus: Capitalism and Schizophrenia*. Trans. Brian Massumi. Minneapolis: University of Minnesota Press.

Dena, Christy. 2007. 'Filmmakers That Think Outside the Film'. *The Workbook Project*. http://workbookproject.com/?page_id=242.

Denby, David. 2007. 'The New Disorder'. *The New Yorker*, March 5. http://www.newyorker.com/arts/critics/atlarge/2007/03/05/070305crat_atlarge_denby.

Derrida, Jacques. 1978. 'Freud and the Scene of Writing'. In *Writing and Difference*, 196–231. Trans. Alan Bass. London: Routledge.

Doane, Mary Ann. 1985. 'Ideology and the Practice of Sound Editing and Mixing'. In *Film Sound: Theory and Practice*, ed. Elisabeth Weis and John Belton, 54–62. New York: Columbia University Press.

———. 2002. *The Emergence of Cinematic Time: Modernity, Contingency, the Archive*. Cambridge, MA: Harvard UP.

———. 2004. '(De)realizing Cinematic Time'. In *Subtitles: On the Foreignness of Film*, ed. Atom Egoyan and Ian Balfour, 259–81. Cambridge, MA: MIT Press.

Draaisma, Douwe. 2000. *Metaphors of Memory: A History of Ideas About the Mind*. Trans. Paul Vincent. Cambridge: Cambridge University Press.

Duncan, Carol. 1991. 'Art Museums and the Ritual of Citizenship'. In *Exhibiting Cultures: The Poetics and Politics of Museum Display*, eds Ivan Karp and Steven D. Lavine, 88–103. Washington, DC: Smithsonian Institution Press.

Eakin, Hugh. 2006. 'The Novelist Walks: Why Did Turkey Drop the Charges Against Orhan Pamuk?' *Slate*, January 24. http://www.slate.com/id/2134828.

Eliot, George. 1988. *Middlemarch*. Oxford: Oxford University Press.

Eskelinen, Markku. 2004. 'Towards Computer Game Studies'. In *First Person: New Media as Story, Performance, and Game*, ed. Noah Wardrip-Fruin and Pat Harrigan, 36–44. Cambridge MA: MIT Press.

Field, Syd. 1994. *Screenplay: the Foundations of Screenwriting*. New York: Dell.

Foucault, Michel. 1972. *The Archaeology of Knowledge*. Trans. A. M. Sheridan Smith. London: Routledge.

Frank, Joseph. 1991. *The Idea of Spatial Form*. New Brunswick, NJ: Rutgers University Press.

Frasca, Gonzalo. 1999. 'Ludology Meets Narratology: Similitude and Differences Between (Video) Games and Narrative'. *Ludology*. http://www.ludology.org/articles/ludology.htm.

———. 2003. 'Simulation Versus Narrative: Introduction to Ludology'. In *The Video Game Theory Reader*, ed. Mark J.P. Wolf and Bernard Perron. New York: Routledge.

Freud, Sigmund. 1961. 'A Note Upon the "Mystic Writing-Pad"'. In *The Complete Psychological Works of Sigmund Freud*, vol. 19, 227–32. Trans. James Strachey. London: Hogarth Press.

Friedberg, Anne. 1993. *Window Shopping: Cinema and the Postmodern*. Berkeley: University of California Press.

Genette, Gérard. 1980. *Narrative Discourse: An Essay in Method*. Trans. Jane E. Lewin. Ithaca: Cornell University Press.

Gere, Charlie. 2002. *Digital Culture*. London: Reaktion Books.

Geuens, Jean-Pierre. 2002. 'The Digital World Picture'. *Film Quarterly*, 55 (4): 16–27.

Gondry, Michel. 2004. Interview by Stéphane Argentin. *Ecranlarge.com*, September 11. http://www.ecranlarge.com/interview-21.php.

Gunning, Tom. 1990. 'The Cinema of Attractions: Early Film, Its Spectator, and the Avant-Garde'. In *Early Cinema: Space, Frame, Narrative*, ed. Thomas Elsaesser, 56–62. London: British Film Institute.

Harris, Neil. 1981. *Humbug: The Art of P.T. Barnum*. Chicago: University of Chicago Press.

Harvey, David. 1990. *The Condition of Postmodernity: An Enquiry into the Origins of Cultural Change*. Oxford: Blackwell.

Hayles, N. Katherine. 1990. *Chaos Bound: Orderly Disorder in Contemporary Literature and Science*. Ithaca: Cornell University Press.

——, ed. 1991. *Chaos and Order: Complex Dynamics in Literature and Science*. Chicago: Chicago University Press.

Heise, Ursula. 1997. *Chronoschisms: Time, Narrative, and Postmodernism*. Cambridge: Cambridge University Press.

Henderson, Brian. 1983. 'Tense, Mood and Voice in Film: Notes after Genette'. *Film Quarterly*, 36 (4): 4–17.

Hodgkin, Katherine and Susannah Radstone. 2003. 'Introduction: Contested Pasts'. In *Contested Pasts: The Politics of Memory*, ed. Susannah Radstone and Katherine Hodgkin, 1–21. London: Routledge.

Howley, Kevin. 2004. 'Breaking, Making and Killing Time in *Pulp Fiction*'. *Scope: An Online Journal of Film Studies* (May). http://www.nottingham.ac.uk/film/journal/articles/making-breaking-and-killing.htm.

Hutcheon, Linda. 1988. *A Poetics of Postmodernism: History, Theory, Fiction*. New York: Routledge.

Huyssen, Andreas. 1995. *Twilight Memories: Marking Time in a Culture of Amnesia*. New York: Routledge.

——. 2000. 'Present Pasts: Media, Politics, Amnesia'. *Public Culture*, 12(1): 21–38.

——. 2003. *Present Pasts: Urban Palimpsests and the Politics of Memory*. Stanford: Stanford University Press.

Jameson, Fredric. 1991. *Postmodernism, or, The Cultural Logic of Late Capitalism*. Durham, NC: Duke University Press.

——. 1992. *The Geopolitical Aesthetic: Cinema and Space in the World System*. Bloomington and Indianapolis: Indiana University Press.

——. 1995. *The Seeds of Time*. New York: Columbia University Press.

——. 2003. 'The End of Temporality'. *Critical Inquiry*, 29 (4): 695–718.

Jenkins, Henry. 2004. 'Game Design as Narrative Architecture'. In *First Person: New Media as Story, Performance, and Game*, ed. Noah Wardrip-Fruin and Pat Harrigan, 118–30. Cambridge MA: MIT Press.

——. 2006. *Convergence Culture: Where Old and New Media Collide*. New York: New York University Press.

Johnson, William. 2004. Rev. of *Russian Ark*, dir. Alexandr Sokurov. *Film Quarterly*, 57 (2): 48–51.

Joyce, James. 2000. *Ulysses*. London: Penguin.

Juul, Jesper. 2001. 'Games Telling Stories? – A Brief Note on Games and Narratives'. *Game Studies*, 1 (1). http://www.gamestudies.org/0101/juul-gts.

——. 2004. 'Introduction to Game Time'. In *First Person: New Media as Story, Performance, and Game*, ed. Noah Wardrip-Fruin and Pat Harrigan, 131–42. Cambridge MA: MIT Press.

Kassabian, Anahid. 2001. *Hearing Film: Tracking Identifications in Contemporary Hollywood Film Music*. New York: Routledge.

Kaufman, Charlie. 2005. 'Why Charlie Kaufman Doesn't Watch Movies Anymore'. Interview by Michael Koresky and Matthew Plouffe. *Reverse Shot Online* (Spring). http://www.reverseshot.com/spring05/kaufman.html.

Kermode, Frank. 1967. *The Sense of an Ending*. London: Oxford University Press.

——. 2002. 'Forgetting'. In *Pieces of My Mind: Essays and Criticism 1958–2002*, 307–26. New York: Farrar, Straus and Giroux.

Kern, Stephen. 1983. *The Culture of Time and Space 1880–1918*. Cambridge, MA: Harvard University Press.

Kinder, Marsha. 1999. '*Doors to the Labyrinth:* Designing Interactive Frictions with Nina Menkes, Pat O'Neill, and John Rechy'. *Style*, 33 (2): 232–45.

———. 2001. 'Violence American Style: The Narrative Orchestration of Violent Attractions'. In *Violence and American Cinema*, ed. J. David Slocum, 63–100. New York: Routledge.

———. 2002a. 'Hot Spots, Avatars, and Narrative Fields Forever – Bunuel's Legacy for New Digital Media and Interactive Database Narrative'. *Film Quarterly*, 55 (4): 2–15.

———. 2002b. 'Narrative Equivocations Between Movies and Games'. In *The New Media Book*, ed. Dan Harries, 119–32. London: British Film Institute.

———. 2003. 'Designing a Database Cinema'. In *Future Cinema: The Cinematic Imaginary After Film*, eds Jeffrey Shaw and Peter Weibel, 346–53. Cambridge, MA: MIT Press.

King, Geoff. 2002. *New Hollywood Cinema: An Introduction*. London: I.B.Taurus.

Klein, Norman M. 1997. *The History of Forgetting: Los Angeles and the Erasure of Memory*. London: Verso.

Kujundzic, Dragan. 2004. 'After "After": The Arkive Fever of Alexander Sokurov'. *Quarterly Review of Film and Video*, 21 (3): 219–39.

Labyrinth Project. 2005. 'The Labyrinth Project on Interactive Narrative'. Los Angeles: University of Southern California. http://www.annenberg.edu/labyrinth/about/about1.html.

Landon, Brooks. 1992a. *The Aesthetics of Ambivalence: Rethinking Science Fiction Film in the Age of Electronic (Re)production*. Westport, CT: Greenwood Press.

———. 1992b. 'Not What It Used to Be: The Overloading of Memory in Digital Narrative'. In *Fiction 2000: Cyberpunk and the Future of Narrative*, eds George Slusser and Tom Shippey, 153–67. Athens, GA: University of Georgia Press.

———. 1999. 'Diegetic or Digital?: The Convergence of Science-Fiction Literature and Science-Fiction Film in Hypermedia'. In *Alien Zone II*, ed. Annette Kuhn, 31–49. London: Verso.

Landow, George P., ed. 1994. *Hyper/Text/Theory*. Baltimore: Johns Hopkins University Press.

———. 1997. *Hypertext 2.0: A Convergence of Contemporary Critical Theory and Technology*. Baltimore: Johns Hopkins University Press.

Landsberg, Alison. 1995. 'Prosthetic Memory: *Total Recall* and *Blade Runner*'. In *Cyberspace/Cyberbodies/Cyberpunk*, eds Mike Featherstone and Roger Burrows, 175–89. London: Sage.

Laurel, Brenda. 1993. *Computers as Theatre*. Reading, MA: Addison-Wesley.

Leibniz, Gottfried Willhelm Freiherr von. 1973. 'The Monadology'. In *Philosophical Writings*, 179–94. Ed. G. H. R. Parkinson. Trans. Mary Morris and G. H. R. Parkinson. London: Dent.

Levin, Thomas Y. 2002. 'Rhetoric of the Temporal Index: Surveillant Narration and the Cinema of "Real Time"'. In *CTRL [SPACE]: Rhetorics of Surveillance from Bentham to Big Brother*, ed. Thomas Y. Levin, Ursula Frohne and Peter Weibel, 578–93. Karlsruhe: ZKM Center for Art and Media.

Lunenfeld, Pater. 2002. 'The Myths of Interactive Cinema'. In *The New Media Book*, ed. Dan Harries, 144–54. London: British Film Institute.

Lupton, Catherine. 2005. *Chris Marker: Memories of the Future*. London: Reaktion.

Lyotard, Jean-François. 1984. *The Postmodern Condition: A Report on Knowledge.* Trans. Geoff Bennington and Brian Massumi. Manchester: Manchester University Press.

Martin-Jones, David. 2006. *Deleuze, Cinema and National Identity: Narrative Time in National Contexts.* Edinburgh: Edinburgh University Press.

McHale, Brian. 1987. *Postmodernist Fiction.* New York: Methuen.

McKee, Robert. 1999. *Story: Substance, Structure, Style and the Principles of Screenwriting.* London: Methuen.

Mamber, Stephen. 1998. 'Simultaneity and Overlap in Stanley Kubrick's *The Killing'. Postmodern Culture,* 8 (2). http://muse.jhu.edu/journals/pmc/v008/8.2mamber.html.

Manovich, Lev. 2000. 'What Is Digital Cinema?' In *The Digital Dialectic: New Essays on New Media,* ed. Peter Lunenfeld, 172–92. Cambridge, MA: MIT Press.

——. 2001a. 'From DV Realism to a Universal Recording Machine'. *Lev Manovich* website. http://www.manovich.net/DOCS/reality_media_final.doc.

——. 2001b. *The Language of New Media.* Cambridge, MA: MIT Press.

McGowan, Todd. 2000. 'Finding Ourselves on a *Lost Highway*: David Lynch's Lesson in Fantasy'. *Cinema Journal,* 39 (2): 51–73.

Metz, Christian. 1974. *Film Language: A Semiotics of the Cinema.* Trans. Michael Taylor. New York: Oxford University Press.

Mitchell, William J. 1995. *City of Bits: Space, Place, and the Infobahn.* Cambridge MA: MIT Press.

——. 1999. *e-topia: 'Urban Life, Jim – But Not As We Know It'.* Cambridge MA: MIT Press.

Mittel, Jason. 2006. 'Narrative Complexity in Contemporary American Television'. *The Velvet Light Trap,* no. 58: 29–40.

Monaco, James. 1979. *Alain Resnais.* New York: Oxford University Press.

Murray, Janet. 1998. *Hamlet on the Holodeck: The Future of Narrative in Cyberspace.* Cambridge, MA: MIT Press.

Naremore, James. 1998. *More Than Night: Film Noir in Its Contexts.* Berkeley and Los Angeles: University of California Press.

Ndalianis, Angela. 2005. 'Television and the Neo-Baroque'. In *The Contemporary Television Series,* ed. Michael Hammond and Lucy Mazdon, 83–101. Edinburgh: Edinburgh University Press.

Neale, Steve, and Murray Smith, eds 1998. *Contemporary Hollywood Cinema.* London: Routledge.

Newman, James. 2004. *Videogames.* London: Routledge.

Nietzsche, Freidrich. 1983. 'On the Uses and Disadvantages of History for Life'. In *Untimely Meditations,* 57–123. Trans. R. J. Hollingdale. Cambridge: Cambridge University Press.

Noé, Gaspar. 2004. Liner Notes for *Irréversible,* dir. Gaspar Noé. 2002. DVD. Accent Film Entertainment.

Nowotny, Helga. 1994. *Time: The Modern and Postmodern Experience.* Trans. Neville Plaice. Cambridge: Polity Press.

Nye, David E. 1997. *Narratives and Spaces: Technology and the Construction of American Culture.* Exeter: Exeter University Press.

O'Sullivan, Carol. 2006. 'The Choice Of An Ending: DVD And The Future(s) Of Post-Apocalyptic Narrative'. *Refractory: A Journal of Entertainment Media,* no. 9. http://www.refractory.unimelb.edu.au/.

Panek, Elliot. 2006. 'The Poet and the Detective: Defining the Psychological Puzzle Film'. *Film Criticism*, 31 (1–2): 62–88.

Pisters, Patricia. 2003. *The Matrix of Visual Culture: Working with Deleuze in Film Theory*. Stanford: Stanford University Press.

Polan, Dana. 2000. *Pulp Fiction*. London: British Film Institute.

Prigogine, Ilya, and Isabelle Stengers. 1984. *Order Out of Chaos: Man's New Dialogue with Nature*. London: Flamingo.

Proust, Marcel. 2002. *In Search of Lost Time*. 6 vols. Trans. C.K. Scott Moncrieff and Terence Kilmartin. Rev. D.J. Enright. London: Vintage.

Ramirez Berg, Charles. 2006. 'A Taxonomy of Alternative Plots in Recent Films: Classifying the "Tarantino Effect"'. *Film Criticism*, 31 (1–2): 5–61.

Ravetto-Biagioli, Kriss. 2005. 'Floating on the Borders of Europe: Sokurov's *Russian Ark*'. *Film Quarterly*, 59 (1): 18–26.

Ray, Robert. 1985. *A Certain Tendency of the Hollywood Cinema, 1930–1980*. New Jersey: Princeton University Press.

——. 2001. *How a Film Theory Got Lost and Other Mysteries in Cultural Studies*. Bloomington and Indianapolis: Indiana University Press.

Ricoeur, Paul. 1984–8. *Time and Narrative*. 3 vols. Trans Kathleen McLaughlin and David Pellauer. Chicago: University of Chicago Press.

Rieser, Martin, and Andrea Zapp, eds 2001. *New Screen Media: Cinema/Art/ Narrative* London: British Film Institute.

Robbe-Grillet, Alain. 1965a. *Two Novels by Robbe-Grillet: Jealousy* and *In the Labyrinth*. Trans. Richard Howard. New York: Grove Press.

——. 1965b. *Snapshots* and *Towards a New Novel*. Trans. Barbara Wright. London: Calder and Boyars.

——. 1977. 'Order and Disorder in Film and Fiction'. Trans. Bruce Morrissette. *Critical Inquiry*, 4 (Autumn): 1–20.

Rombes, Nicholas. 2005. 'Avant-Garde Realism'. *CTheory.net*, January 19. http://www.ctheory.net/articles.aspx?id=442.

Rosenberg, Martin E. 1994. 'Physics and Hypertext: Liberation and Complicity in Art and Pedagogy'. In *Hyper/Text/Theory*, ed. George P. Landow, 268–98. Baltimore: Johns Hopkins University Press.

Rosenstone, Robert A. 1995. 'Introduction'. In *Revisioning History: Film and the Construction of a New Past*, ed. Robert A. Rosenstone, 3–13. Princeton, NJ: Princeton University Press.

Roth, Michael S. 1995. '*Hiroshima Mon Amour:* You Must Remember This'. In *Revisioning History: Film and the Construction of a New Past*, ed. Robert A. Rosenstone, 91–101. Princeton, NJ: Princeton University Press.

Russell, Catherine. 1995. *Narrative Mortality: Death, Closure, and New Wave Cinemas*. Minneapolis: University of Minnesota Press.

Rutsky, R.L. 1999. *High Techne: Art and Technology from the Machine Aesthetic to the Posthuman*. Minneapolis: University of Minnesota Press.

Ryan, Marie-Laure. 2001. 'Beyond Myth and Metaphor – The Case of Narrative in Digital Media'. *Game Studies*, 1 (1). http://www.gamestudies.org/0101/ryan.

——. 2006. *Avatars of Story*. Minneapolis: University of Minnesota Press.

Sassen, Saskia. 2001. 'Spatialities and Temporalities of the Global: Elements for a Theorization'. In *Globalization*, ed. Arjun Appadurai, 260–78. Durham, NC: Duke UP.

Schrader, Paul. 1996. 'Notes on *Film Noir*'. In *Film Noir Reader*, ed. Alain Silver and James Ursini, 53–64. New York: Limelight Editions.

Shaw, Jeffrey. 2003. 'Introduction'. In *Future Cinema: The Cinematic Imaginary After Film*, ed. Jeffrey Shaw and Peter Weibel, 19–27. Cambridge, MA: MIT Press.

Smith, Evan. 1999. 'Thread Structure: Rewriting the Hollywood Formula'. *Journal of Film and Video*, 51 (3/4): 88–96.

Smith, Murray. 1995. *Engaging Characters: Fiction, Emotion, and the Cinema.* Oxford: Clarendon Press.

——. 1998. 'Theses on the Philosophy of Hollywood History'. In *Contemporary Hollywood Cinema*, ed. Steve Neale and Murray Smith, 3–20. London: Routledge.

Sobchack, Vivian. 1997. *Screening Space: The American Science Fiction Film* New Brunswick, NJ: Rutgers University Press.

Sokurov, Alexandr. 2001. 'Plane Songs: Lauren Sedofsky Talks with Alexander Sokurov'. Interview by Lauren Sedofsky. *Artforum International*, 40 (3): 124–8.

Talen, Julie. 2005. '*24*: Split Screen's Big Comeback'. *Salon.com*, May 14. http://dir.salon.com/story/ent/tv/feature/2002/05/14/24_split/print.html?pn=1.

Telotte, J.P. 1989. *Voices in the Dark: The Narrative Patterns of* Film Noir. Urbana and Champaign: University of Illinois Press.

——. 1995. *Replications: A Robotic History of the Science Fiction Film*. Urbana and Chicago: Illinois University Press.

——. 2001. *Science Fiction Film*. Cambridge: Cambridge University Press.

Thanouli, Eleftheria. 2006. 'Post-Classical Narration: A New Paradigm in Contemporary Cinema'. *New Review of Film and Television Studies*, 4 (2): 183–96.

Thompson, Kristin. 1999. *Storytelling in the New Hollywood: Understanding Classical Narrative Technique*. Cambridge, MA: Harvard University Press.

Tobias, James. 2004. 'Cinema, Scored: Toward a Comparative Methodology for Music in Media'. *Film Quarterly*, 57 (2): 26–36.

Tryon, Charles. 2003. 'Virtual Cities and Stolen Memories: Temporality and the Digital in *Dark City*'. *Film Criticism*, 28 (2): 42–62.

Turim, Maureen. 1989. *Flashbacks in Film: Memory and History.* New York: Routledge.

Virilio, Paul. 1991a. *The Aesthetics of Disappearance*. Trans. Philip Beitchman. New York: Semiotext(e).

——. 1991b. *The Lost Dimension*. Trans. Daniel Moshenberg. New York: Semiotext(e).

Weinbren, Grahame. 1995. 'In the Ocean of Streams of Story'. *Millennium Film Journal*, no. 28. http://www.mfj-online.org/journalPages/MFJ28/GWOCEAN. HTML.

White, Hayden. 1996. 'The Modernist Event'. In *The Persistence of History: Cinema, Television, and the Modern Event*, ed. Vivian Sobchack, 17–38. New York: Routledge.

Williams, G. Christopher. 2003. 'Factualizing the Tattoo: Actualizing Personal History through Memory in Christopher Nolan's *Memento*'. *Post Script*, 23 (1): 27–37.

Wilson, Rob and Wimal Dissanayake, eds 1996. *Global/Local: Cultural Production and the Transnational Imaginary*. Durham, NC: Duke University Press.

Wolf, Mark J.P. 2001a. 'Narrative in the Video Game'. In *The Medium of the Video Game*, ed. Mark J.P. Wolf, 93–111. Austin: University of Texas Press.

——. 2001b. 'Time in the Video Game'. In *The Medium of the Video Game*, ed. Mark J.P. Wolf, 77–91. Austin: University of Texas Press.

Woolf, Virginia. 2000. *Mrs. Dalloway.* London: Penguin.

Wyatt, Justin. 1994. *High Concept: Movies and Marketing in Hollywood.* Austin: University of Texas Press.

Yates, Frances A. 1966. *The Art of Memory.* Chicago: Chicago University Press.

Young, Kay. 2002. 'That Fabric of Times'. *SubStance*, 31 (1): 115–18.

Zizek, Slavoj. 2000. *The Art of the Ridiculous Sublime: On David Lynch's* Lost Highway. Seattle: Walter Chapin Simpson Center for the Humanities.

Index